The Norway Channel

The Norway Channel

The Secret Talks That Led to the Middle East Peace Accord

Jane Corbin

Atlantic Monthly Press
New York

Picture sources: Jane Corbin: pages 4 *top*, 8 *top*; Sidney Harris: page 3 *bottom left*; Popperfoto: page 6 *top*; Press Association: page 4 *bottom*; Scanfoto: pages 1, 6 *bottom*, 8 *bottom*; Sygma: pages 2 *top left* and *bottom*, 3 *top*

Map on p. viii by Neil Hyslop

First published in Great Britain as *Gaza First* by Bloomsbury Publishing Limited, 1994
First Atlantic Monthly Press edition, February 1994

Printed in the United States of America

FIRST EDITION

Library of Congress Cataloging-in-Publication Data
Corbin, Jane.
The Norway channel: the secret talks that led to the Middle East Peace
Accord / Jane Corbin.--1st ed.
Published in Great Britain in 1994 by Bloomsbury under the title: Gaza first.
ISBN 0-87113-576-0
1. Declaration of Principles on Interim Self-Government Arrangements (1993) 2. Jewish-Arab relations--1973- 3. Israel-Arab conflicts. 4. Munazzamat al-Tahrir al-Filastiniyah. 5. Israel. 6. Mediation, International. I. Title.
DS119.7.C665 1994 956.04--dc20 94-1028

The Atlantic Monthly Press
841 Broadway
New York, NY 10003

10 9 8 7 6 5 4 3 2 1

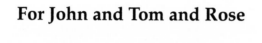

For John and Tom and Rose

Acknowledgements

I would like to thank the members of
the Oslo Channel for sharing so much
of their time and so many of their recol-
lections with me. I am also grateful to
many others in Jerusalem, Tunis and
Oslo, and to the *Panorama* team, in
particular Glenwyn Benson, Ruthie
Drewett and Judy Groves, for their help
and support.

Contents

Prologue   1

1   Images of War and Terror   10

2   The Creation of the Oslo Channel   29

3   Brainstorming at Borregaard   42

4   The Sarpsborg Document   51

5   The Walls of Jericho   64

6   The Diplomat and the Lawyer   78

7   Strawberries at Gressheim   95

8   A Trip to Tunis and Jerusalem   114

9   Crisis by the Fiord   127

10   Ménage à Trois   137

11   A Night in Stockholm   148

12   The Oslo Spirit   161

13   A Surprise for the Superpower   172

14   The Handshake   188

     Epilogue   205

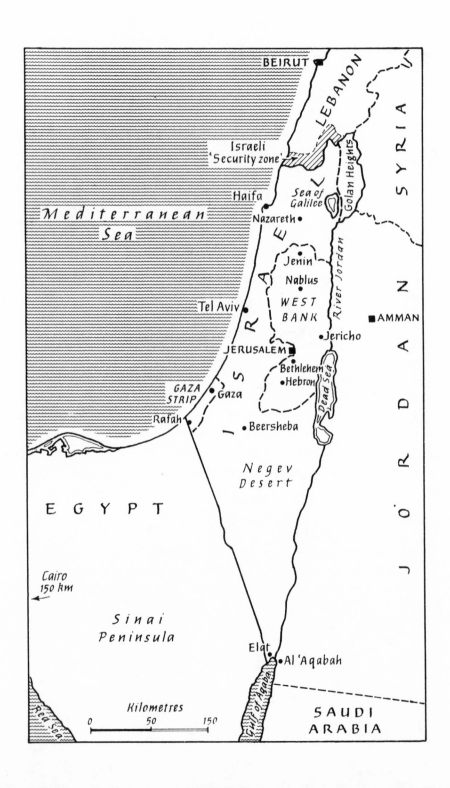

BEIRUT

LEBANON

SYRIA

Israeli
'Security zone'

Golan Heights

Haifa

Sea of
Galilee

Mediterranean
Sea

Nazareth

Jenin

Nablus

WEST
BANK

River Jordan

AMMAN

Tel Aviv

ISRAEL

Jericho

JERUSALEM

Bethlehem

Hebron

Dead Sea

GAZA
STRIP

Gaza

Rafah

Beersheba

J O R D A N

Negev
Desert

EGYPT

Cairo
150 km

Sinai
Peninsula

Elat

Al 'Aqabah

Red Sea

Kilometres

0   50   150

Gulf of Aqaba

SAUDI
ARABIA

Prologue

The young, clean-cut marine, in peaked cap and sparkling white gloves, peered in anxiously through the long windows of the White House. Behind him, on the green expanse of lawn, in warm autumnal sunshine, a vast crowd waited expectantly; its murmuring rose and then fell away on the still air. It was 13 September 1993. In front of three thousand international dignitaries the white columns of the portico glittered under a blue and cloudless sky. Behind the glass, in shadow, Bill Clinton waited, two men beside him. The voice of the master of ceremonies rang out and the three men stepped forward, past the saluting marine, into the brilliant light beyond.

'Ladies and Gentlemen, Mr Arafat, Chairman of the Executive Council of the Palestine Liberation Organization; His Excellency, Yitzhak Rabin, Prime Minister of Israel; the President of the United States.'

Before a hundred cameras, one of the defining dramas of twentieth-century history began to unfold. Yitzhak Rabin, leader of Israel and veteran of all her wars, walked stiffly forward. His military bearing, his characteristic look of resignation, signalled his discomfort with pomp and ceremony. Just feet away Yasser Arafat, leader of the PLO and veteran of his people's fight for self-determination, smiled confidently as he crossed the grass beside the President of the United States. This was recognition he had scarcely dreamt were possible. Clinton began his speech, with a tribute to the brave gamble taken by those who believe the future can be better than the past.

'Now the efforts of all who have laboured before us bring us to this moment, a moment when we dare to pledge what for so long seemed so difficult to imagine: that the security of the Israeli people will be reconciled with the hopes of the

Palestinian people, and there will be more security and more hope for all.'

The still fragile promise of peace the two sides had come to Washington to sign was their own achievement. But the moment of glory, it seemed, was Clinton's too. This high-profile ceremony at the White House was a clear American statement: America had set the parties on the road to peace and it would undertake to ensure they reached their journey's end. Before the podium sat those who had laboured long and hard in the interests of peace: the former power brokers whose years in office had been marred by the violence and the intransigence that characterized relations between Israel and her Arab neighbours. George Bush and Henry Kissinger were there; beside them sat Jimmy Carter, the last Democrat President, who had mediated between Egypt and Israel. He gazed at the oak table on the lawn, the very one at which he had put his name to the Camp David accords in 1979. Carter's face contracted as the name of Anwar Sadat was invoked. The Egyptian President had been murdered for his historic initiative.

The columnists and the TV anchormen who ringed the lawn were calling this signing a historic moment too: an accord between two peoples whose enmity had lain at the heart of the conflict in the Middle East for half a century. For nearly two years the United States had sponsored talks aimed at bringing the Israelis and the Palestinians to some agreement. The talks had come to nothing, just empty words and sterile posturing. The presence of Rabin and Arafat at the White House was a tribute not to America's might, but to the efforts of a small country with a gentler touch. The President acknowledged this in one brief sentence: 'Let us salute also, today, the government of Norway for its remarkable role in nurturing this agreement.'

Warm applause rippled through the crowd, directed at a tall and rangy figure seated amongst the former American presidents. Johan Jorgen Holst, the Foreign Minister of Norway, tried to suppress a grin at Bill Clinton's words. Holst was now the man publicly associated with a most extraordinary diplomatic coup: his government had secretly hosted nine months of talks, in log cabins and country manor-houses, which had resulted in the gathering on the White House lawn. Holst had been denied a place alongside the protagonists and their American host on the podium. This was Clinton's hour. But basking in reflected glory, in the front row, was some consolation for this clever and ambitious politician, thrust suddenly into the international limelight.

The President concluded his opening speech by describing the peace deal he had come to witness as 'the peace of the brave, yearning for the quiet miracle of a normal life'. And then two men stepped forward to sign the blue-bound documents embossed with gold that lay upon the table. Shimon Peres, the Foreign Minister of Israel, and Abu Mazen, the number three man in the PLO, had been the ones to recognize and to respond to the yearning of their peoples for that quiet miracle. Together they had been the architects of the so-called 'Oslo Channel', the secret talks in Norway that had led to this agreement. Now Shimon Peres took the microphone to speak of his dream of a new Middle East, a vision which had driven the Israeli negotiators. Peres's cultured face was grave, his voice gravelly and compelling as he spoke about another Genesis:

'I want to tell the Palestinian delegation that we are sincere, that we mean business. We do not seek to shape your life or determine your destiny. Let all of us turn from bullets to ballots, from guns to shovels. We shall pray with you, we shall offer you our help in making Gaza prosper and Jericho blossom again.'

The early political achievement of Shimon Peres had been to create a fearsome nuclear arsenal for his country. Now, aged seventy, he had effected the even greater accomplishment that was this peace deal on the table.

Listening beside Peres stood the little-known figure of Abu Mazen. A stocky, dynamic man in his late fifties, he had fled from Palestine in 1948, a boy of thirteen destined for a life in exile. Forty-four years later, this realistic and moderate voice within the top ranks of the PLO had negotiated a deal to set his people free. Gaza and Jericho had been the key, the signal that part of Palestine, at least, could now be governed by the PLO. It was an irony that the philosophy of Abu Mazen and the early Zionists had been the same, to take whatever land was offered and expand on small beginnings.

Back home in Gaza, the squalid and violent streets of the coastal strip were at this moment filled with the red, green and black of Palestinian flags, no longer banned. Exultant youths in cars plastered with pictures of Arafat careened along the narrow alleyways of the refugee camps as Abu Mazen and Shimon Peres solemnly signed the four documents before them containing the

Declaration of Principles on Interim Self-Government in Gaza and the West Bank.

Behind the men who signed the deal stood their political masters, Yitzhak Rabin and Yasser Arafat. It was they who had taken the decision to back the agreement forged in Norway. They were risking the future of their peoples and their own lives by doing so. As the signing was completed the tension in the air increased. The crowd on the White House lawn and millions around the world were waiting to see if two lifelong enemies would set the seal on their uneasy truce.

In one fluid movement President Clinton shook Rabin's hand, then Arafat's. With his arms outstretched to encompass the two men, yet without physical contact, he firmly ushered them together. Arafat's response was instantaneous, a decisive movement forward with his arm extended. Rabin, his body language spelling resistance, visibly hesitated before taking his opponent's hand. It was an unmistakable beat in the ceremonial rhythm, and it touched many hearts in Israel. Arafat, outwardly undeterred by his partner's lack of enthusiasm, pumped Rabin's arm strenuously as if to invest it with energy and purpose. The historic, if less than heartfelt, contact was over in a few seconds but its significance was clear. The message was that peace is made with enemies, not friends. For nine months, throughout the secret negotiations, both men had harboured the deepest suspicions about each other's motives. But, in the end, they knew peace was the only answer to the many problems both faced at home. They were staking their political futures on the deal; for commitments given in the glare of the media's lights, with the endorsement of the most powerful nation on earth, would have to be adhered to. Rabin knew that, if Israel was to have a prosperous future, the continued occupation of the Palestinian territories was an impossibility. The spectre of militant Islam, and the spiral of violence it created, gave new impetus to the moral imperative for withdrawal.

'Enough of blood and tears. Enough!' Rabin spoke slowly and deliberately. His speech, full of grief and anguish, struck an austere note very different from the vision of Shimon Peres. 'We are today giving peace a chance and saying to you, "Enough!" We wish to open a new chapter in the sad book of our lives together, a chapter of mutual recognition, of good-neighbourliness, of mutual respect and understanding.'

Yasser Arafat, dressed in his customary style – olive green fatigues and black and white keffiyeh head-dress, the garb associated with the guerrilla war he had launched in 1968 – spoke too of giving peace a chance. He had realized it was the only option for the PLO. Financial ruin beckoned, extremist rivals were undermining his political support and the Chairman's back was, once more, against the wall. The great survivor had taken his biggest gamble and had lived to fight another day:

'Let me address the people of Israel and their leaders, with whom we are meeting for the first time, and let me assure them that the difficult decision we reached together was one that required great and exceptional courage. We will need more courage and determination to continue the course of building peace and coexistence between us.'

Amongst the thousands on the White House lawn, there was a small and special group of people who knew just how difficult those decisions had been, how much courage and determination had been needed. These people were not prominently placed, not lauded or even recognized by the roving cameras. These Israelis and Palestinians, who listened intently to their leaders' words, did not acknowledge each other's presence but there were strong, unspoken bonds between them. For they had pitted their wits against each other, had hated and loved, laughed and cried together.

Just yards apart sat a sophisticated Arab banker in his fifties and an urbane young Jewish diplomat: Abu Ala, the financial brains behind the PLO; and Uri Savir, the Director-General of the Israeli Foreign Ministry. These men, who had been at the heart of the secret negotiations, were both driven by the certainty that their peoples wanted and needed peace above all else. That certainty had inspired their debates and rekindled their efforts, even in the darkest hours when it seemed they could progress no further.

Abu Ala had left his small village near Jerusalem in 1968 after the Six Day War with Israel. In Jordan, Saudi Arabia and Lebanon he learned the hard lessons of life on the street and honed the financial skills which were to make him both a successful businessman and a wily operator in the cutthroat world of Palestinian politics. His pragmatism and his personal charm combined uniquely with hard-headedness and a ruthless bargaining style to wrest a triumphant peace deal for the PLO from the jaws of financial and political oblivion.

Amongst the Israeli officials sat Abu Ala's opponent, Uri Savir. On the surface, he appeared a very different kind of man. A forty-one-year-old high-flyer, son of a famous ambassador, he had led a privileged and much-travelled life. Savir, a trained negotiator, was promoted young, showing wisdom beyond his years. He is an intellectual prepared to exhibit flexibility and to play the cunning and tortuous games of bluff that lie behind the making of an international peace deal.

Between these two men there had developed an intensity of feeling, fuelled by the tense negotiations. There was respect and kinship but, ingrained with the legacy of hate and bloodshed, they hesitated to call it friendship. The special chemistry they created became a vital part of the character and the success of the Oslo Channel.

While Uri Savir and Abu Ala had much in common, other members of the secret delegations were poles apart politically and personally. Yet they too, against all the odds, had managed to reach an accommodation and a real understanding. That morning in Washington, a lawyer, Joel Singer, came briefly to the podium to help Shimon Peres turn the pages as he signed the Declaration of Principles. Singer, the legal adviser to the Israeli Foreign Ministry, had been responsible for the drafting of the agreement. A formidable performer in the courtroom, he had been a colonel in the Israeli army for twenty-seven years. He had written many of the laws by which the Israeli military governed the Palestinians in the Occupied Territories. His tough and unsentimental attitude had thrown the secret talks into crisis but, despite his uncompromising approach, he had never doubted that a deal would be reached.

From within the crowd, Hassan Asfour watched Singer leafing through the Declaration of Principles, the agreement both sides had argued over syllable by syllable. An up-and-coming figure in the PLO, Asfour had, like Singer, been a hard-liner in his government. A Moscow-trained member of the Palestinian Communist Party, Asfour came from the slums of Gaza and believed in cold war ideology. He and Singer had faced each other many times in anger, but they had grown to respect each other for the plain-speaking, direct manner they both shared. Asfour had recognized by the end of the negotiations that all his fundamental beliefs had changed: as his perception of the enemy had been transformed, so had his political views. He and Singer had experienced the steepest learning curve in Norway, and they had forged the unlikeliest of alliances.

Outside the White House gates, kept well away from the distinguished gathering, the voices of those opposed to the peace process were raised in protest. Arabs accused Arafat and the PLO of treachery and swore that more blood would be spilt. Black-hatted Jews accused their leaders of betraying their birthright, Judea and Samaria, the land of Greater Israel. Inside, on the lawn, sat a young Israeli politician who had been prepared, right from the start, to risk both the condemnation of his people and his own career. Yossi Beilin, a quiet individual with a decisive manner and a deadpan sense of humour, had been the man to initiate the Oslo Channel. For years this idealistic Labour MP had been a voice in the political wilderness, consistently urging dialogue with the PLO. And he had dared, when his country's laws forbade it, to explore a way to open discussions with the enemy. He had sent two emissaries to establish contacts with the Palestinians and to persuade them to join the Israelis and seize the opportunity to make a lasting peace.

Beilin's messengers were at the White House too that day, but they were seated at the back, not part of any official Israeli delegation. Yair Hirschfeld and Ron Pundak, two academics, shunned the well-cut suits worn by their Israeli and Palestinian colleagues. Hirschfeld, an emotional man, bearded and rotund, had devoted himself to the cause of peace. He and his friend and fellow peace campaigner, Ron Pundak, had been the ones to go to Oslo first, to risk the contacts with the PLO. Their willingness to be denied by their political backer, if the talks failed, was crucial to keeping the negotiations secret. Hirschfeld and Pundak had had to accept a back seat as the discussions became more serious, and the big players moved centre stage. It was not easy but they managed it with good grace. Now they listened as the President drew the ceremony to a close.

'The children of Abraham, the descendants of Isaac and Ishmael, have embarked together on a bold journey. Together, today, with all our hearts and all our souls, we bid them Shalom, Salaam, Peace.'

To prolonged applause, Rabin and Arafat, with President Clinton at their side, walked along the front row to receive admiring messages from the representatives of many nations.

The Israeli leader warmly greeted Norway's Foreign Minister, Johan Jorgen Holst, and Arafat embraced him. Holst was the only one of his countrymen to be officially recognized that day. But far behind him, in the furthest reaches of the diplomatic enclave, seated behind the ambassador for Trinidad and Tobago, sat three other Norwegians: Jan Egeland, Mona Juul and Terje Larsen. They were all but ignored that day, although they had been the moving spirit behind Norway's nurturing of the agreement, a nurturing acknowledged, if only briefly, by the Americans. The will of these three individuals, their faith and their conviction, had brought the Oslo Channel into being and kept it going to the very end.

As a student, Jan Egeland, Norway's Deputy Foreign Minister, had written an academic paper comparing the achievements of superpowers and small states like his own in the human rights arena. This thirty-five-year-old social scientist argued that a small free-thinking country, without colonial baggage and interventionist impulses, could engineer success denied the leading powers. Egeland had been Norway's official link between Israel and the PLO at the beginning of the secret negotiations. Though it had to be a closely guarded secret, he had committed the necessary facilities and public money – a risk in a country renowned for open government. Now he had the satisfaction of knowing that he had proved his thesis: the little country had achieved the seemingly impossible, even if the superpower was claiming all the credit.

Beside Egeland sat his good friends Mona Juul and her husband Terje Rod Larsen. Egeland had been at the student meeting fifteen years before where these two had met and fallen in love. Mona Juul, a young dark-haired, attractive woman, is a Norwegian diplomat, an expert on the Middle East. The Oslo Channel, which she had helped to set up and run, had dominated her whole life – her work, her marriage, her career – for nearly a year. She had watched her husband change from a successful academic, running a prestigious research institute, to a man possessed, body and soul, by the elusive goal of peace. For it was Terje Larsen who created the magic of the Oslo Channel, the unique atmosphere that fostered respect and friendship and ultimately made the agreement possible. He had never sought to influence the outcome of the negotiations, beyond a passionate appeal to both sides never to walk away. He was, they said, the orchestrator of their music without knowing the lyrics or their meaning. But he knew more than they had told him and, in this knowledge, his wife was his partner and his foil, her caution and her understanding of the Middle East tempering his instinct and his desire to direct the show.

It was Larsen who, more than a year before, had realized the grip of history was weakening: the two warring sides were ready to bury their enmity if a way could be found beyond the speeches, the politicians, and the strait-jacket of public pressure. That morning on the White House lawn Larsen heard Rabin quote from Ecclesiastes:

'"To everything there is a season, and a time to every purpose under heaven. A time to be born, a time to die. A time to kill, and a time to heal. A time to weep, and a time to laugh. A time to love, and a time to hate. A time of war, and a time of peace" – the time for peace has come.'

The Israelis and the Palestinians had known this long ago but had been unable to achieve that peace unaided. They needed the good offices of an honest broker, and the dedication of people from a country far away, to reach beyond the bloodshed and the recriminations. The story of the Oslo Channel is the story of a small group of Jews and Arabs who came together, with the help of outsiders, to build a better future.

1

Images of War and Terror

It was appropriate that a peace agreement built on the notion of first returning Gaza to Palestinian control should have had its beginnings in that narrow sliver of land along the Mediterranean coast. For it was Gaza that first drew a Norwegian social scientist to investigate the suffering and the humiliating and hopeless existence of nearly a million Palestinian refugees. And by doing so, both he and his country became the conduit to peace between Israel and the PLO.

Burning tyres, rusted cars and boulders blocked the squalid streets of the Gaza Strip; blood-red graffiti dripped from walls, its grim message the exhortations of Islamic mullahs, crying death to Israel. A Norwegian academic, Terje Rod Larsen, was touring the alleys of the Palestinian refugee camps in June 1990. With him was his wife, Mona Juul, assistant to the Foreign Minister of Norway and a specialist in Middle East affairs. Their escort that day was a UN officer, also from Norway, Colonel Zacharias Bakker. Larsen was preparing to begin an extensive social survey of the living conditions of people in the most densely populated spot on earth and, despite the dangers, was determined to witness for himself the precarious existence of nearly a million people crammed into a slice of land barely twenty-five miles long and seven miles wide.

Suddenly, in front of their armoured car, Larsen, Mona and their escort witnessed an incident – just one of many repeated daily in Gaza's fearful, battle-scarred streets. A patrol of young Israeli soldiers and a gang of Palestinian youths faced each other, the former armed with weapons, the latter with stones. Larsen, not a man of great physical courage, had no time to run and hide, or to protect his wife; the rocks were bouncing around them and they heard the ricochet of bullets. Colonel Bakker jumped out and tried to restrain the soldiers and, as he remonstrated with their leader, Larsen and Mona stared in fascination at the antagonists before them. What Larsen saw when he gazed into their eyes was to haunt him for months to come and to inspire him to undertake a seemingly impossible mission. In the faces of the Israeli teenagers, recruited against their will into an army of occupation, he saw fear and longing – to be anywhere but Gaza. And in the Palestinian youths, who were of the same age, physique and appearance as their enemy, he saw defiance and despair – and in their eyes the selfsame fear.

That night, back in their room at the Gaza Strip UN Club, the grandly-named barracks with bar and terrace used by UN personnel, the Norwegian couple thought about what they had seen and what they could do to help. Larsen had come to the Occupied Territories to set up a social study to assess the living conditions of the inhabitants. He resolved that he must not just dissect their lives without addressing their aspirations too. And so he determined that his study would have a strong political base. He would not shirk from addressing the real problem, the battle of two peoples for the same piece of land. And although he did not have a concrete plan, he determined that he would do everything he could to bring like-minded people from both sides together, to work towards a common future. Mona Juul, thirty-two years old at that time and just beginning her career as a diplomat, felt passionately that the Norwegian government should do whatever it could to foster better relations between Israel and the Palestinians, to try and improve the wretched lot of the people of Gaza.

The outlook was not encouraging. Decades of peace initiatives had led nowhere and the lot of Palestinians in the Occupied Territories had worsened with the passing years. No one knew exactly how many people were crammed into the camps and shanties round the decaying city of Gaza. Nearly a million, maybe more, three-quarters of them refugees and almost one-quarter under the age of five. Gaza was a demographic and political time bomb whose population was expected to double in just seventeen years. With only one in four adult males currently employed, the future was worse than bleak, it was terrifying.

Gaza was the land that no one wanted. A part of Palestine under the British Mandate, it borders on Egypt and, after the war of 1948, was administered by Cairo. But Egypt had no desire to annex this impoverished neighbour with its scanty agricultural resources and nothing else to recommend it. With the Suez War of 1956, Gaza was occupied by the Israelis, and it was during this conflict that the Palestinians acquired their first experience of armed resistance. It was in Gaza that most of the leaders of Fatah – Arafat's faction in the PLO – hammered out their ideas of Palestinian nationalism.

In 1957 the Israelis evacuated the Gaza Strip. In 1967 they once more occupied the coastal territory and fought for years to subdue the population until, in 1971, the iron hand of General Ariel Sharon achieved a conclusive military victory in Gaza. Jewish settlements were established and the area was integrated, uneasily, into the Israeli economy. Almost half the population crossed the military checkpoints into the Jewish state daily to underpin industry, the public services and the building trade. But Gaza has always fought against the yoke of occupation. The militant Islamic movement Hamas was born there and, in October 1987, the Intifada, or Palestinian Uprising, began in the narrow, filth-choked alleyways of Gaza.

Over the years Gaza has become a byword for squalor and violence. The gross overcrowding has defeated the sanitation system, piles of garbage line the streets and sewage flows along the alleyways where swarms of children play. Since the great exodus from Palestine in 1948, which filled Gaza to bursting point, Palestinian leaders have been accused of having no great desire to alleviate the suffering in this vast refugee camp. Gaza, the argument goes, serves as a convenient reproach to the international community for its refusal to act to end the stateless limbo in which the Palestinians are trapped.

Surprisingly, given the well-known problems of Gaza, no one had carried out a proper scientific study of the lives of the inhabitants until, in 1989, Terje Larsen arrived to begin discussions with local Palestinian leaders and with the Israeli government. He wanted to carry out a comprehensive survey of the living conditions of Palestinians in Gaza and also on the West Bank and in East Jerusalem.

Larsen had been living in Cairo with Mona, who had been posted to the Norwegian embassy in Egypt. It was her first foreign appointment and her husband went with her to investigate the possibilities of setting up social projects in the Middle East. He was the director of a Norwegian think-tank called

FAFO, the Institute for Applied Social Sciences which Larsen had founded in 1981. In the spir1it of his country, one of the world's most generous donors of aid, Larsen was always open to suggestions to quantify need in developing countries. From the moment of their arrival in the lively and cosmopolitan city of Cairo, Larsen and Juul were fascinated by the Middle East and quickly made influential contacts. One of these was Fathi Arafat, a doctor and the brother of the Chairman of the PLO. He was the head of the Palestinian Hospital in Cairo and of the Palestinian Red Crescent – the local equivalent of the Red Cross. Fathi suggested that FAFO take on the challenge of a socio-economic survey in the Occupied Territories.

Larsen, with characteristic gusto, seized on the suggestion despite the daunting task. He would have to negotiate political approval to implement complex field operations in the midst of the Intifada, the war of stones and strikes and assassination being waged against the occupation. Larsen embarked on a series of visits to Gaza, the West Bank and Israel to negotiate access with local Palestinians and with the Israeli military government in the area. His enthusiasm and his determination soon brought him into contact with well-connected people in Jerusalem and Tel Aviv, and in Tunis, home to the PLO.

The survey became a springboard for Larsen. It informed his ideas about the conflict and it strengthened his initial desire to become involved in more than just a social study. From the start he determined the research should stimulate an identification of common interests between Palestinians and Israelis. As he met more and more people from both sides, he realized the gap between them was not as great as they, or the outside world, felt it to be. It was their hostile image of each other, forged by war and terror, which prevented any real understanding. Larsen decided that what was needed was a forum to bring the two sides together, to foster trust and common interests in place of suspicion and enmity. Only then might they begin to discuss a meaningful way to progress towards peace.

His friends describe forty-six-year-old Terje Larsen as an entrepreneur. It is perhaps an odd word to use to describe a social scientist who founded and runs an academic institute funded mainly by Norway's trade unions. The description reflects not his business acumen but rather his complete conviction that anything that is worth doing can be done. Larsen is self-confident but without aggression. He is supremely persuasive and his charm and social dexterity mask an iron determination. He simply ploughs ahead despite the obstacles.

The obstacle in this case was a formidable one: nearly fifty years of bloodshed and retribution since the founding of Israel, and before that many decades of strife between Jew and Arab in the region. There had been four wars and countless skirmishes, laced with sustained campaigns of terror that had indelibly marked the psyche of both peoples. The history of Israel and the Palestinian diaspora since 1948 is dominated by a roll-call of tragedy, the stuff of headlines and shocking television broadcasts. In 1948 Israel's War of Independence drove nearly half the Arab population of what had been the British-ruled territory of Palestine from their homes to the West Bank of the Jordan, to Gaza, or into exile. Out of a total of 1.3 million about 700,000 fled, spurred on by fear of massacre, like the killing by the Irgun, the Jewish underground movement, of 250 people in the village of Deir Yassin.

In June 1967, as Arab forces threatened, Israel, in a preemptive strike, grabbed the Sinai Peninsula and Gaza from Egypt, and the Golan Heights from Syria. Six days later the Arabs had been roundly defeated and Israeli forces, under the command of General Yitzhak Rabin, had swallowed up the West Bank and East Jerusalem – all that was left of Palestine. Fatah stepped up guerrilla attacks on Israel and gained in popularity until its young leader, Yasser Arafat, controlled the Palestine Liberation Organization and a full-scale war of terror was unleashed. The extremists of Black September struck in Munich at the Olympics, massacring eleven Israeli sportsmen. King Hussein of Jordan expelled Arafat and his fighters who sought refuge in Lebanon. PLO commando units struck south, at beaches, towns and buses in Israel, while abroad hijackings and bombings sought to keep the world's attention focused on the Palestinian cause. In 1982 the Israeli army struck back, invading Lebanon and forcing Arafat and the PLO once more to flee, this time to Tunis. And in the wake of their departure came the horror of the Sabra and Chatila massacre. Hundreds of defenceless Palestinian families in these refugee camps were killed by Christian militiamen, allowed into the area by the Israeli army, who seemingly turned a blind eye while the atrocities were committed. And then in 1987 the Intifada, the Palestinian Uprising, erupted in protest at the continued occupation of the West Bank and Gaza. Palestinians killed Jewish settlers and soldiers and each other, and the Israeli army killed and imprisoned youths and children in the war of stones.

These were the images that would-be peacemakers had for years fought unsuccessfully to erase from the collective memory of Israelis and Palestinians. The images of war and terror, masked gunmen, soldiers firing in the precincts of Jerusalem's sacred mosque, a small child in a shroud, a body casually dropping on the tarmac, an old man in a wheelchair pushed overboard from a cruise liner.

No one can count the toll, or prove conclusively who was behind which killings. But it is believed that at least 540 Israeli civilians and 770 troops have died in terror attacks since 1964 when Fatah was founded. Hundreds of Palestinian civilians have died in bombing raids by Israeli jets, and more than a thousand have been killed by Israeli troops in the Occupied Territories since the Intifada began. Twice that number have been assassinated by their own side, vengeance exacted against informers in the never-ending war.

And, in this battle, one of the most potent images burnt into the minds of people in the region is that of the Palestinian leader, Yasser Arafat. To Jews he is a demon of their modern mythology, the perpetrator of terror, an artful, slippery, mendacious wearer of the chequered head-dress, who seems to rise inexorably from the ashes of everything he touches. To his own people, Arafat is Palestine, a figurehead, but one with mysterious, all-consuming power. The Israeli people regard him as 'Hitler in his lair', as Menachem Begin put it. For years they have known in their hearts that he was the only one who could deliver peace but, paradoxically, he could never be trusted to do it.

These were the images that Terje Larsen sought to break, although he did not know how to do it. But the Norwegian found himself in the Occupied Territories at a critical moment, when several factors came together fortuitously – not least of which was the relationship his country, Norway, enjoyed with both sides in the conflict. In addition, there was the waning of the conservative Likud government in Israel and its replacement by a new Labour administration. In Tunis, Arafat's power was declining too, his organization beset with financial crisis. The famous survivor had never been at such a low ebb. He desperately needed to reach an accommodation with the enemy to stave off his political obituary. In Washington the set-piece talks, heralded with such fanfare at Madrid in 1991, had degenerated into stalemate: no peace accord was emerging there, just a meaningless war of words. Perhaps the most important factor was the rise to prominence and political influence, on both sides, of a group of individuals who believed coexistence was not only desirable but a necessity. The interplay of all these circumstances, laced with a large dose of luck, would mean that Larsen could find a role to play, one that would make an enormous contribution to peace in the Middle East.

Larsen's interest in the Occupied Territories coincided with the peace process launched with such optimism in the aftermath of the Gulf War. George Bush had proclaimed the region's problems would be resolved by America and its new partner, Russia. At the heart of the hostility between Israel and her Arab neighbours was the thorny question of a Palestinian homeland – 'self-determination', as it was known in political jargon. That hung on the fate of the territories occupied by Israel since the Six Day War in 1967. The Occupied Territories had remained in Israel's hands for nearly a quarter of a century, despite United Nations resolutions calling for withdrawal, and in defiance of international opposition.

But Bush's concept of a 'new world order' had a magic ring to it and great things were expected of the Middle East in the aftermath of Iraq's defeat at the hands of the Allies. Now, warned America, Israel would have to play its part. Despite the determination of Yitzhak Shamir, the right-wing Likud Prime Minister, not to concede an inch of territory, there were high hopes that the Palestinian problem could be solved, and that Syria, Lebanon and Jordan would then be able to resolve their differences with Israel.

The aim of the Madrid peace process, which quickly shifted from the Spanish capital to the real centre of power in Washington, was to work towards an agreement on interim self-government for the Palestinians. The participants were fully aware that it would be impossible to agree immediately on the permanent status of the Occupied Territories. It would be more fruitful to decide upon the shape and functions of an interim Palestinian government in the area for the next five years, and then go on to address the most difficult question: could Israeli and Palestinian states coexist on the old territory of Palestine? To reach an interim agreement, therefore, two complex sets of talks were convened simultaneously. The main ones, centred at the State Department in Washington, were the bilateral talks between three Israeli teams and three Arab delegations – one from Syria, one from Lebanon, and a joint Jordanian/Palestinian group. The subsidiary, or multilateral talks, took place at various locations around the world and involved thirty countries from Canada to China acting as advisers and sponsors. These multilateral talks concentrated on the more practical problems in the region: water-sharing, arms control, the economy, the environment and the fate of refugees.

Shamir's government refused to negotiate directly with the PLO and so surrogates had to be found. A group of academics, doctors and representatives from powerful Palestinian families inside the Occupied Territories were thrust into the spotlight in Madrid when the conference opened in November 1991. A few of them, notably Faisal Husseini, scion of a prominent East Jerusalem family, and Dr Hanan Ashrawi of Beir Zeit University, quickly became the darlings of the media. Israel encouraged and built up this alternative leadership as a way of shutting out the Palestinian Liberation Organization. Shamir's government considered Yasser Arafat, and his PLO government-in-exile in Tunis, renegade terrorists who could not be trusted to do a deal and stick to it. The Israeli government chose to ignore the reality – that the new Palestinian group took all its orders from Arafat – and maintained the fiction that it was not dealing with the PLO. As the months wore on it became apparent that the Palestinians at the peace talks had no independent mandate to negotiate; they were travelling back and forth via Tunis where Arafat authorized every dot and comma.

As the months passed, successive rounds of talks degenerated into sour name-calling by both sides. Yet the media circus and public expectations grew in inverse proportion to the progress being made. A war of microphones was being waged. Each side took its stand and refused to compromise, despite the sticks and carrots alternately wielded and proffered by the American co-sponsors of the talks.

The problem for the Americans was that while their power and influence had been essential to persuading, and even strong-arming, the parties to the table, that very power and influence stood in the way of settling the dispute. The special relationship with Israel, whose economy was shored up by massive injections of American aid, worked against the fundamental requirement that the sponsor be unbiased. Whilst the Russians were nominally co-sponsors, the turmoil in their own country meant their participation could never be on a par with that of the United States. The Arab delegations were suspicious and the Israelis often resentful of the pressure exerted by the Bush Administration. To Larsen, and to many others watching from Israel and the capitals of the Arab world, a weary stalemate seemed to be the only thing emerging from the talks. Larsen began to consider what a different negotiating framework might achieve, and what a small country like Norway might be able to offer in place of the American model.

Norway already enjoyed a unique position between the opposing parties, being independent but trusted by both. Under Nazi occupation, Norway's small Jewish community was almost wiped out. The horror and the guilt felt by Norwegians was a strong factor in the country's decision to back the creation of the State of Israel after the Second World War. Successive socialist governments in Norway forged strong links with the Israeli Labour Party. The powerful trade union organizations in both countries were close, and two-thirds of Norway's MPs belonged to the influential lobby group Israel for Peace.

On the other hand, Norway also maintained excellent links with the Palestinians. This was a tribute to Thorvald Stoltenberg, Norway's long-standing and statesmanlike Foreign Minister. In the 1980s he realized that Norway risked becoming too one-sided in the Middle East debate. His predecessor had almost been forced to resign, so strong was public displeasure in Norway at the government's vote in favour of Arafat speaking at the United Nations in 1974. Stoltenberg thought it was important to take a more balanced stand, and on 31 December 1981 he – then the Deputy Foreign Minister – went to Tunis to meet Yasser Arafat. They had dinner together, visited a Palestinian orphanage and, a gesture of symbolic importance, saw in the New Year together. That night Arafat appealed to Stoltenberg to use his influence to help the PLO establish direct contact with the Israeli Labour Party.

The response from the Israelis was not encouraging but the Norwegian diplomat persevered. In April 1983 he tried to engineer secret contacts between Israeli Labour Party members and Dr Issam Sartawi, a prominent and outspoken Palestinian moderate. But his initiative ended in tragedy. Stoltenberg and Sartawi were at a Socialist Congress meeting in a Portuguese hotel, the Montechoro in Albufeira, where the Norwegian hoped he could discreetly facilitate a get-together. But instead Thorvald Stoltenberg witnessed the assassination of the Palestinian, gunned down in the hotel lobby by a member of Abu Nidal's terror group. This was a terrible warning that extremists would not tolerate contacts with the enemy – a warning too for would-be go-betweens.

In 1987 Stoltenberg became Norway's Foreign Minister and introduced his young protégé, and Deputy Minister, Jan Egeland to his plans for helping to build bridges between Israel and the PLO. The slim, blond-haired Egeland, an earnest academic and boyish idealist, had international credentials earned with the human rights group Amnesty International, with the Red Cross in Geneva, and at the Hebrew University in Jerusalem.

The two men made sure that Norway, while maintaining its strong links with Israel, gave generous aid to Palestinian medical and humanitarian projects in the Occupied Territories. The Foreign Ministry was amongst the backers of, and had contributed funds to, Larsen's study in the Palestinian areas. Egeland had been a contemporary of Mona Juul's at university and he and Larsen had become close friends.

Norway is unique in the closeness of its political and academic circles, and the personal relationships between individuals who move in them. In a country of just four million it is perhaps inevitable, though some would regard it as questionable nepotism. But the reality is that this intermingling of politicians and social scientists – and their wives and husbands too – was an important factor in enabling the Norwegians secretly to form a close-knit group designed to bring the warring sides together.

Stoltenberg, an imposing and genial figure, renowned for his kindness and easy manner, had picked out the promising young diplomat Mona Juul to be his assistant. Juul was Egeland's friend and Larsen's wife. Larsen in turn had many important Labour Party and trade union connections. One of his researchers on the Palestinian study was Camilla Stoltenberg, the Foreign Minister's daughter. The co-author of Larsen's survey was

Marianne Heiberg, a sociologist married to Johan Jorgen Holst. Holst, who was then Defence Minister, would later take over as Foreign Minister from Thorvald Stoltenberg, who was his brother-in-law – they had married two sisters. This small-scale, informal character of Norwegian political and public life was in direct contrast to the large, hierarchical and impersonal structure of the US Administration and the State Department.

Terje Larsen and Mona Juul move with ease and skill through Norway's tight academic and political circles. They are a golden couple, attractive, intelligent, devoted to each other yet with separate and successful careers. Larsen was brought up in Bergen, a seaboard town on the west coast of Norway, geographically remote from the capital, Oslo. Bergen people have a reputation as independent and adventurous spirits and the Larsen family fitted that description. Terje's father was a sailor, and as a boy Terje had travelled abroad, to London and other European cities, before he had ever been to Oslo. Mona Juul comes from a close-knit and prosperous farming family living near Trondheim, in rural Norway. A student with radical left-wing views, she first met Larsen in 1978 at a debate where he, a teacher, was one of the speakers. She spoke out strongly against him. They argued passionately that night; Larsen soon fell in love with Mona and later married her.

Now thirty-four, dark-haired and vivacious with a strong, attractive face, Mona Juul has something wild and mysterious about her. Yet in her work she is cautious, thorough and very diplomatic. Terje Larsen has a good-looking, lived-in face and an air about him that raises protective instincts in women. He dresses with casual insouciance but always looks stylishly at home in any setting. He has a warm manner and an immediately disarming quality; men find him engaging and intelligent but not threatening. Meanwhile Larsen is analysing their words, their every move: for sociology and psychology are both his academic and his personal obsession.

By May 1992, the fieldwork for the Norwegian study was about to get under way and Larsen made yet another trip to Jerusalem. The country was in the grip of election fever. Shamir's ruling Likud Party was under attack from Labour whose leader, Yitzhak Rabin, had promised a speedy solution to the faltering peace talks. As he campaigned around the hot and dusty streets of the Israeli working-class areas, Rabin publicly declared his party would tackle the intractable issue of the expanding Jewish settlements in the Occupied Territories. The issue of the settlements had blocked US loans and the economy of the whole country was suffering.

An acquaintance of Larsen's told him he must meet a kindred spirit, Yossi Beilin, a controversial young MP and rising star in Labour's ranks. Larsen took a taxi from Jerusalem to Tel Aviv to the Tandoori Restaurant in Dizengoff Square where they had arranged a rendezvous. Beilin, who was busy on the campaign trail, nearly cancelled the lunch but decided at the last minute to come. When the two men met they experienced an immediate rapport – the 'click', they called it. They had an instantaneous understanding, an interest and enthusiasm for each other's ideas. They talked for three hours, ignoring the third man at the table, the Israeli trade unionist who had introduced them.

They both agreed that there was a historical momentum pushing towards peace in the Middle East. The fall of the Berlin Wall and the collapse of the Soviet Union, followed by the Gulf War, had sent shock waves through the region. The PLO's socialist-revolutionary principles and its long-standing links with the Soviet Bloc made Arafat look distinctly outdated now. However, the frustrating fact was that the Washington peace process had not been able to seize the opportunity presented by a changing world. 'But we need a two-track system,' said Larsen. 'Washington and the second track – secret negotiations.' Beilin agreed and he went further. He talked about the inevitability of a two-state solution, or some kind of loose confederation between Israel, Jordan and the Palestinians. For Larsen it was refreshing to meet an Israeli politician whose views so closely matched his own.

Yossi Beilin had for many years encountered ridicule and hostility for his public statements that the Israeli government should be prepared to talk to the PLO. He had even introduced a bill to revoke the law forbidding contacts between his countrymen and the PLO. But Beilin, a low-key intellectual, was a man with determination. He had a toughness about him, and yet also a self-deprecating air and dry sense of humour. Carefully dressed and bespectacled, at forty-five he was a man whose youthful look belied his political awareness and his experience. A former journalist, on the ideological left of his party, Beilin had been appointed Cabinet Secretary by Shimon Peres when the latter became Prime Minister in 1984.

Beilin was, like Larsen, an academic by training and, like the Norwegian, he had founded a research group, his own small think-tank dedicated to finding ways to advance the cause of peace by direct links with the Palestinians. Beilin's Economic Cooperation Foundation in fact contained just two other men, Dr Yair Hirschfeld and Ron Pundak, left-wing intellectuals who shared their mentor's beliefs. Enthusiasm and passion were Dr Hirschfeld's guiding principles. This historian from Haifa University had spent long hours driving Beilin down potholed tracks on wild-goose chases looking for Palestinian community leaders who might prove to be useful contacts. Hirschfeld built up the personal relations with West Bank Arabs, a risky business for an Israeli. Beilin, more at arm's length, used those links to develop political activities dedicated to furthering his aims.

In the Indian restaurant in Tel Aviv in May 1992, as the animated conversation flowed between the Israeli MP and the Norwegian visitor, Beilin made it clear that he was interested in thinking of ways to act quickly on the peace process if Labour won the coming election. Larsen immediately suggested that Norway could use its good offices to set up some sort of secret contacts – a 'second track', he called it – which would be a useful sideshow to the Washington talks. It might develop ideas and establish behind-the-scenes relations with the Palestinians. Beilin's response was enthusiastic. He immediately thought that he could make use of such an offer from an academic whose independent institute had close links with Norway's Foreign Ministry. Larsen's suggestion was to build bridges with local Palestinian notables from inside the Occupied Territories, people like Faisal Husseini and Hanan Ashrawi, rather than making direct links with the PLO in Tunis. Husseini had already suggested to Larsen that Norway might help in setting up a second track. Larsen quickly arranged a meeting at his hotel – the American Colony, a beautiful and tranquil villa in East Jerusalem, formerly the residence of the Husseini family. This oasis of blue and turquoise tiling and trickling fountains, with its discreet and welcoming staff, is the favourite haunt of journalists in the city. Larsen was, as yet, new to the game of secret meetings; but he knew enough to stagger the arrival times by half an hour so that no one would observe the well-known figures of

Beilin and Faisal Husseini, one of the most prominent Palestinians in East Jerusalem, heading for the same room, Number 16. At the meeting the three men discussed two things: the possibility of setting up a second track and the way in which the Palestinians could help the Labour Party come to power, by supporting its candidates in the coming election.

Three days later Labour won a narrow but significant victory in the Israeli election. After the usual horse-trading with minority parties, Yitzhak Rabin became Prime Minister. He appointed his old rival Shimon Peres Foreign Minister, and Peres in turn appointed Yossi Beilin his Deputy Minister. Larsen was quick to re-establish contact and this time he brought the authority of the Norwegian government with him. Thorvald Stoltenberg was as keen to help as Larsen, and in September, when the new Israeli government was secure in office, Jan Egeland made an official visit to the country. He was accompanied by Mona Juul, the Foreign Ministry's Middle East expert. Terje Larsen, who had made the contact with Yossi Beilin, was in Israel too. They all had instructions from Thorvald Stoltenberg to see if they could pursue a secret agenda and establish Norway as a go-between, in the interests of peace.

On 12 September, in a Tel Aviv hotel, Yossi Beilin hosted an official dinner for Egeland and Juul, and a number of other Norwegians from the embassy. During the meal the talk was all of Syria: Egeland had been visiting that country and the Israelis were curious to know what his assessment was. The Palestinians were hardly mentioned but what most of the people around the table did not know was that a secret meeting on that subject, the first such get-together at an official level, had been planned for later that night.

After dinner the guests all said their cordial goodbyes and expressed their hope to meet again. Beilin got into his car, drove a few times around the block, re-entered the building and rushed into a lift to avoid bumping into the Norwegian ambassador who was still in the lobby. He made his way to Egeland's room where Terje Larsen had now joined Mona Juul and the Norwegian Deputy Minister. Egeland was somewhat embarrassed. His 'junior suite', the only one available, was neither large nor luxurious and he was afraid the Israelis would think Norway an even more inconsequential diplomatic player than it already was. Larsen, his keen social antennae attuned to the situation, immediately stepped in, solicitously offering drinks and joking with Yossi Beilin.

Beilin had asked Yair Hirschfeld to come along that evening. He had promised Larsen he would send him an intermediary, someone who could make the face-to-face contacts with Palestinians which were too sensitive for a man who was now a government minister. Larsen had already had several discussions with the enthusiastic lecturer.

Egeland came straight to the point; the Norwegian government could offer any kind of contact with the Palestinians, at any level, under any disguise. He asked Beilin himself to come to Norway for a direct meeting with the other side. Beilin, in his typical businesslike way, made it very clear that, despite his personal convictions, meeting with the PLO was breaking the law and a new government could not be seen to do that. He was, however, prepared to meet Husseini and he welcomed Norway's offer. Egeland said he would fix it so that both Beilin and Husseini were in Oslo at the same time, on separate missions, and that they could meet in secret. The Norwegians agreed with Beilin's choice of one of the new-style Palestinian leaders; they considered them more moderate and forward-looking than the hard-liners in Tunis whose attitudes were growing increasingly out of touch.

However, their assessment of the PLO was not entirely accurate. For in the shady villas behind the tree-lined streets of the Palestinian enclave in Tunis, important figures in the PLO government-in-exile were watching closely the changing face of the Israeli political scene. Their interest was born of necessity. Yasser Arafat's unwise decision to support Saddam Hussein in the Gulf War had had disastrous political and economic consequences for his people. Outraged Arab leaders in the Gulf, afraid that Iraq's seizure of oil-rich Kuwait was just the prelude to more predatory attacks across the region, abhorred the action of the PLO leader. They abruptly cut off their generous financial backing for the organization and began expelling Palestinian workers.

The PLO was faced with hardship; its bureaucracy, its schools, and its hospitals depended on the generosity of its Arab brothers. Within the Palestinian community Arafat found himself under increasing criticism for his mishandling of the Iraqi situation and his dictatorial style of government. The mood around him grew acrimonious and divisive. The PLO's weakness at the end of the Gulf War had let the Americans push successfully to set up peace talks. Arafat had no option but to back them, yet he and the PLO had been effectively sidelined, excluded from the process. New Palestinian leaders were being groomed to take over and he suspected the motives of this new, younger breed of moderate professionals. They cleverly trod the tightrope of loyalty to the PLO while seeming independent to the outside world, but the whole set-up was basically flawed. Arafat knew the only long-term solution was to negotiate with Israel. He had an interest in bypassing the Washington forum, which was trying to ignore him, yet any alternative hidden track carried the risk of blowing up in his face. He had no time to waste. The PLO's finances were a closely guarded secret, an intricate and impenetrable web known only to Arafat himself, but it was public knowledge that they were dwindling fast and, like the money, the Chairman's luck was running out.

For some years, as Norway's contacts with the PLO in the early 1980s had made clear, Arafat had known there would have to be a deal with Israel, and that meant real coexistence with a Jewish state. Since the Palestinian National Council implicitly recognized Israel by its acceptance of UN Security Council Resolution 242 in 1988, the general course of PLO policy had been based on compromise and a piecemeal strategy towards the establishment of a truncated state. But the Chairman, juggling diverse factions in the cutthroat world of Palestinian politics, blew hot and cold, his motives always a mystery, even to those supposedly close to him. Yet in 1992 the signals sent by the changing climate in Israel, and indeed the world, convinced one of the highest-ranking moderates in the PLO, Mahmoud Abbas, that there was an opportunity to be seized.

A shrewd, silver-haired intellectual in his late fifties, Abbas, known as Abu Mazen, had risen to the number three position in the PLO largely owing to his ability to survive. As close confidants around the Chairman succumbed to the assassin's bullet or fell from favour, Abu Mazen became one of the few senior figures from the old days who was still around. This energetic and straight-talking man of stocky build, who chain-smokes stylishly from an ebony and gold holder, was a Fatah stalwart but had a reputation as a man of reason and moderation. In 1977 he had had the courage to appeal to the ruling body, the Palestinian

National Council, to allow contact with the enemy. Following his speech a resolution was passed permitting tentative links with what were termed 'democractic forces' in Israel, and Abu Mazen became the PLO's official Israel-watcher.

It was his responsibility to run the campaign known within the PLO as 'dividing the enemy camp', that is, trying to maximize the emerging feeling in some sectors of Israeli public opinion that the Palestinian problem had to be dealt with constructively. Abu Mazen's portfolio was to try to make contacts among anyone in Israel – peace campaigners, academics, left-wing politicians – prepared to flout the law of the country and meet members of the PLO. Abu Mazen knew the enemy well: his doctoral thesis was on Zionism, he had written books about Israel's political parties, and was well versed in the public statements Israel had made and the hints those statements gave of changing views.

When Labour was elected in June 1992, Abu Mazen noted Yitzhak Rabin's indication that he was ready to negotiate autonomy for the Palestinians. He also saw with interest that the former general was prepared to differentiate between Jewish settlements with a military or strategic purpose and those which had been established for political reasons, to maximize the Jewish population in parts of the West Bank. The latter, he said, he would halt. Most significantly Rabin did not pointedly refer to the disputed areas in biblical terms as Judea and Samaria, as his Likud predecessors had – so stressing Israel's historical claim. Instead he called them, factually, Gaza and the West Bank, the names by which the areas were known to the Palestinians and the outside world. To Abu Mazen these were hopeful signs that a tentative approach by the PLO might not be rebuffed, as all approaches had been hitherto. He decided to use a mutually acceptable intermediary, the government of Egypt, to act as a go-between. On 9 October 1992 he wrote a letter to Amr Moussa, the Egyptian Foreign Minister who enjoyed cordial relations with Rabin, suggesting he approach Israel with a view to setting up a secret channel for negotiations. The answer came back and it was negative; it was too premature and Rabin was not in favour.

While Abu Mazen pursued links through the Egyptians, another member of the PLO, Ahmed Qurei, was also thinking about the future, the economic rather than the purely political outlook. Qurei, known as Abu Ala, was the financial brains of the PLO, the director of Samed, the investment fund underpinning the PLO's economy.

From a body founded to provide work for the families of guerrillas killed in action, Samed had developed into one of Lebanon's major industrial employers. Its network of thirty-six factories produced everything from shoes and clothes to furniture and foods. Under Abu Ala, Samed had also built up a significant investment portfolio, trading in commodities and land in African and Arab countries. Ultimate control of this empire rested with Arafat, who insisted on retaining control over even the minutest details, but Abu Ala had built a reputation as a shrewd and discreet financial manager, in his running of the fund's affairs.

Samed means 'steadfast' in Arabic but the PLO's finances in 1992 were anything but steadfast. Although no one but Yasser Arafat really knew just where the money came from, where it went and what the balance sheet looked like, Abu Ala was the next best placed to appreciate the dire economic forecast. With his experience of international finance and the practicalities of running a large factory complex, Abu Ala was that rare combination: a banker and a street-smart operator. Sophisticated, a warm and charming companion, he could be tough and ruthless too. He had been working with Palestinian economists on a detailed plan for the difficult years to come. And he had written an unusually pragmatic document looking ahead to the peace dividend to be reaped once the central dispute over land was settled. In this paper Abu Ala advocated economic cooperation on a regional basis in the Middle East, and included Israel in the picture. It was a far cry from the usual pariah status accorded to the Jewish state by many Arabs, and Abu Ala's work was read with interest in many European countries, including Norway. On 28 February 1992 he had been to Oslo on a visit to try and prise more money out of Jan Egeland, specifically for the PLO. Egeland politely pointed out that Norway would aid only humanitarian, not political, appeals but he was impressed with Abu Ala and so was his colleague Mona Juul.

That February afternoon the telephone rang at FAFO's headquarters in a quiet street in Oslo: 'Terje, it's Mona, you have to meet this man who just came here to the Ministry. He's called Abu Ala from the PLO in Tunis and I just know you'll have a lot in common.'

Mona Juul proved to be right. When Larsen met Abu Ala there

was the 'click', just as there later would be with Beilin. Larsen explained about his Palestinian survey and his desire to develop links between the two sides. Abu Ala was immediately alerted to the possibilities. He urged Larsen to do his best to persuade the Israelis, and assured him that he and other high-ranking PLO officials would back him. Larsen felt the energy of the man and he recognized that, although he was in his late fifties, he thought and spoke intuitively, unlike the old guard of the PLO. He communicated superbly in accented but fluent English and his charm could bowl you over, his laugh was hearty and he had a twinkle in his eye. He was short and balding but always immaculately dressed in dark, well-cut suits, subdued ties and expensive shoes. In short, said Mona, he was a perfect gentleman. She and Terje both decided that Abu Ala was someone they would like to see more of, and soon. How soon and how much more of him they would see in the months to come was something they could scarcely have imagined.

In Israel copies of Abu Ala's paper on regional development circulated at government level. Yossi Beilin and others in the Foreign Ministry were impressed; not only was this a realistic document, it implicitly supported the idea of economic coexistence and cooperation with Israel.

In the autumn of 1992, while Prime Minister Rabin was rejecting Abu Mazen's overtures through Egypt, Yossi Beilin went ahead with his plans to meet with Faisal Husseini in Oslo. Egeland's office tried to set up dates in October, November and December, but Beilin was busy and the Norwegians found it impossible to pin down Husseini's rather chaotic schedule. They concluded that there was still a reluctance on both sides. In fact there was no need for the Norwegians to be involved in establishing links between Beilin and Palestinian figures from East Jerusalem. Those contacts already existed and, through Yair Hirschfeld, could be explored in Israel. It was becoming clear to Yossi Beilin that real progress could only be made if the Israelis and the PLO engaged in a direct dialogue. He was pushing hard to remove the biggest hurdle, the law against contacts with Arafat and his people in Tunis. He had worked behind the scenes to change his project from a Labour Party into a government issue, and on 2 December 1992 a bill to revoke the statute received its first reading in the Knesset, the Israeli parliament.

2

The Creation of the Oslo Channel

The scene now shifted to a wintry London. On 3 and 4 December 1992 the British capital played host to the multilateral talks that were part of the Madrid peace process. The subject was economic issues and the coordinator of the Palestinian delegation was Abu Ala. The rules oᶠ the game dictated that as a PLO man he could not be seen to be directly involved, although everyone, including the Israelis, knew that he was masterminding the Palestinian response, sitting in his hotel room and issuing orders down the phone in his usual autocratic style.

Three other key players were in London too. Yossi Beilin had come for the multilaterals and he had asked Yair Hirschfeld to be present in order for him to meet and talk with Arab delegates to the talks. Terje Larsen was also in London, he had agreed to meet Hirschfeld to discuss funding for academic projects in the Palestinian areas. The small research unit set up under Beilin's patronage was permanently strapped for cash, and Hirschfeld hoped Larsen could help him get a grant. Besides these three men, Dr Hanan Ashrawi, the elegant and feisty academic from the West Bank, was in London as the spokeswoman for the Palestinian delegation. Ashrawi now became the catalyst to get secret talks going, the one to give both reluctant sides the critical shove to get them moving in the right direction.

Hanan Ashrawi was determined that Hirschfeld and Abu Ala should meet each other. Both men were active in the economic field, and Ashrawi knew of Hirschfeld's links with Beilin and thought the contact would be useful. She rang them both to try and persuade them. Hirschfeld was reluctant; it was against the law and Yossi Beilin had been most explicit on that subject. He agreed to give Hanan the phone number of his cousin's house where he was staying. Meanwhile Ashrawi told Abu Ala that the

Israeli wanted to speak to him and that with his government links he might prove a valuable contact. Although Abu Ala was hesitant, he was persuaded by Ashrawi and that evening he called Hirschfeld.

Hirschfeld had great doubts about the wisdom of a meeting with a PLO official. He thought it could prove useless anyway, and if it got out it would compromise Yossi Beilin. Moreover, he was not happy about breaking the law. But being a naturally impulsive, emotional character, when the PLO got in touch Hirschfeld decided to take the plunge. He said he would get back to them with a time and place to get together. Now came the problem of how to arrange a secret meeting, maybe more than one. He naturally thought of Larsen, the Norwegian academic who seemed so keen to help, the man to whom Beilin had introduced him. Larsen was a man who inspired confidence, and the Israeli trusted him. So he called to ask Larsen what he knew about Abu Ala and when and where they should meet. Larsen suggested 10.00 a.m. the next day at his hotel, the Cavendish near Piccadilly Circus, where he had been going to see Hirschfeld that morning anyway.

The next morning a very excited and anxious Yair Hirschfeld, who had had a sleepless night, sat for hours with Larsen in the window-seat of the first-floor coffeeshop in the Cavendish. The elegant, pale green façade of Fortnum and Mason's department store across the street was reflected in the large hotel window. Beneath them Christmas shoppers bought hand-made shirts and fancy toiletries in the emporia of Jermyn Street. Larsen reassured Hirschfeld that he would be of service, wherever and whenever he was needed.

'Don't worry, you'll get along just fine. I'm sure there'll be a personal rapport between you, he's that kind of man. I cannot speak officially for the Norwegian government but, as you know, my contacts are pretty good and if you want to hold further meetings I can help you, facilitate your contacts and so on.'

Larsen suggested that he should not be present at the meeting. If it did not go well, then that would be the end of it and Hirschfeld would be able to deny the contact more easily if no one else had witnessed it. Fifteen minutes before Abu Ala was due to arrive, Larsen slipped away, praying that he had built up the Israeli's confidence sufficiently to prevent him from bolting at the last minute. Just after ten Abu Ala arrived with Afif Safieh, the eloquent and ebullient PLO man in London, whom Abu Ala had brought along for moral support. Hirschfeld introduced himself and began to talk of Abu Ala's economic paper, saying he liked the concept of it. Then they began to discuss the situation in Washington.

'There just isn't any progress, don't you agree? What can we do? Both sides must come up with something,' said Hirschfeld.

The two men agreed that the talks sponsored by the State Department seemed futile. Hirschfeld found Abu Ala outspoken and dynamic, with lots of personal charm. He seemed determined to reach some understanding and, although his thinking was clearly influenced by the usual ideological concepts of the PLO, this man seemed to distinguish between dreams and reality. Hirschfeld sensed that he wanted to explore what was really possible.

'Can we meet and talk again? Perhaps in Oslo?' he ventured.

'Why Oslo?' Abu Ala was somewhat mystified. 'And I have to ask you who you really are and who you speak for.'

'I am no one official,' said Hirschfeld firmly. 'I am not authorized by anyone and I am only speaking to you informally. It's my own idea, no one else's.'

'To be frank, what's the point, then, of further talk, in Oslo or anywhere, if you have no official status?' said Abu Ala bluntly.

The talk turned to more general matters but Hirschfeld deliberately let it slip that he was due to have breakfast with Yossi Beilin the next day. That aroused Abu Ala's interest. Beilin was the Deputy Foreign Minister, close to Peres, one of the circle of doves inclined to accommodation with the Palestinians.

The two men agreed to talk again that evening and Hirschfeld went to find Yossi Beilin to tell him what he had done. He had not informed him beforehand that he intended to meet a high-ranking PLO official. It was still illegal and Hirschfeld was prepared now to be told, as he put it, to 'go to hell' if Beilin thought the risks too great. But Yossi did not forbid him to meet the PLO again. He was confident that the bill legalizing contacts would become law within weeks and he knew that, with Larsen and the Norwegian government poised to act as go-betweens, it was an opportunity they could not afford to miss. So with Beilin's approval, Hirschfeld made another rendezvous with Abu Ala, this time at the Ritz Hotel. Before they met, another chance encounter strengthened Hirschfeld's hand. He bumped into Dan Kurtzer, top official at the State Department responsible for the multilaterals on the US side. He told him about his contact with Abu Ala; Kurtzer asked to see Hirschfeld the next day and told him he would ascertain the American reaction to this new development.

Hirschfeld and Abu Ala met at the Ritz at 8.00 p.m. The cocktail hour was in full swing beneath the ornate gold and pink ceiling of the Palm Court. Couples were dancing as the waiters in dark green tailcoats took orders from the crowded tables. Yair Hirschfeld, feeling rather awkward in this glamorous place, was afraid they might attract undue attention. He was all for going to a small Italian restaurant round the corner. But Abu Ala, a cosmopolitan traveller with a taste for luxury hotels, felt quite at home and he insisted they stay. They found a corner and sat down to talk. Hirschfeld mentioned he had seen Dan Kurtzer and had fixed a meeting with him for the next day. Abu Ala was impressed with the Israeli's contacts and told Hirschfeld he would think about the idea of establishing an unofficial channel for communications through Oslo.

Abu Ala, who had been taken by surprise by the sudden request from an Israeli for a meeting in London, had not had an opportunity to get instructions from Tunis. On his return he went to see Abu Mazen, the man in charge of relations with Israel, and also a personal friend. Abu Ala explained what had happened and gave his analysis. Things were at a very early stage, he warned, but perhaps a secret contact could be developed. Hirschfeld was obviously a friend of Beilin's and had been in touch with him in London – he even knew Peres. Abu Ala thought the Americans either were involved or had given their blessing because of the Kurtzer connection which Hirschfeld had been careful to point out. And lastly the fact that Norway seemed to be included in the picture was encouraging. Abu Ala did not believe this small country would create diplomatic problems for the USA; Norway had no ambitious global policies and was an ally of the United States and a NATO member. Both men also knew that Norway was in a unique position with regard to both Israel and the Palestinians. Perhaps the Americans were even using Norway to explore contacts with the PLO, as the US had formally broken off relations with Arafat in 1990 following an abortive terrorist raid.

Two weeks later Terje Larsen went to Tunis. His fieldwork in

Gaza and the West Bank was over. He had wanted to visit the PLO earlier but was afraid that if he did so the Israeli authorities would make difficulties for his researchers on the ground. So he had waited until the long process of interviewing 2,500 large Palestinian families was over. Yossi Beilin encouraged him to go, saying he was very interested in Larsen's evaluation of the people there. In Tunis, Abu Ala was one of the PLO officials on Larsen's itinerary. There were others present at their meeting, but it was clear to Larsen that Abu Ala had little interest in his survey and was anxious to talk to him about something else.

'I'd like to speak to Mr Larsen alone.' Abu Ala's voice was abrupt.

Everyone left the room, except the PLO representative in Oslo who had been invited to the meeting. He assumed he should stay. Now Abu Ala glared at him and, rather bewildered, the man withdrew. He did not dare to ask Larsen later what had taken place after he had left the room.

Abu Ala began by asking whether Norway could facilitate contacts with the Israelis. He was interested in Yossi Beilin. He told Larsen that when he had met Hirschfeld in London they had talked about setting up a series of contacts through Oslo. The Palestinian wanted to know more about Hirschfeld and his links.

Larsen vouched for him, stating that the Israeli was well connected and that he was 'Beilin's man'.

Then Abu Ala came directly to the point. 'Clearly, if there were to be contacts it would be absolutely necessary to keep them secret, to have a secret channel. Can FAFO help? You have access to facilities and I know about your connections with your Foreign Ministry. Can they set something up using FAFO as a front?'

Abu Ala was remarkably candid with Larsen. He told the Norwegian that Abu Mazen knew of the London meeting but he warned him not to speak about this matter with anyone in the PLO. Larsen knew the risk that Abu Ala was taking: powerful figures within the PLO were staunchly opposed to this kind of initiative. Larsen assured the Palestinian that he would follow up his request as soon as he got home.

That evening Larsen had his first encounter with the Chairman of the PLO. It was a somewhat bewildering occasion, for Arafat had suffered a minor stroke two weeks before and had not fully recovered. Abu Ala was in the room too; he indicated to Larsen that he should sit in one of the deep armchairs in the corner of Arafat's spacious office. Arafat was sitting on an upright chair a few feet higher than Larsen; he seemed stiff and distracted, staring off into space. Larsen tried to introduce himself, using Arafat's more familiar name in Palestinian circles: 'Abu Ammar, I am a close friend of your brother Fathi, in Cairo ...' He tailed off as the Chairman continued staring past him. Again he tried, with no response, and Abu Ala motioned him to continue. The third time he had no more luck; then suddenly the Chairman roused himself, pushed a button on the desk and a terrified-looking man appeared in the doorway, saluted and clicked his heels. Arafat yelled at him in Arabic and the man looked more and more frightened. Then he almost ran from the room. Abu Ala was looking discreetly at the floor.

Larsen recovered his voice: 'Abu Ammar, what has that man done to make you so angry with him?' he ventured.

'Mr Larsen,' came the answer, 'I am a democrat. I always let anyone speak, whatever he wants to say. But when it comes to implementing things I am a dictator. That man has done great wrong. He will be punished.'

For Larsen this was a salutary lesson in Arafat's style of government, and the careful path that those around him must tread. The evening went better after that. Arafat regaled Larsen, always a sympathetic listener, with tales of his early political career, his admiration for Zhou Enlai, the Chinese Communist leader, and his views of Fidel Castro's problems. Then he spoke of his disappointment that the Swedish socialist government, sympathetic to the PLO, had recently been defeated at the polls. His next words seemed to have a special meaning. 'Mr Larsen, Norway must now take over Sweden's role. I hope you will convey this message to your government when you return.'

There were others in the room apart from Arafat, Abu Ala and himself. Larsen sensed that Arafat did not want to be more specific, but he felt the Chairman was asking him to establish a role for Norway as a go-between. However, Arafat's behaviour earlier on had also left his visitor with an uneasy feeling that he might be losing his grip. Larsen was concerned that the PLO might be drifting and he feared therefore that Abu Ala and Abu Mazen might be taking the decision to open clandestine talks with the Israelis on their own initiative. Later he learnt otherwise.

By now Larsen had realized the PLO was the only body who could negotiate for the Palestinian people. The new leaders in the Occupied Territories were not the answer; they had no muscle. At grass-roots level it was Arafat who still exercised power over his people's minds and hearts. Over the months, he had noticed, as he tried to arrange things with Husseini, that Tunis always called the shots. His conclusion was that however outdated the top echelons of the PLO might be, however divorced from reality they seemed, there would be no solution without them. In his four-hour meeting with Abu Ala he was again charmed by this man who was a light in the dark compared to the old-style *apparatchiks* in the PLO.

Despite Larsen's fears, Abu Mazen had consulted Yasser Arafat after Abu Ala had informed him of what had taken place in London. He told him that someone connected to the Israeli delegation at the multilaterals had made an approach. And he bluntly advised the Chairman that this was an opportunity they could not afford to miss. They had been rebuffed too often. Abu Ala should go to Oslo for further talks. Yasser Arafat agreed; it was just one of many leads he was pursuing and at this stage there was no reason to think the Oslo initiative would come to anything.

In Norway Larsen, Juul and Egeland hit the phones to Jerusalem to cajole Beilin into following up the ideas he had discussed with Larsen and taking the London meetings further. Beilin assured Jan Egeland that Hirschfeld was authorized by him. But Beilin insisted he had to have what he called 'full deniability'. If news of the secret meetings leaked, Beilin would have to be able to deny having any knowledge of them. For Beilin there were considerable risks. He had decided to keep to himself, for the time being, the idea of a secret channel parallel to the Washington talks, a channel run from Oslo. If Hirschfeld, an Israeli citizen, was prepared to meet a PLO official with a view to discussing the many sensitive issues that divided them, that would suit his purpose but it could not be seen to have been set up by the Deputy Foreign Minister.

But while the calls went to and fro between Oslo and Jerusalem, a huge international row erupted over an Israeli action that made peace an even more distant prospect. On 18 December Yitzhak Rabin, just six months into office, decided to show his renowned iron fist. He deported 417 Palestinians accused of supporting Hamas, the Islamic resistance movement. The expulsions were in retaliation for the murder of an Israeli border guard. The Palestinians were escorted by the army over the northern border into Israel's self-declared security zone in southern Lebanon. It was a bitterly cold desert winter and they had little food or shelter. 'Deportations Kill Peace Talks' screamed the headlines; there was international outrage and Israel was warned that it was jeopardizing the Washington peace process. Arab delegates boycotted the final session of the current round of negotiations and the PLO said the talks would not continue unless Israel revoked its order. It was clear that the Palestinian delegation would not be allowed by Tunis to attend the next round in January.

For both the Palestine Liberation Organization and the Israelis, Hamas casts the militant spectre of Islam over a conflict already complex and intractable enough as a fight between competing nationalisms. In the refugee camps of Gaza, the bedrock of despair proved fertile ground for Hamas to breed on. By 1992 the movement had grown in strength and was threatening the mainstream secular Fatah movement of the PLO. Hamas allows no accommodation with Israel and therefore rejects the peace process. The message of Hamas is that the whole of former Palestine must be for the Palestinians alone, and that ultimately Israel must be driven into the sea. While the PLO may have been, privately, not unhappy with Rabin's uncompromising stand on the deportation of its political rivals, it could not afford to admit publicly to any splits in Palestinian ranks. Arafat was concerned to present as broad a front as possible – national solidarity in the face of Israeli repression. And so the threat to boycott the peace talks.

In the early 1980s the Israelis, in an attempt to undermine the PLO, had allowed Islamic activists to open a network of mosques and welfare associations. But they could no longer control the monster they had helped to create. Inexorably support for Hamas grew amongst the young and dispossessed. And now, with alarm, Israel watched Hamas taking over; the PLO was being forced to bow to pressure from grass-roots activists to take a harder line. Some in Israel realized that it might not be long before a weakened Arafat and his PLO would no longer be there to do a deal with. The nightmare scenario whereby the Islamic hard-liners would become the dominant force began to haunt them. Voices on the Left of Mr Rabin's coalition government began to urge that the only way to deal with the fundamentalist tide was to negotiate directly and openly with the PLO.

In Jerusalem, as 1992 drew to a close, Yossi Beilin was faced with the considerable international fallout from Rabin's deportations. He remained insistent that any meeting with the PLO could not be seen as negotiations, or even talks. Rather, it must be a wide-ranging discussion of the issues. Hirschfeld was not official and he could not speak for the Israeli government, therefore the notion of negotiations was premature. By the time the Norwegians succeeded in persuading Beilin to sanction the first meeting in Oslo, 1993 had dawned.

The Oslo Channel had its first, tentative, green light. Now Larsen had to devise a cover story, organize the meeting-places and the logistics – and find the money to pay for it all. He did not know whether there would be just one meeting, how long it would last and whether enough progress would be made to justify a follow-up. He had no clear idea of what he was getting into.

Larsen decided that the FAFO living-conditions study would provide a good cover. The visitors from both sides could be academics taking part in the survey. He did not inform the Board of FAFO that its organization would be fronting secret talks between Israel and the PLO; he took the risk that these meetings would not arouse much attention. Jan Egeland at the Foreign Ministry approved the plan and agreed to find public funds to pay for hiring meeting-places, providing hospitality and all the other myriad expenses.

Yair Hirschfeld and an assistant were put on the FAFO payroll. They had no money to pay their own way and could not raise any. They had agreed with Yossi Beilin that, at this stage, it was vital their actions should not be traced either to him or to the Israeli government. They had to be willing – and it had to be possible – for their involvement to be denied if things went wrong. Therefore they could not be paid for by official sources.

Larsen was taking a considerable risk. His left-of-centre institute was run on scrupulously democratic lines. Everything was normally above board, and openly discussed. If what he was doing were discovered, he was sure he would be accused of crazy irresponsibility. He would probably lose both his job and the institute he had founded and worked for years to build into Norway's premier think-tank. But Larsen was convinced that the only way to keep the meetings secret was to limit the number of people in the know to just a handful.

Foreign Minister Thorvald Stoltenberg had already informed the Prime Minister of Norway, Gro Harlem Brundtland, of his initiative and had received her approval. He decided to leave the details to Jan Egeland who kept him briefed on progress. Mona Juul was the only other person in the Foreign Service who was involved. She and Egeland knew they would have enormous difficulties keeping it from their colleagues, professional diplomats used to reading volumes of meaning into every chance word or meeting behind closed doors.

It was perhaps presumptuous of this small group of Norwegians to think they could help solve one of the world's long-standing and most intractable problems. If any Scandinavian government was identified with attempts to mediate in the Middle East, it was Sweden rather than Norway: for many years Sweden had enjoyed very public relations with the PLO. But in 1991 the Socialist government in Sweden was ousted and Foreign Minister Sven Anderson, who had strong PLO connections, acknowledged that the incoming Conservatives would shift their policy to a more equal footing between Israel and the Palestinians. Anderson told Egeland at the time that he was handing over the torch, as he put it, to Norway. The Socialist government in Oslo was uniquely placed because it had run a carefully balanced Middle East policy for years now, and was trusted by both sides.

But there was nervousness in the Norwegian Foreign Ministry about the reaction of the Americans. They were the pre-eminent player in the region, widely seen as the protectors of Israel and the only power with sufficient influence to sway the Arabs. In November 1992 Egeland had taken the precaution of informing Dan Kurtzer of the State Department that Norway was in a position to establish links between some Israeli and Palestinian figures. Kurtzer was not disapproving; he admitted the progress of talks in Washington was slower than he had hoped and asked Egeland to keep him informed. He said America would not oppose the secret meetings in Oslo as long as it was clear they had not encouraged Norway to involve the PLO directly. This contact between the Americans and the Norwegians was the first of several in which the small Scandinavian country played a clever hand: clearing its actions without revealing any details that would alarm the Americans, or even alert them to what was really happening.

Right from the start the Norwegians recognized that secrecy was the number one requirement for the kind of negotiations they were setting up. They knew the failure of the talks in Washington was in large part due to the intense publicity which surrounded them. From the moment the Madrid peace process began in the Spanish capital, and as the circus moved to Washington, with appearances in Moscow and other cities, discussions had been conducted before the cameras of the world. Both sides took great care to choose their spokesmen and women for their media-friendly qualities. Every day the ritual of arrivals and departures at the State Department was broken several times for press conferences and set-piece statements. This had the effect of hardening each side's position. Once Israelis or Palestinians revealed what the hitches were, and defended their stance before a worldwide audience, it was difficult to change it or even to exhibit flexibility, for fear of being seen to back down. So the talks degenerated into sterile posturing and formulaic insults, presented day after day on the television and in the papers. As a result, little or no progress was being made.

Larsen had observed this and decided that the talks in Norway had to be kept secret. Shielding the participants completely from the media was the only answer. Both sides knew that other behind-the-scenes meetings, which might have borne fruit, had been blown apart once the press got to hear about them. Publicity also alerted special interest groups on both sides, groups which had often been deliberately kept in the dark to prevent sabotage attempts. The PLO was particularly sensitive to this. It was notoriously faction-ridden and its attempts to establish discreet contacts had often been derisively rejected by the Israelis because of the near impossibility of maintaining secrecy.

In putting such emphasis on a secret channel for discussions, Larsen was drawing on his own experience of trade union politics in Norway. In his country the political structure between capital and labour is very different from that in Britain, America, France or Italy. Both sides see that there are conflicting interests, but there is also common ground. In Norway a negotiating structure exists, which means there are few strikes. Compromise and a recognition of the national interest are the country's guiding principles. Larsen argues that the result of this has been responsible wages bargaining, sustaining a steady growth economy, which in turn has supported the country's extensive welfare state. The tradition has always been that, when the going gets tough, the chairman of the Congress of Trade Unions and the chairman of the Businessmen's Union get together over a quiet dinner and resolve the problems. There is thus a permanent clandestine channel in Norwegian labour relations acting as a safety valve.

It was natural, therefore, for Larsen to think in terms of front, or public, channels and back, or secret, channels when it came to the problem of the Middle East. The Oslo Channel was envisaged by the Norwegians as the back channel to the public Washington negotiations. Their aim was to build confidence and respect in private, and perhaps suggest some solutions that could be implemented through the public channel.

As well as the secrecy, there was another essential difference between the American and the Norwegian approach. Egeland and Larsen were determined their country would play the role of facilitator, not mediator. The Norwegians would bring the parties together, use their good offices to promote trust and explain the difficulties each side faced to the other party. If the meetings developed into negotiations they would not take a position on the substance of the talks, or suggest the routes that should be taken. They would, therefore, not actually negotiate or even actively participate in negotiations, but they would be there at all times to help smooth the way. For the Norwegians, the most important precondition to the setting up of their secret channel was the willingness of both the Palestinians and the Israelis to approach the talks in good faith. They had to be ready to do a deal; then the Norwegians would be prepared to help them reach an accommodation, by building trust and using their unbiased stance to interpret and clarify positions when the going became difficult.

The prerequisite of secrecy would present numerous logistical difficulties for all concerned. The Norwegians would have to get Israelis and Palestinians in and out of the country by the normal routes without activating diplomatic channels. Any VIP party would raise interest and curiosity and that meant the risk of leaks. The Israelis and Palestinians would have to make their way unobtrusively, by randomly chosen routes, from Tel Aviv and Tunis to Oslo – hardly, like Frankfurt or London, the hub of European air connections. Once in Norway they would have to be accommodated in a discreet location suitable for meetings, not too remote and with good phone links back to their respective capitals.

Terje Larsen's personal contacts yielded the first location for the meetings. A friend of his, Jens P. Heyerdahl, is Managing Director of the Orkla Group, a large industrial conglomerate. Its pulp-producing factory is at Sarpsborg, south of Oslo: the company owns an old mansion there, called Borregaard. Larsen had been to parties and seminars at the house and thought it would be perfect. He called his friend and asked to hire it for some unspecified international political activity. Heyerdahl said that he trusted him, he would not enquire any further, and the house and its small staff were put at Larsen's disposal.

Having found a location, Larsen decided to let one more person in on the secret, someone who could act as driver and help him with the arrangements. He chose one of the young researchers at his institute, Even Aas. Two days before the Israelis and Palestinians were due to arrive, Larsen took Aas aside and explained what they were going to do, swearing him to secrecy and asking him to help. It would be difficult for Even. As well as a full-time research post he also had an unusual and time-consuming after-hours job – training the Norwegian women's speed-skating team. And he was caring alone for a small daughter. But this slim, handsome twenty-six-year-old, who sports an earring, agreed to become the unlikely Chief of Protocol for the Oslo Channel. He hired two anonymous-looking cars in which to ferry the visitors around, he checked and rechecked the flight times and connections. Then, with trepidation and uncertainty, masked behind smiles and a reassuring air, Terje Larsen and Even Aas set off on a freezing Wednesday evening for the airport.

3

Brainstorming at Borregaard

The Israelis were the first to arrive that evening, 20 January. The day before, the Knesset had finally legalized contacts with members of the PLO but the idea of such a meeting was still a very alien and risky one. The row over the expulsions was still raging, with the deportees stranded in no man's land, on a hillside in southern Lebanon, in bitter wintry conditions. Yitzhak Rabin refused to relent as he waited for a High Court ruling to determine whether to reverse his decision. On the day that two very ordinary-looking Israeli academics turned up at Oslo's Fornebu Airport, the Arab nations and much of the Western world were protesting over Israel's harsh action.

Larsen had informed Yair Hirschfeld that the Palestinians would have a three-man delegation and suggested that the Israelis match this. But Hirschfeld brought only one companion, Ron Pundak, a close friend and associate who shared his ideals. He had already confided in Pundak the details of his meeting with Abu Ala in London, and felt that he was therefore the natural choice to accompany him. But, in the interests of secrecy, he resisted widening the Israeli group.

The two men had worked together for many years. Hirschfeld had once taught Pundak at university. After returning from his doctoral studies in London, Pundak had been persuaded to join his mentor and Yossi Beilin in their small research group. After Labour won the election, Pundak had been aware of the feelers extended by Hirschfeld, with Beilin's backing, and he was eager to come to Oslo to help Hirschfeld in any way he could. The two professors made an unlikely pair. Hirschfeld, absent-minded and permanently dishevelled, was at forty-nine the older of the two but at heart an enthusiastic youngster, always rushing hither and thither with some mad scheme in mind. Pundak, thirty-eight years old, was a small, bright, birdlike man with owlish spectacles and pronounced opinions. The Norwegians immediately christened them, privately, Laurel and Hardy, and it was an apt description. In public they were usually referred to as 'the professors', a reflection of their academic status and a slightly tongue-in-cheek reference to their less than slick appearance.

The Palestinian group arrived late the same night. Abu Ala had been careful to cover his tracks. He had bought a return ticket from Tunis to Geneva. Once in Geneva he purchased another ticket for a side trip to Oslo. With him came two men, Maher El Kurd and Hassan Asfour. Maher El Kurd, an economist, had worked in Abu Ala's office and was trusted to be discreet. His English was also excellent. More recently he had been working for Arafat: his purpose in the delegation was to be Arafat's eyes and ears. Hassan Asfour was Abu Mazen's trusted assistant, an agricultural engineer by training. He came from Gaza, had been to university in Iraq and had studied Marxist doctrine in Moscow. A good-looking man aged forty-two, Hassan was slim and dark-haired with a moustache. A member of the Palestinian Communist Party, with a keen political sense, he spoke somewhat limited English but his eyes missed nothing. Abu Ala had chosen these men but their presence also reflected the authority of those in Tunis who were backing him.

The first hitch occurred even before the Palestinians met their Norwegian hosts. The immigration officials at Fornebu were suspicious of these three Arabs. Norway is a small and very homogenous country, with a tiny immigrant population. It is not an international hub and foreigners are noticeable and often treated as outsiders. Through the auspices of FAFO, it had been arranged that because the so-called academic visitors had no entry visas they would be granted emergency visas on their arrival and no fuss would be made. But the message was not passed on and the officials on duty kept the party waiting while they took away their passports and photocopied them.

When the Palestinians finally emerged to find Larsen waiting for them, a furious Abu Ala threatened to go straight home. Larsen was solicitous and conciliatory. He explained that in order to maintain strict secrecy they could not be given any special treatment or have their entry and their exit cleared in advance. It was a humbling experience for Abu Ala, a man who sets great store by rank and expects to be accorded proper respect. He had visited Norway several times before, but always officially, with red carpet treatment. Abu Ala was not convinced that Larsen's approach was the best way to handle things but decided to keep his criticisms to himself for the time being – after all, he reflected, the Norwegians were just learning the business of international negotiations.

Now the Palestinians embarked on a long drive through the snowy night to an unknown destination, the small town of Sarpsborg, two hours south of Oslo by car. They arrived at a large white house at the end of a long drive flanked by pine trees. It was now the early hours and after brief introductions they all went to bed.

The visitors awoke to find themselves in a beautiful old Norwegian wooden mansion called Borregaard, rich in Viking history. The saga writer Snorri tells how in 1016 a Viking king, Olaf the Holy, built a simple fortress on the promontory at the great waterfall called Sarp. Inside the fortress he established the basis of a town, Borg. His manor was the Manor of Borg, or Borregaard, and for three hundred years it was the residence of Norwegian kings, especially in winter. In the thirteenth century the estate lost its royal status and in 1702 it was hit by an even greater disaster. A landslide swept the whole estate into the river, killing fourteen people. It had to be rebuilt – this time on a safer, more solid site. In the nineteenth century a British architect, Sir John Henry Pelly, added a wing when the property came under English ownership. The mighty waterfall was still half owned by the estate and at the end of the nineteenth century a paper-mill was established down-river. And so the mill and Borregaard Manor eventually passed into the hands of the Orkla industrial group who, in 1988, restored it sympathetically to its former glory.

The agenda for the first morning had been arranged by the Norwegians along the lines of an academic seminar. Jan Egeland, Mona Juul and Marianne Heiberg, the co-author of the FAFO study, were due to arrive at noon by chauffeur-driven car. Heiberg and Larsen had travelled together many times to the Middle East while carrying out the FAFO survey. Heiberg's contacts in the Palestinian community were excellent but she had not been informed as to the real purpose of this gathering or the background of the people there. She was told that she was coming to talk about the FAFO study to a group of Israeli and Palestinian academics.

Before the other Norwegians arrived the two groups assembled somewhat awkwardly in the sitting-room. The Palestinians, with the exception of Abu Ala, seemed ill at ease. They looked very formal in immaculate suits and ties. The Israelis were more friendly and more casually dressed; Ron Pundak was wearing his favourite blazer with a golfer embroidered on the pocket. Hirschfeld's ample frame was squeezed into a jacket and baggy trousers. Larsen asked them to sit down. He wanted to establish the ground rules the Norwegians had decided on:

'If you two are going to manage to live together, you've got to solve this problem between you. You own the problem. If you need some help from us, please ask for it. We can provide money, houses, services – and we can be intermediaries on the phone. After lunch you should go into the meeting room and I will wait for you outside – unless you get into fisticuffs!'

His final comment raised a laugh, as he intended it to.

After lunch Marianne Heiberg outlined the progress of the survey to the assembled group. The Israelis and Palestinians listened politely but, as one of them said later: 'We couldn't give a damn.' During the talk Mona pushed little notes across to her husband: 'They're just going through the motions, try and cut it short!'

Heiberg was in full flow but Larsen broke in with thanks, and asked if there were any questions. Two rather unenthusiastic queries ensued and then the seminar broke up. Then Egeland, Juul and Heiberg returned to Oslo, leaving Terje Larsen with the Israelis and the Palestinians. Although Egeland was only at Borregaard for a few hours, both parties were impressed that Norway's Deputy Foreign Minister had devoted time to them and entertained them over lunch. It was a sign that their meeting was sanctioned at a high level and that Egeland would be expecting a report back on the progress made. For the Israelis it put the entire endeavour on a significant plane. For although Yossi Beilin, the Israeli Deputy Foreign Minister, was not physically present at Borregaard, he was there in spirit, and they felt that somehow Egeland's presence established a connection between political decision-makers.

That afternoon the five Israelis and Palestinians adjourned with Larsen to the comfortable sitting-room on the first floor. They lit a fire and settled down on the large red velvet sofas either side of a low coffee table. Behind them, above the piano, a large portrait of Jens Werenskield, who had rebuilt Borregaard in

1702, gazed benignly down on the group meeting with the task of rebuilding trust and understanding between their peoples. The group tried to insist that Larsen stay, but he quietly left the room. Then Abu Ala, in his typical, rather formal, style, launched the proceedings with a carefully prepared speech in Arabic. Hirschfeld understood a fair bit of Arabic and listened attentively to the words and then to the English translation provided by Maher.

Abu Ala had resigned himself to the fact that the PLO could not be part of any negotiations on an official level with Yossi Beilin or the Israeli government. His instinct for politics told him, however, that he had to accept this academic exercise they had embarked on, and use it as a means to create something more significant. Now he began by telling Hirschfeld and Pundak that they must first draw lessons from Washington and the impasse there. That meant rejecting any historical approach to their problems.

'We have to deal directly with the issues,' he said, 'not go back to history – to repeat our history over and over again. We have our point of view – that Palestine is for the Palestinians. You have your point of view – that Israel is for the Jews. If we go back into history we will spend years arguing – without any achievements. We must go directly to the substance, to the points where we can agree and where we can't. We must take what we can agree and put it down and then go to where we have different points of view and find a way to deal with them. That's what we must do. We are not here to compete, to show who is cleverest or most intelligent. So many seminars end up as a competition between Israelis and Palestinians. We are here to find solutions.'

Hirschfeld replied in English, giving an impromptu speech without the aid of notes. He agreed with the Palestinian approach: they should decide which issues could be resolved now and identify those where flexibility was possible. Those where agreement seemed impossible should be postponed. Hirschfeld stressed, as he had before, that he was not an official representative and that therefore this meeting could in no way be seen as an exercise in negotiations. It was a chance to identify the common ground and the sensitive issues in order to work out what both sides called 'the mobiles and immobiles of negotiations'.

Although he gave no outward indication of the fact, Hirschfeld's attention had been drawn immediately to one concrete proposal Abu Ala had made: the peace process would have to start with the withdrawal of Israeli forces from the Occupied Territories. Abu Ala had suggested that this withdrawal should occur first in Gaza. The coastal strip would be a testing ground in which to work out the mechanics of returning control to the Palestinians. It was a concept that was bound to be attractive to the Israelis, something they could start to move on, and the PLO knew it. The fact that Abu Ala had proposed it at this early stage was a sign to Hirschfeld that he meant business and that something significant could grow out of this academic exercise at Borregaard.

The notion of handing back Gaza first had been publicly proposed by Shimon Peres in 1980. It had even been on the table at Camp David but the Egyptians had not been willing to consider it. Until now the Palestinians had flatly rejected it. They knew the Israelis were keen to rid themselves of the security nightmare and the enormous social problems of the overcrowded, violent piece of land, but they had not been prepared to accept what was called the 'Gaza First' option lest it become a trap. Gaza first could mean Gaza last, the only piece of land the Israelis would be willing to concede.

In that first meeting, which continued all afternoon and long into the night, the most significant decision of all was taken – one that would provide a framework for all the contacts and meetings yet to come. Abu Ala declared that this should not just be an academic meeting of minds, it should have an aim, a purpose. He proposed they work towards a 'Declaration of Principles'. Hirschfeld and Pundak agreed. Both sides knew it was a masterly suggestion; the idea was not to make a peace accord as such, but an agreement on how to reach agreement.

Hirschfeld considered the task before them, the 'mapping of the Rubicon', as he put it, an exploration of the whole terrain of their many and complex problems. For the Israelis a Declaration of Principles would be a very effective way of checking the details of the Palestinian position on each and every point at issue. Washington had proved there was no comprehensive settlement to be had, no overarching agreement. The best they could hope for was an interim accord to build trust, cooperation and mutual interests in order to help both sides agree on the final status of the disputed land. Step by step progress was the only answer. But even a Declaration of Principles would not be easy.

48

In Washington the delegations had been trying to grope towards such a statement but had had no success in bridging the gaps on many different points. Now this small group would attempt to begin that task, in the tranquil surroundings of Borregaard.

Over the next two days and nights both sides discussed this basic proposition. On the first day they talked right through the night and went to bed at 5.00 a.m. Larsen sensed that progress was being made but at this early stage was careful to stay well back from the proceedings. He had decided that the Norwegians would not go into any of the meetings unless the parties asked them to. They would stay outside, fetch and carry papers and arrange typewriters, computers and telephone links as they were needed. And his own role would be to build a feeling of trust and even relaxation by getting to know the individuals and helping them to know each other.

Larsen hovered endlessly in a state of ever-readiness to antici-pate any desire or whim that might suddenly strike one of the five men: coffee at 2.00 a.m., breakfast at three in the afternoon – nothing was ever too much to ask of him. It would become a per-manent way of life for Larsen in the coming months. His greatest contribution was made between the meetings when, four or five times a day, people came out for food or drinks and wanted to unburden themselves to a sympathetic ear. Larsen used his knowledge of Palestinian and Israeli fears and aspirations, not to arbitrate or put forward solutions, but rather to encourage the parties by convincing them that Norway understood their diffi-culties. He was reassuring and, to the amusement of both sides, confident that their discussions would bear substantial fruit. His conviction was flattering for his guests, even though they were privately very sceptical.

Larsen concentrated on creating a unique atmosphere around these and subsequent encounters. It was a combination of his personal charm and warmth and the all-important physical details. At Borregaard many of the meetings, particularly those late at night, took place in the comfortable sitting-room before a roaring fire. Sometimes the meetings split into small groups around the house. A favourite place was the small library at the end of the house, painted in a traditional and very restful shade of green. The room was lined with books, at its centre a massive grey slate chimney-piece. On the walls a nineteenth-century painting depicted a snowy Norwegian landscape, with men hauling logs. The scene outside the window that January in 1993 was much the same, as inside five people from far away argued over the fate of a small piece of sunbaked land in the Middle East.

Borregaard was to prove an extremely successful setting for the Oslo Channel. An ambience envelops the house which, although large and comfortable, is not ostentatiously luxurious or grand. The main rooms on the first floor are flooded with light and painted in bright and jewel-like colours – yellow, blue and green. The bleached floorboards are covered with large rugs and the furniture is upholstered in soft Nordic shades of blue and grey.

Food played an important role both in establishing the hospitality of the Norwegians and in introducing a social element into the proceedings. Larsen paid meticulous attention to seating plans, and Even Aas supervised the menus produced by the housekeeper, Palme Ericsen. Certain foods, like pork, were unacceptable to the dietary restrictions of both groups. Fish was popular, except with Hassan Asfour, as Even discovered at that first lunch when they all sat down to eat grilled Norwegian salmon with cream sauce and steamed potatoes. Asfour was picking at his food, and Even asked if he disliked it. Asfour grinned and said: 'In Gaza, you know, we are all fishermen and cannot stand the sight of fish.'

There was always good wine on offer, which pleased the connoisseurs amongst the guests. And there was plenty of whisky too; Johnnie Walker Black Label was the preferred brand. All these elements contributed to the atmosphere of a country house weekend: good food and company and stimulating discussion late into the night. The Israelis slept in bedrooms in the main house, the Palestinians in a small guest wing beyond. Larsen sat with the PLO men on the first night, while they drank endless cups of coffee, chatted, smoked and watched the news on the satellite channel CNN. It was his first introduction to the nocturnal hours the PLO keep. At last, at 4.00 a.m., he could stay awake no longer. He excused himself and went to bed.

Many of the brainstorming sessions actually took place in the wintry landscape, under the trees surrounding the house. All the participants, sometimes accompanied by Larsen, took long walks in the woods, arguing and discussing as they went.

Within the PLO delegation Abu Ala was clearly the boss, and

the other two deferred to him. Maher appeared to be an assistant. He said little but, when one of the Norwegians got him quietly into a corner for a chat, his views came across as moderate and his outlook seemed realistic.

Hassan Asfour was quite a different matter. Observing him at dinner the first night, Larsen felt his spirits sink. Asfour was clearly an unreformed communist with rhetoric to match. He represented the more traditional PLO view, referring in stern tones to the need to implement those UN resolutions flouted by Israel. He also talked frequently about the heroic struggle in which his people were engaged. Asfour seemed typical of the more thuggish elements of the PLO, and the Norwegians were not optimistic that he was the right choice for this mission. He seemed the opposite of the pragmatic, personally warm and charming Abu Ala. Though Abu Ala treated Hassan as a subordinate, there was clearly a more complex relationship between the two men.

Asfour was extremely well informed about every aspect of the Palestinian position on the various issues raised by the peace process. As Abu Mazen's assistant he was responsible for liaising with the official Palestinian delegation to the talks in Washington. He kept the records in the PLO computer of all the details of the negotiations, what had been proposed, agreed, disagreed and conceded. His help was vital for Abu Ala who, though a canny operator, lacked the detailed political knowledge that Asfour had at his fingertips.

The intensity of the talks at Borregaard was in marked contrast to the situation in Washington where formal meetings had often hardly got under way each day before it was time to break and return to the delegates' separate hotels for lunch and endless internal discussions. Several days could pass without there being any protracted period of negotiation. The Oslo Channel at this stage was little more than brainstorming, but the important fact was that the opposing sides were living, eating and above all working together. And there was an intensity to the discussions. Throughout the meals and the walks and late into the night the discussions ebbed and flowed. The two days allotted passed quickly by and it was time to leave.

4

The Sarpsborg Document

The three Palestinians returned to Tunis, the two Israelis to Jerusalem, to report their impressions of this academic exercise and to decide whether another meeting in Norway was justified. At PLO headquarters Abu Mazen was most anxious to hear Abu Ala's report. He wanted to know who the two Israelis were and for whom they spoke. The crucial factor was the authority behind the professors. How far up the chain of command did it extend? The PLO was gambling on a hunch that the Oslo discussion group would come to have more substance than its appearance suggested. Abu Ala told Abu Mazen he had come to the conclusion that Hirschfeld not only acted as Beilin's messenger but reported back to Peres too. The Israeli had been sent to test the waters for Peres and his group, who since the election had been openly pushing the peace process to the top of the Israeli political agenda.

Abu Ala had another intriguing theory, that Ron Pundak was Yitzhak Rabin's man, probably an operative from Mossad, the Israeli intelligence service, with orders to report back to the Prime Minister. Pundak's function was not only to assess the opposition but to spy on Hirschfeld, Peres's man. The rivalry between the two best-known political figures in Israeli life was common knowledge in Tunis. At Borregaard the Palestinians, watching the two men closely, had decided the Israeli delegation mirrored the two factions in Labour Party ranks. The truth was that this theory, while undoubtedly a reflection of Israeli political in-fighting, was also a mirror of the rivalry and suspicion endemic in PLO ranks. Arafat and the coterie around him would, all too frequently, plot to thwart each other. Lesser men were used, and then discarded, in the constant power struggles that characterized Palestinian politics.

Back in Norway, Larsen was, for the next two weeks, on the

receiving end of innumerable phone calls from both sides. Abu Ala demanded:

'Who are these men? Are they reporting to Peres or are they reporting to Beilin? Does Rabin know about it?' And then, conspiratorially:

'Because you know I notice that Pundak ... he is always watching Hirschfeld. He's reporting directly back.'

And then, a few hours later, an abrupt reversal:

'These Israelis are too adventurous, they're just setting us up. They have no contacts whatsoever. They are nothing.'

On the other side the Israelis were sceptical that the top figures in the PLO were really behind the initiative:

'Who is Abu Ala? Is he really handling this thing on his own? Is he really reporting to Arafat? Does Arafat know about this and do you believe him when he says he does?'

Then, five minutes later, another call:

'Does Abu Mazen know about this? Who is Abu Mazen anyway? And who's this extra Palestinian who turned up – Hassan Asfour? Check them out!'

Larsen could do little but offer reassurances. The Norwegians themselves were almost equally in the dark. Egeland had doubts about the Israeli professors. Larsen felt sure both sides were serious, but he had to admit that Hirschfeld and Pundak looked unlikely spearheads for a clandestine, and politically audacious, Israeli contact with the enemy, the PLO. And it was impossible to figure out who was the influence of the moment in the machiavellian manœuvrings that were the stuff of PLO politics. Abu Ala was a discreet technocrat rather than a well-known political figure, and the Norwegians knew almost nothing of Abu Mazen's background. But from the start they were determined to create trust, and that meant that everyone involved had to take the chance of backing unknown quantities. Larsen, Juul and Egeland determined to give both sides the benefit of the doubt.

In the modest two-storey building in Jerusalem housing the Israeli Foreign Ministry, Yossi Beilin received Yair Hirschfeld's verbal report of the January meeting in Oslo. The professor said the Palestinians had been most anxious to pass on the message that Gaza First was an option on the table.

As soon as he heard that, Beilin knew it was time to inform the Israeli Foreign Minister, Shimon Peres, of the secret channel. Peres was the man who had publicly voiced the notion of Israeli

withdrawal from Gaza as a first step towards Palestinian autonomy, and Beilin knew the Palestinian proposal would interest
him.

Shimon Peres was Israel's most prominent 'dove', a man who
had consistently pursued pease with his Arab neighbours. He
had long had a vision of what he called 'the new Middle East', of
an Israel at peace, in a union with Jordan and the Palestinians,
three countries cemented together by the fruits of economic
cooperation. In 1992, as Labour stood on the threshold of power
once more, Peres feared his country would be engulfed by the
sort of ethnic conflict that had torn apart the former Yugoslavia.
Terrorism still haunted his people, and the local Arab population
was expanding fast. Israelis risked being outnumbered, in the
land between the Mediterranean and the Jordan river. It was
now, in the twilight of his career, aged sixty-nine, that he was
appointed Israel's Foreign Minister by his old foe Yitzhak Rabin.

Everyone assumed that once Shimon Peres regained high
office the peace process would become his top priority. But the
big question remained his relations with the Prime Minister.
Would Peres pursue his own agenda alone, or would he involve
Rabin? On that question hung the likelihood of success. Once
before Peres had stood on the brink of a historic breakthrough. In
1987, when he was Foreign Minister in the government of
National Unity, he and King Hussein of Jordan, in secret negotiations, nearly established an agreement over the future of the
West Bank. But the Likud Prime Minister, Yitzhak Shamir, sabotaged the accord; Peres had kept him in the dark and he resented
it. Thus Peres had good reason not to embark on another clandestine peace mission. But he also had plenty of reason not to
trust Rabin, or to feel that he could work closely with him on this
secret mission.

Since the 1970s the two men had continually contested both
the Labour Party leadership and the premiership of the country.
An intense and bitter rivalry had developed between them, one
that thrilled and sometimes horrified the nation. In 1976 Peres
replaced Rabin after a political scandal forced the Prime Minister
from office. But a year later Peres led the Labour Party to defeat,
the first loss by the party since the founding of the state. He was
to become Prime Minister again and lose once more. In 1984 he
formed a coalition with the Likud Party in order to stay in power.
And in 1992, after a bruising fight, he again lost the Labour

leadership to Rabin. After the election in the summer of 1992, there were many who advised Rabin not to have Peres back in his Cabinet. Peres, who had been Defence Minister before, coveted that portfolio; but Rabin decided to make his old sparring partner Foreign Minister instead.

Yitzhak Rabin and Shimon Peres, the hawk and the dove, are poles apart. Rabin is a tough, austere ex-general shaped by forty years of soldiering, a brilliant military tactician, who laid the plans for Israel's dramatic victory over the combined Arab armies in the Six Day War. Many Israelis find Rabin's toughness reassuring; they believe they are safe with him. His iron-fisted reputation was enhanced during the Intifada when he called for the uprising to be met with 'force and might and beatings'. A lone wolf, with no time for small talk, Rabin is straightforward and direct: his mind engages on the details. Peres could not be more different. He is an intellectual and a dreamer, with a vision of the future and a love of the complex games of power and negotiation. In an account of his years in office, Rabin described his rival as 'an inveterate schemer', a tag that haunted Peres and fuelled the enmity between them. But Rabin, though hawkish, was not opposed to peace. He had made it his election pledge and had promised to deliver it within a year of taking office. 'Peace through security' had always been his motto. If the security of Israel could be assured, he would be prepared to give up land.

The Israeli press, who waited with bated breath to reveal the newest instalment of the country's most gripping political soap opera, were quick to note that Rabin kept the responsibility for the high-profile Washington talks for himself. He delegated to Peres the more mundane multilateral talks involving all the Arab countries and many Western nations. The Foreign Minister, all the commentators decided, had been effectively sidelined in the peace process. But Peres bided his time, and bit his tongue, when it came to questions about his relegation from the scene of negotiations with the Palestinians. It took him some months to reconcile himself to his position in the government hierarchy. Rather than fretting over the loss of influence, he decided to look ahead to the place he, and indeed his country, might occupy in history. He resolved to devote his energies not to undermining Rabin but to achieving a lasting peace. He knew that if the leadership appeared divided, it would be impossible to persuade the Israeli public to back a peace plan. It was essential that his past relationship with Rabin did not overshadow his operational freedom.

Peres was not overly concerned that he had been distanced from the American-sponsored bilateral talks in Washington: he considered the focus there was on old views and differences between the parties. In contrast, the multilaterals looked to the future, to establishing a foundation for a new regional framework. As a European-oriented Jew, Peres had no convictions that the Americans should, or even could, be the prime movers in the action. Neither did he share the belief of both the previous Prime Minister, Yitzhak Shamir, and Rabin that the way to make peace was to build up the local Palestinian leadership and freeze out Arafat and the PLO in Tunis. He thought this approach was just a way to divert Israeli public attention from previous failures. He believed it would be more productive to create a situation whereby Israel could negotiate with the PLO without trying to reshape it. But unlike Beilin, who had been driving towards direct negotiations between Israel and the PLO almost from the start of his career, Peres chose a different *modus operandi*. He had great faith in the ability of the Egyptians, the only Arab government to enjoy cordial relations with Israel, to sway the PLO. At the end of 1992, Peres asked President Mubarak, his adviser Osama El-Baz and Foreign Minister Amr Moussa to revitalize the peace process by acting as a conduit for his proposals to the PLO.

Peres knew that any dialogue with the PLO would have to be based on tempting Arafat with real estate – the lure of land. Allowing the Chairman back into the Occupied Territories would be an offer he could not refuse. For years Peres's thinking had centred on the notion of Israeli withdrawal from the Gaza Strip as a first move to draw the PLO into the peace process. Gaza was a security and social nightmare for the Israelis. The joke, in government circles, was that a bonus would be awarded to anyone who could work out how to get rid of Gaza. And the process of divesting Israel of Gaza would be relatively straightforward. The West Bank had developed an 'omelette demography', as Peres called it, a scrambled mixture of Jewish settlements interspersed with Arab villages. Whereas Gaza had a relatively small Israeli population.

However, the Palestinians had always rejected any Israeli suggestion of handing back the strip. Peres knew there would have to be a sweetener, the offer of part of the West Bank, the larger, more prosperous and more strategic part of the Occupied Territories. That would also allay Palestinian fears that accepting Gaza first could prove to be Gaza first and last – their only gain. Peres explained his theory to the Egyptians and asked them to sound out the PLO. He mentioned that a West Bank town might be included in the deal, Tulkarm, perhaps, or Jericho. He hoped that ideas which came via Mubarak would be more acceptable to Arafat; the Palestinians might even suggest those ideas back, through the Egyptians to the Israelis, as their own.

With the start of the new Labour government, in the autumn of 1992, Peres informed Rabin about the Egyptian connection he was forming, and of his conviction that the concept of Gaza First would be the key. In early January 1993 the two men had a meeting in which Peres tried to persuade Rabin that there needed to be a radical change in the Israeli approach towards the peace talks. It was no good imagining that the new-style leaders in the Palestinian delegation in Washington could ever deliver a peace agreement. 'We need to make a big step towards the PLO,' he told Rabin. 'As long as Arafat remains in Tunis he represents the Palestinian diaspora – and he will block the negotiations.'

Rabin listened but did not seem enthusiastic. Peres was not dismayed, Rabin had not rejected the idea out of hand. The Foreign Minister had laid the groundwork and he would wait to see what happened next.

He did not have to wait long. A couple of weeks later Yossi Beilin came to see him. He told Peres that he had initiated, through Hirschfeld, a direct dialogue with a high-ranking PLO official and that the Norwegians had arranged the first meeting, which had taken place in January. It had been an interesting exercise and not just an academic one. The Palestinians had put a proposal on the table which he knew would interest his boss. That proposal was Gaza First: it looked as if the PLO was on the hook. Beilin had taken a risk by not consulting Peres at the very start. But he knew the man and his way of thinking; indeed Beilin had been the creator of a magic circle around Peres.

Shimon Peres had always considered himself, as had many others, a man with a natural Presidential style. He collected like-minded acolytes around him. In 1984, when he became Prime Minister, the American press started referring to the 'Peres Boys', the young, bright élite who staffed his office. Yossi Beilin, who was the ringleader, introduced a new, American-style management. Uri Savir, Peres's press spokesman, created a slick, media-wise approach. Avi Gill, Peres's policy adviser, was another, later, recruit. Unlike their counterparts in other Israeli ministries, casually clad in sandals and open-necked shirts, the Peres team were snappy dressers, always sporting smart jackets and ties. And so the Peres Boys became known as the 'Blazers'. They attracted compliments, jealousy and criticism. Their low point came when Peres lost the 1988 election – people said the Blazers had put him out of touch with ordinary Israelis. But the Oslo Channel was to be their finest hour.

The Foreign Minister was interested to learn of his protégé's initiative. Peres already had a clear concept of the way to peace, made up of three components. First, Israeli withdrawal from Gaza as an opening gambit. Secondly, postponing the very difficult issues to the future, when the final status of the Occupied Territories would have to be decided. Thirdly, building a strong foundation of economic cooperation. He now saw that the Oslo Channel could be the vehicle to carry these concepts to a conclusion, a peace accord. He would marry his ideas with Beilin's secret channel and become the Israeli architect of an agreement reached in Oslo.

Within a fortnight of learning of the initiative in Norway, Peres had informed Rabin. And so, from the outset, both men knew what had happened at Borregaard and what its significance might be. These were early days but, remarkably, there was no backstairs intriguing in the corridors of power. Peres had decided to play it straight, and Rabin was listening: it was an indication of how the relationship between the two might change and it would have an impact on the future of the channel.

Although the Prime Minister listened to Peres, he did not greet the news with great enthusiasm. He was prepared, however, to allow the Oslo contacts with the PLO to continue. His own inclination was to believe that an agreement with Syria, not the Palestinians, would be the real key to peace in the region. At this time the Washington talks were stalled and the row over the deportees was still unresolved. But Rabin had promised the electorate peace, and since he had taken office his hawkish public acts – the deportations, the security clamp-down – had been privately paralleled by more conciliatory moves. Rabin also had his links with Egypt, and he too was secretly testing the PLO waters through informal contacts. A study group had been set up in October 1992, under the auspices of the prestigious American Academy of Arts and Sciences, to explore issues of security in the Occupied Territories, in the context of a possible peace agreement. Over the course of five meetings in Rome and London, Israeli defence experts, including General Shlomo Gazit, former head of military intelligence, met a number of Palestinian representatives, amongst them Nizar Ammar, a member of the PLO. The Palestinians emphasized that they, and not the Israeli military, had to have control over their own security. They would not accept being relegated to a civilian police force, limited to traffic control and other municipal duties. The study group under American academic auspices was still in operation when Peres and Rabin first talked about the Oslo Channel at the beginning of 1993. It showed that the Prime Minister with the iron fist was clearly prepared to listen to what the PLO had to say, even on sensitive issues such as security. And he was prepared to allow Israeli members of the defence establishment to meet with them.

With the backing of Peres and Rabin, a second meeting in Norway was approved and the team in Oslo received the go-ahead. The word from Tunis was that Abu Mazen and Arafat also supported the channel, and so on 12 February the five men again arrived at Fornebu Airport. The Norwegian ground rules were that each group would be treated with scrupulous equality regarding accommodation and even who would meet and accompany them between the airport and their destination. On this occasion Terje Larsen met the Israelis, who came first, and drove with them up to Borregaard. Even Aas and Mona Juul went to meet the Palestinians later that evening. On the way back the two teams would swap drivers so that neither side would feel it was somehow less important.

This time Mona Juul had booked the airport VIP lounge through the Foreign Ministry, and they hoped that there would not be another hitch. It was not to be. The immigration officials were most interested to find the same three mysterious Arab gentlemen passing through. On this occasion the visitors had passports in different names – the PLO is used to travelling incognito. Abu Ala was adamant, he did not want his passport photocopied again. Mona Juul stayed with him and the others in the VIP lounge while downstairs Even Aas tried to negotiate with the suspicious officials. Aas grew desperate, but suddenly help arrived from an unexpected quarter. A group of attractive Filipino girls presented themselves to immigration. A flashily dressed young man was waiting nervously for them on the other side. It was clear to the passport officials that these girls were prostitutes arriving from Manila to work in Oslo. A huge row erupted and in the confusion the three Palestinians were quickly hustled through.

A rattled Even Aas drove the grimly silent Abu Ala and the others through the driving rain towards Sarpsborg. The leader of the delegation was obviously offended by his treatment, his pride somewhat injured. It was nearly one in the morning when suddenly they were pulled up by a police patrol on the outskirts of Oslo. Everyone in the car was convinced the airport authorities had changed their minds and radioed ahead to have the Palestinians stopped. It turned out to be a random breathalyser test for Even. The three others sat wordless as he dutifully blew into the bag. When they were allowed to proceed the tension broke and the first jokes were bandied about in the back of the car. 'Now they're on to us – they're right behind us! They'll be waiting for us at Borregaard!' This was the beginning of camaraderie, the sense of shared danger and excitement. In the weeks to come, the closeness, and the humour, would grow.

At the second meeting at Borregaard the PLO came with a plan – based on one that had already been unsuccessfully presented to the Israelis through a mediator. It contained terms of reference for an interim agreement on autonomy for the Occupied Territories, and also for implementation of a final accord settling the status of the disputed land. It set aims for negotiations leading towards that end and laid down what jurisdiction the Palestinians would have in that interim period. It also made provision for a 'Marshall Plan for Gaza', a massive international aid effort – the PLO calculated that this rather visionary concept would appeal to Shimon Peres. However, it also contained references to the most difficult question of all: the future of Jerusalem – the Holy City claimed by both Arabs and Jews as their capital. In essence, it was the Palestinian version of the Declaration of Principles the group had talked about in January at Borregaard.

Hirschfeld also arrived with his proposal, a six-page paper he had written. This was a daring move for him. He had repeatedly said he was not an official representative, not even authorized and certainly not in any position to negotiate for Israel. Yet he felt that the academic exercise they were supposedly involved in warranted a discussion paper, setting out all the issues at stake. Hirschfeld's paper was a Declaration of Principles written from the Israeli point of view. It echoed the concept of Gaza First and contained ideas about economic cooperation. And it also included new elements which Hirschfeld knew were likely to appeal to the Palestinians.

The most important of these new proposals was what he called 'graduality' – a gradual transfer of power in the Occupied Territories. This idea was not as obvious as it seemed. The 1979 Camp David accords, which established peace between Israel and Egypt, had been negotiated on a different basis. There the territory of Sinai was handed back to Egypt in one piece at the agreed hour; it was an instant transfer, virtually lock, stock and barrel. Hirschfeld now suggested a transfer of one authority after another to the Palestinians, month by month. In that way matters like health and education and cultural affairs could be handed over one by one. And in conjunction with this there was also a proposal for what Hirschfeld called 'institution building': the Palestinians would be allowed to build and run utilities in Gaza such as an electricity company, a water authority and a seaport. Such important and practical institutions would be developed in preparation for the future negotiations to determine the status of the Occupied Territories. It would be a clear signal that the Israelis were prepared to allow the infrastructure of a state to be built up by the Palestinians.

Overall, there were encouraging developments on both sides during that weekend at Borregaard. Again the food, the atmosphere and the Norwegian presence all combined in a productive way. Jan Egeland again joined them for a meal, and this time Mona Juul spent the whole weekend at the house, joining Larsen in his attempts to help the guests relax and to encourage them to explore new avenues of discussion. The Norwegians were still careful not to intrude, while at the same time being available whenever they were needed. 'We consider this your business,' Larsen told the group. 'We don't want to intervene at all. If you want us to participate in the meeting later, then it's your initiative. Maybe you're just being polite when you say we should sit in.'

Sometimes the group did invite Larsen or Mona Juul to sit in with them, sometimes the negotiatiors came out to report the conflicts that were going on inside, and sometimes they gave no hint of what was happening. On other occasions they handed the Norwegians copies of documents. In the evening Abu Ala, his formality relaxed, donned a very English-looking pair of velvet slippers to wear about the house. Ties were loosened and so were tongues. The dinner was excellent: prawn cocktail followed by venison garnished with vegetables, with vanilla parfait and raspberries for dessert.

By the second day both sides had moved on to talk about how their concepts might be transferred to a forum for real negotiations. The obvious outlet was the Washington talks. Now the five participants began to voice openly the idea that they were creating a secret back channel, behind the front channel where the official negotiations were taking place. The Norwegians had thought along these lines ever since they first suggested they play a role in bringing the two sides together, but only now did the Israelis and the Palestinians begin to think in these terms too. They believed they could augment the Washington process. But they still thought they were very much a subsidiary group. The main drive would continue to come from across the Atlantic.

The February meeting ended on a high note. The two groups sat together and hammered out a joint Declaration of Principles, synthesizing their two versions into one. In a downstairs room, set up as an office, on a computer brought from FAFO's headquarters, Ron Pundak typed up the first draft of the Declaration of Principles they all agreed should be their framework. Yossi Beilin had given his team strict instructions to make sure they only committed words to paper on FAFO stationery. That way if anything leaked they could claim that these new ideas had merely been spawned by an academic seminar. The two groups christened their proposal 'the Sarpsborg Document' and they gave a copy to Terje Larsen, who was to pass it on to Jan Egeland and Thorvald Stoltenberg. When each group left Fornebu Airport, bound for Jerusalem and Tunis, they carried with them the seven-page document for their political masters at home. It seemed a small step but, as the Norwegians realized, it was enormously significant – joint papers on any matters concerning the Israelis and the PLO were rare indeed.

Back in Jerusalem, Yossi Beilin read the paper with growing

interest. It was clearly a rough-and-ready draft, and he winced at some of the proposals, which were very risky as far as Israel was concerned. But Beilin could see beyond the words and phrases, to the ideas which had inspired the paper. Thus he suggested Peres see Yair Hirschfeld for a full run-down of the activities in Norway. But Peres was disinclined and kept putting off the meeting. He already knew Yair, who was not like his own Blazers, quickfire individuals who got things done immediately. Yair was clumsy and took a long time coming to the point; Peres was impatient with such people. Beilin gave him Hirschfeld's paper but Peres took days to get around to reading it, despite Beilin's constant badgering. When he did finally read it, Peres, like Beilin, felt that the language and the structure of the Declaration of Principles left much to be desired, but he too recognized the message contained between the lines: the PLO was signalling that it could do a deal. 'It's an awful paper,' Peres told Beilin bluntly, 'but it looks like something serious is going on.'

Rabin was given a copy of the Sarpsborg Document. He was no more enthusiastic than he had been about the January meeting, but the Foreign Ministry was beginning to take the Oslo Channel seriously. Shimon Peres formed a working group with Yossi Beilin and the two professors. The other members were Peres's policy adviser, Avi Gill, and Beilin's assistant, Shlomo Gur. They took the draft Document of Principles – or 'DOP', as they all now called it – and began to work through the dozen or so points it contained. Much time was spent on the Gaza First option. The draft DOP from Borregaard proposed that Gaza become a United Nations Trusteeship. The Israelis did not like the sound of this. They looked up its precise meaning in books of constitutional history and found a somewhat arcane proposition: the UN would become the sovereign entity and bridge the period between the departure of the colonizing power and the assumption of control by the local inhabitants. Peres was not impressed.

'Is this your idea or the PLO's?' he demanded of Yair Hirschfeld.

Hirschfeld hesitated, then replied: 'It's mine.'

'Then take it out!' snapped Peres.

In Tunis Abu Ala and Hassan Asfour reported to Abu Mazen's office, where the Sarpsborg Document was subjected to minute dissection. Then Yasser Arafat was consulted. Abu Ala was loath to let the Gaza First option become the central tenet of the agreement. He felt it would be dangerous for the Palestinians to single out parts of the Occupied Territories, insisting they should discuss the whole area, including Jerusalem. But Arafat and Abu Mazen knew that Gaza was a magnet to Peres. And so it remained a major concept in the DOP.

In March the parties met again at Borregaard, their third get-together. By now Hirschfeld and Pundak knew Peres was behind the project, although they were not aware that Rabin had been informed. But the PLO did not know, despite repeated attempts to find out, whether the channel was authorized from the top. So far both sides had persevered with the secret contacts, despite the harsh reality of events back home. But now a wave of terror, and a responding security clamp-down, hit Israel and the Occupied Territories, and the channel was buffeted by the backlash.

5

The Walls of Jericho

On 2 March 1993 a Palestinian youth from Gaza ran amok in the streets of Tel Aviv, killing two Israelis and wounding eight others. Rabin announced that the army would seal off the Gaza Strip until further notice, throwing 30,000 inhabitants who earned their living in Israel out of work. On 13 March two Arabs were killed, one by the army, another by a bomb. An Israeli woman settler was hacked to death and soldiers shot dead two demonstrators in Gaza. Rabin cut short a visit to the new US President, Bill Clinton, aimed at restarting the Washington talks.

At Borregaard, still in the grip of winter snows, the proceedings mirrored the stand-off in the humid, dusty streets of Gaza. The Palestinians, feeling they had been flexible and accommodating until now, began to dig in their heels on the issues where there was disagreement. They had decided to make the Israelis fully aware of the many differences which still existed between them: the question of Jerusalem, who would take responsibility for security, who would have jurisdiction in the Occupied Territories and how the arrangements for self-government would be implemented.

This new air of realism was to be expected, for the discussions were entering a more significant phase. Although the Israelis had been prepared for a hardening of the Palestinian stance as the channel gathered momentum, Hirschfeld and Pundak were worried that their success in overcoming Palestinian opposition on many issues was still not enough to achieve a real agreement. They began to fear that this meeting would be the last one, that they had gone as far as they could go. They did, however, redraft the DOP and took it home for further consultations. The Palestinians were frustrated at the lack of identifiable official involvement in the talks. After three rounds they felt that, if the

Israelis were serious about starting real negotiations, they should now send a government figure to meet them in Oslo. By now they had realized that Ron Pundak had no links with Yitzhak Rabin and they were afraid there was no authority behind the channel.

Egeland and Larsen were afraid that Abu Ala wanted to break out of the channel altogether because he did not believe that the talks could progress any further with an unofficial representative such as Hirschfeld. Larsen was sent to Israel to talk to Beilin. He met him in the small villa in Tel Aviv where the Foreign Minister, Shimon Peres, and his deputy had their secondary offices – just two small suites with secretaries. Beilin kept Larsen waiting while in the next room he discussed with Peres whether the Foreign Minister himself should receive the Norwegian coordinator of the secret channel. They decided it would be too risky for Peres. If he was to be fully protected should the channel be discovered and blow up into a public row, he had to be in a position to deny he had ever met Larsen.

Terje Larsen understood this and began to talk to Beilin about Abu Ala's demands for an authorized representative. After half an hour he needed to go to the toilet. The entrance to the bathroom was right next to Peres's door; suddenly Peres emerged, with the same destination in mind. Ron Pundak, who was in the hallway, unaware of the delicate game of blind-man's buff, immediately stepped forward smiling. 'This is Mr Larsen,' he helpfully explained. Peres looked dumbstruck, for once at a total loss for words. He abruptly shook Terje's hand, turned on his heel and retreated back inside his office. At least he could say they had never spoken.

The Oslo Channel was about to lose its Norwegian mentor, Thorvald Stoltenberg. Although he had deliberately kept at arm's length from the proceedings, he had been briefed about every aspect of the discussions and he had read the draft document produced at Borregaard in February. In March the UN Secretary-General, Dr Boutros Ghali, asked Stoltenberg to become the mediator in an equally intractable conflict – the war in the former Yugoslavia. Though Stoltenberg was reluctant to take on the job of UN Special Envoy, he felt it was his duty and he prepared to leave Norway.

Stoltenberg had already informed the Americans of what was going on in Norway. On 28 February, at a Nato meeting in

Brussels, he had given the US Secretary of State, Warren Christopher, a copy of the Sarpsborg Document. He had the consent of both the Israelis and the Palestinians to do this. With thirty years of political experience Stoltenberg felt it was a wise precaution. He was concerned that the key country in the Middle East peace process should not feel that anyone was doing anything behind its back. That would be a sure-fire way to torpedo any peace accord. Christopher was non-committal; he thanked Stoltenberg and asked to be kept informed. Just two months into his job he had many other important matters on his mind. One of his officials, Dan Kurtzer, had already been informed by Egeland that there had been a meeting in January. Kurtzer did not attach much importance to what the Norwegians were doing. It seemed just like other informal academic contacts that had been made between Israelis and members of the PLO. From the start Abu Ala had been keen to get the Americans involved in the Oslo talks, to draw them into direct contacts with Tunis. Egeland passed on the message in this January call but Kurtzer flatly turned down the offer. He only gave Egeland one piece of advice – to make sure that Rabin was involved, or the whole exercise would be meaningless.

The Americans were preoccupied with the lack of progress in Washington. The next round of talks would be the ninth since Madrid, eighteen months before. The Palestinians, still protesting at the deportations, would not even commit themselves to returning to the negotiating table. There had also been the usual hiatus between administrations as Bill Clinton put together his team. Now the new President and his advisers decided to show their determination to solve this difficult foreign policy issue. In March they announced they would become 'full partners' in the talks – in effect, there would now be three parties instead of two trying to reach a settlement. The Russians, nominally the co-sponsors of the process launched in Madrid, had almost disappeared from the scene. The American announcement further eroded the Madrid rules, which stated there should be direct negotiations between the two parties. The Palestinians were not happy as they watched the machinery of US government grinding from lassitude to overkill, almost overnight.

Israel was preparing to celebrate Pesach, the Passover. Family and friends from abroad arrived for the holidays, amongst them Dan Kurtzer of the State Department who came on a private visit to see relatives in Jerusalem. Whilst there he met Beilin and Hirschfeld and they showed him the Sarpsborg Document. Hirschfeld confided in him that the Norway meetings, which had gone so well at first, were now in difficulties. He listened and then, to their surprise, he said: 'You're on your way to an agreement. You feel now it probably won't work but, as in the Washington negotiations, there'll be many ups and downs. And in the end we may both end up with much the same product.'

Kurtzer's words were a tremendous psychological boost for Hirschfeld. He would go to the next meeting fired with vigour and determination. But privately, Dan Kurtzer had dismissed the Norway initiative. The document, though creative, did not have authority. It was just an academic exercise and there was no indication that Yitzhak Rabin was involved.

That same Easter weekend, in Norway, a new and important player made his entrance on to the stage. Thorvald Stoltenberg had left his government post in Norway and Johan Jorgen Holst, the former Defence Minister, had been named as Foreign Minister. On Easter Monday, 12 April, the day before he took up his new appointment, Holst and his wife Marianne Heiberg, the co-author of the FAFO study, were invited to dinner with their good friends Terje Larsen and Mona Juul in their fourth-floor apartment in Oslo. Marianne Heiberg is a striking blonde, a strong, determined woman and a well-known social scientist. Fifty-seven-year-old Holst, a capable and intelligent politician but somewhat lacking in humour, is known to be an ambitious man. But he lacks the status and popularity of his predecessor. Thorvald Stoltenberg would be a hard act to follow. He and Holst are very different, both in personality and in the way they operate on the political scene.

That evening, at Terje and Mona's apartment, their Easter dinner of roast lamb was constantly interrupted by the ringing of the telephone – the usual nightly calls from Tunis and Jerusalem. The guests were obviously intrigued by the snatches of conversation they heard; Larsen and Mona told them briefly what was going on. Marianne already had suspicions that the living-conditions seminar she had attended at Borregaard in January was not all it seemed and she had told her husband so.

The next day Johan Jorgen Holst moved into his new fourth-floor office in the Foreign Ministry, overlooking the gaunt statue of Norway's founder, King Haakon VII, which dominates the square. He asked the Deputy Minister, Jan Egeland, and Terje Larsen to brief him fully on the secret talks. From now on the Foreign Minister himself would take political responsibility and seek a more active role. Stoltenberg, like Beilin in Israel, had been concerned to distance the talks from his government, using FAFO as the cover. Now that three rounds had been completed, despite the recent difficulties, the channel had begun to develop its own momentum. Holst decided that, while the talks should remain a closely guarded secret, there should be political involvement on a higher level; his decision was a reflection of his personal style, so different from Stoltenberg's low-key approach. But it was also a reflection of the seriousness with which the Oslo Channel was now being taken in Israel.

That same week, on 22 April, Yitzhak Rabin made an important public declaration while on an official visit to Egypt: 'Territorial compromise is part of our policy,' he told the journalists accompanying him. This was a strong hint that Israel would be willing to withdraw from part of the West Bank and Gaza Strip. Rabin also made another significant gesture towards the Palestinians, lifting the ban on residents of East Jerusalem taking part in the Washington talks. Faisal Husseini, the prominent Palestinian from Jerusalem, would now be able to head the delegation. In Tunis, Abu Mazen and Abu Ala noted this development. They still did not know if Rabin was informed about the secret channel but these developments were a hopeful sign. In April, Yasser Arafat, Abu Mazen and Abu Ala also made a visit to Egypt, to tell Amr Moussa about the Oslo Channel. The Egyptians encouraged the PLO to continue talks but told the three men they did not think Rabin knew about the secret contacts.

In April 1993 another name began to surface in the secret Oslo Channel and through the Egyptian intermediaries, too. That name was Jericho, a place resonant with history and biblical allusion, the oldest city in the world. Gaza was not the prize, both sides knew that, but the offer of an important West Bank town like Jericho would be a lure to the PLO. Arafat was not the first man to be tempted by Jericho. According to tradition it was in a cave on the Mount of Temptation, near Jericho, that Jesus fasted for forty days and forty nights, resisting Satan's suggestion that he turn stones to bread. The Bible records:

Again, the devil taketh him up into an exceeding high mountain, and sheweth him all the kingdoms of the world, and the glory of them; and saith unto him, All these things I will give thee, if thou wilt fall down and worship me. Then saith Jesus unto him, Get thee hence, Satan: for it is written, Thou shalt worship the Lord thy God, and him only shalt thou serve. (Matt. 4: 8–10)

Today, from the gates of the Greek Orthodox monastery on the mount, there is that same awesome view across the Jordan valley and the town of Jericho. The strategic importance of Jericho is immediately apparent. The PLO regards it as the gate to the West Bank. The roads from Jericho lead to Jordan and to Jerusalem. For Arafat, Jericho would truly be the bridge to the Holy Land. Today the biblical city is a dusty town of 14,000 inhabitants; its famous walls, once brought down by the trumpets, are no more. But Jericho has a wider significance, one that was not lost on either the Palestinians or the Israelis. Peres believed its proximity to the River Jordan opened up the solution he preferred for the future: a confederation between the Jordanians and the Palestinians. Such an arrangement might be the basis for a permanent answer to the problem of a Palestinian homeland. And there were no Jewish settlements in the immediate vicinity of Jericho so there would be no need to discuss their fate.

At the end of 1992, in his approaches to the Palestinians through the Egyptian intermediaries, Shimon Peres had suggested that Jericho or another West Bank town might be included with the Gaza First option, but there had been no response from the Palestinians. Now, through the Oslo Channel, Arafat asked Abu Mazen and Abu Ala to put Jericho firmly in the picture. The idea was that the Israelis should withdraw from both Gaza and Jericho simultaneously. The meaning was clear: the West Bank, the more vital territory, would be included in the interim agreement and if things went well other towns would be vacated by the Israeli army. There would be no danger that Gaza would be the only piece of land to be conceded. Now Arafat began to test the waters; he floated the idea of Jericho in public, on a visit to Vienna. No one fully understood the significance at the time, but Abu Ala noticed the remark, which confirmed in his mind the Chairman's commitment to Jericho. If the town could be included in the Norwegian discussions, then the secret channel might really take off.

On 27 April the Palestinian delegation returned to the Washington talks after a four-month absence. Some of the deportees had been permitted to return home, Rabin had made concessions and the atmosphere had improved markedly. Two days later, the members of the clandestine channel flew into Fornebu Airport for their fourth encounter. This time Larsen had chosen a small hotel, the Holmenkollen Park on the outskirts of Oslo, overlooking the famous Holmenkollen ski-jump. The guests who closeted themselves in the Nansen private conference room were hardly the usual types to check into this elegant sporting centre. Some of them, dressed in formal suits, looked like businessmen, two were in jeans and sweaters, and they were accompanied by a few Norwegians. The group took all their meals in a private room and they seemed uninterested in the superb hiking and other recreational pursuits available, limiting themselves to strolling in the grounds of the hotel. The waiters were curious – too curious – and Larsen grew nervous.

Another Norwegian had joined the secret channel, Geir Pedersen, a Foreign Ministry official and an old and trusted friend of Mona's. Pedersen had been posted to China for several years and was now completing a stint in Bonn, in Germany, before joining FAFO to head the institute's international section. He would travel back and forth as necessary to help with the arrangements. Pedersen, a tall, thirty-seven-year-old with longish hair and a moustache, looked more like a sociologist than a professional diplomat. The soul of discretion, with polished manners and alert to every nuance of word and look, Pedersen was to be a safety-valve for Larsen, someone he could lean on and confide in.

At the Holmenkollen Park the group continued to work on the DOP, which was taking shape around three main principles: Israeli withdrawal from Gaza; 'graduality', a step by step transfer of power; and economic cooperation. Terje Larsen took long walks with Abu Ala. The Palestinian was now asking for one copy of the Sarpsborg Document to be signed secretly by both sides and deposited by Holst in a safe in the Foreign Ministry. It was not to be released without the consent of both parties. Abu Ala requested that an official from Jerusalem come to sign for the Israelis.

The Palestinians were pushing for a clearer indication of how far up the Israeli chain of command knowledge and approval of the channel's activities extended. They wanted to be sure Peres was behind it; Abu Ala seemed to have a strong liking for him and his ideas, and he was clearly a man the PLO could do business with. But Abu Ala was torn over the issue of Rabin's involvement. In his analysis of the power play in Israel, he had decided Peres lacked political clout. He wanted the top man to be involved, but he was afraid that Rabin was as hard-line as his Likud predecessor, Shamir, and that the Declaration of Principles would get short shrift from him.

Larsen himself did not know if Rabin had been informed, but he told Abu Ala: 'I know it's got the backing of Peres. Even if I'm not sure about Rabin, I know that no one can run a thing like this – take this kind of risk – without telling the Prime Minister. It's impossible.'

Despite the Norwegian's intentions to stay on the sidelines, he was being drawn further in. And he was starting to become a target for Abu Ala's frustrations. The Palestinian had realized the contact with Hirschfeld had gone as far as it could. Unlike Abu Ala himself, Hirschfeld had no real authority and, in the absence of a government figure from Jerusalem, Larsen was the only one he could pressurize into taking action. He said to Larsen: 'I can't convince these Israeli academics; it's your obligation to make them understand. You've got to go to Tel Aviv and ask for a meeting with Peres. I'm losing credibility in Tunis. I need concrete proof of who's involved and only you can get it. You've got to persuade them to set up this signing. Go to Holst! Is he willing to do it? Call Yossi Beilin and tell him we're not happy. Either Peres or Beilin must come and sign it.'

In long walks around the Holmenkollen ski-jump with Larsen, Abu Ala grew more and more agitated. 'I'm leaving,' he threatened. Larsen begged him to stay. It was becoming clear to all of them that the channel was creating its own momentum. The Palestinians had the idea that by signing the draft DOP, they would make it an unofficial official document, a secret surety. With both parties' imprimatur on the dotted line, the paper could be made discreetly available by the two leaders through the Washington talks and provide a basis to kick-start the deliberations there. This was an idea attractive to the Israelis too, although they were not yet ready to commit the government figure to make it possible.

But Larsen interpreted the possibility of a signed document

differently, as he informed Holst. He realized that if the draft was signed it meant there would no longer be separate back and front channels. The Oslo Channel would, although still secret, become in effect the front channel. There would be no need for Washington with all its problems.

After receiving many phone calls from Norway, Beilin conceded that Abu Ala's request might be met.

'OK, we'll consider upgrading. But he has to prove he can deliver and that Yasser Arafat is really behind him. Maybe Abu Ala isn't just a minor figure but he's got to prove he's in the kitchen and has the power to negotiate with the full backing of the top group within the PLO.' 'The kitchen' was a term that Abu Ala had used to describe the group around Arafat, a kind of kitchen Cabinet.

'Right, Abu Ala,' Larsen reported back. 'I think you can make it – but you've got to prove yourself first.'

'How can I do that?' snapped the Palestinian.

Within a fortnight Abu Ala was to have two chances to prove his influence and to create some goodwill in the process. The multilaterals were still regularly convening around the globe, and Abu Ala continued to chair the Palestinian steering committee, working discreetly from his hotel room. He had been set a test by the Israelis, working through Terje Larsen. There were two multilaterals scheduled for May, one in Rome, the other by coincidence in Oslo. The Israelis wanted the Palestinians to agree to certain texts to be presented at the multilaterals, to prove the PLO could compromise and to show that Abu Ala had sufficient authority to make it worth Israel raising the secret Oslo Channel to an official level.

The first meeting, in Rome, ended on an optimistic note. The Palestinians and Israelis agreed a text and the usual skirmishing over the protocol of the conference was quickly resolved by Abu Ala behind the scenes. A week later the second multilateral convened, to discuss the issue of Palestinian refugees. The venue was Oslo and this time the Foreign Ministry was the official host. The Norwegian delegation to the multilaterals were, however, completely unaware that their country was also the force behind a secret channel. Holst opened the conference at the SAS Hotel, with Mona by his side. Larsen was there under the pretext, once again, of a presentation of the FAFO study, and Abu Ala was installed upstairs in Room 817.

This time it was not so easy. Abu Ala could not tell his delegation what he was doing, nor could he be seen to back down too much. Larsen, Mona and Geir Pedersen were much in evidence, which aroused suspicion from the other Palestinians. Abu Ala had agreed in principle to compromise over the text which was to be hammered out during the conference. Larsen went through the wording the Israelis wanted. Abruptly Abu Ala declared it was not exactly what he had agreed to. If he was to get his delegation to accept it then a couple of words would need to be changed. He was in a combative mood, accusing Larsen of favouring the Israelis and shouting at any hapless Palestinian who ventured into the room.

Larsen was in despair, the talks were grinding on below them in the hotel's conference room and they faced a deadline. He tried to find Yossi Beilin but the latter was on a plane *en route* to Washington. He urged Beilin's aide, Shlomo Gur, to contact him over the plane's communications system to get authority to change the words. It was useless. The Israeli ambassador was sent, with a mobile phone, to Dulles International Airport to meet the plane as soon as it arrived. But that would be too late, the meeting would be over. The Norwegians were getting desperate. Then Gur called back. They could not reach Beilin but they would authorize the word change anyway. Larsen ran down into the hall and stood behind the Norwegian chairman, who was at this moment starting to read the text. It was the version that the Israelis wanted but Larsen knew that, without the alterations that Abu Ala was demanding, the whole text would be rejected by the Palestinian delegate on the floor. Abu Ala would fail the test and the Israelis would refuse to continue with the secret channel.

And then the situation turned to farce. The Palestinian delegate was exhausted and somehow missed the crucial sentence. Abu Ala phoned down to find out if the word had been changed in time and what had happened. No one knew, there was complete disarray. After some argument a five-minute break was called. Larsen ran back to Abu Ala's room and told him, in no uncertain terms, that the change had been agreed by the Israelis and that he must hurry to inform his delegation. Abu Ala, clearly enjoying this fraught game of negotiation, insisted that he now wanted to add another reference, to UN Resolution 242. He claimed it had been included in a previous conference. Mona, with the knowledge at her fingertips, was able to dig out the minutes from that occasion and prove that 242 had never been included. Abu Ala now had less than a minute to get his delegation into line.

Larsen lost his cool. 'Do something quickly!' he shouted.

'I can't be seen on the floor,' was Abu Ala's reply. 'You go down and tell them you are empowered by me, on behalf of the PLO leadership, to give them the amended text.'

Larsen and Pedersen ran downstairs again. The Palestinians were meeting behind closed doors. The five-minute break was ending. The Norwegians pushed past the guards and physically lifted the leader of the Palestinian delegation out of his chair and dragged him into the corridor.

'What on earth are you doing, who do you think you are?' he spluttered.

'I am empowered by Abu Ala, on behalf of the leadership of the PLO, to give you this, which you are to present as the agreed text,' shouted Larsen, thrusting the troublesome document into his hand.

And so the meeting ended successfully. Everything was agreed. When Larsen, drained and limp, got back upstairs he found Abu Ala sitting there, laughing his head off with the sheer audacity of what he had done. The text itself, which dealt with the issue of refugees, was almost irrelevant. The significance of the incident was that it confirmed that Abu Ala was a force to be reckoned with on the Palestinian side. No one could do what he had done that day unless Arafat was behind him.

The official Norwegian delegate, unaware of the drama behind the scenes or the real reason for the sudden acceptance of the slightly amended text, was delighted. He announced to the media that the multilateral meeting had been 'an important milestone in the peace process.'

Larsen then called Beilin who by now had landed. The Israeli's response was typically dry: 'So he did it. OK, he can call the shots now.'

That evening Abu Ala laughed all the way to dinner as he sat in the back of the car with Larsen and Mona. He was openly affectionate with Terje, as if to make up for his behaviour earlier. Larsen forgave him and they all had an excellent meal. Holst and his wife were there, along with other delegates from the multilateral talks. They were all in a euphoric mood, the conference had been a success. That night the phrase 'the Oslo spirit' was coined, but only a handful of people in the room understood how it had been created.

But though the Oslo refugee conference improved the outlook for the secret channel, ironically it nearly blew the whole undertaking wide open. Dan Kurtzer usually headed the American delegation at the multilaterals. However, he was unable to attend the Oslo conference and the man who took his place alarmed Larsen by asking openly, in a crowded room, how the secret talks were going. The American insisted on being briefed about developments even though Larsen pretended he did not know of any secret meetings. The Norwegians had always tried to impress upon the Americans the need for the utmost secrecy, and they assumed that only Warren Christopher, Dennis Ross, his top-ranking Middle East official, and Dan Kurtzer knew about the channel. Jan Egeland and Terje Larsen had twice used the US embassy to pass information down the secure telephone line to Washington. They concluded the leak must have come from a source within the embassy.

The Norwegians became nervous after this experience. They dediced that there would be no more visits to the embassy. They would convey no further details to the Americans unless there was a one-to-one conversation at Foreign Minister level. The leak caused consternation in the Israeli camp as well, and they thought seriously about closing down the secret channel immediately, before the news got out. However, with the talks about to take off, they decided to run the risk and carry on.

Peres was impressed with the way Abu Ala had handled the Palestinian side at the Rome and Oslo multilaterals. Until now the Israelis had been unclear about the rank and stature of Abu Ala. But their new assessment was that he did have the necessary influence. Peres kept Rabin informed and there were twice-weekly meetings between them with Beilin present. They always met outside the office to put staff and journalists off the scent. The mere sight of Peres entering Rabin's office could have aroused considerable speculation. They often discreetly entered Rabin's house by the back door at lunch-time, to talk and to exchange the documents that were flowing from the Oslo Channel.

Beilin proved an effective manager, with a talent for putting teams together to work on projects. His choice of Yair Hirschfeld and Ron Pundak had already proved his skill in picking people for the delicate task of starting up the Oslo Channel. During March and April Beilin had been working on the next phase of his plan. The job of Director-General, the top non-political post at the Foreign Ministry, was due to be filled. Beilin was determined to find the right man for the job, someone sympathetic to his and Peres's aims, someone dynamic and quick-thinking with whom he could work closely. Beilin also had a hunch the Oslo Channel could be affected by the choice of candidate. He wanted his best friend and fellow Blazer, Uri Savir, who was now enjoying life in New York as Israel's Consul-General. But there were other strong contenders and Peres favoured another man. He admired Savir, who had been his press spokesman, but Savir was only forty years old and Peres thought it too soon to promote him to run the Foreign Ministry, with responsibility for all Israel's diplomatic efforts around the world.

But Beilin worked on Peres and managed to prevent him from nominating his own first choice. The business proved awkward for Beilin when the story got into the press, though the reasons for his championing of Savir were not guessed. On 1 May Uri Savir was appointed Director-General of the Israeli Foreign Ministry in Jerusalem and moved into his new office down the corridor from Beilin. The Blazers were back in charge and from this moment on things really began to move.

Abu Ala was pushing hard, through both Larsen and Hirschfeld, for official Israeli participation in the secret talks. His tactics were at once threatening and cajoling: one minute he was vowing to break the channel, the next reminding them how he had orchestrated the multilateral talks. Two days after the break-through at the Oslo refugee conference, Peres suddenly decided to act. He was disillusioned with the impasse in Washington. As they read the top-secret cables emanating from the US capital, his team in Jerusalem did not know whether to laugh or cry, the talks were such a farce. Ten hours spent arguing over one insignificant word was all the reports had to offer. Peres's conviction that Gaza and Jericho would be the key was becoming an obsession.

On 15 May Peres asked Rabin for a private meeting, just the two of them, no aides, no record of what was said. Outside, their assistants, unused to these convivial tête-à-têtes, joked that it was really a conference of six ministers: two prime ministers, two defence ministers, a foreign minister and a chief of staff. For such was the combined experience of the two old rivals. Inside the room Peres dramatically told the Prime Minister that he intended to go to Norway himself and meet Abu Ala. Peres was typically overenthusiastic about the Oslo Channel. Rabin, as usual, showed no enthusiasm whatsoever. But together they reached a compromise; a new relationship of grudging respect was developing between them, though it was difficult to shake off the bitterness of the past. They agreed that Peres should not go – the risks were too great. But Uri Savir would be sent instead, Israel's top-ranking diplomat, an official at the highest level. The decision was not one lightly taken by the two men. For this would be the very first time a senior Israeli official had met a member of the PLO, still regarded as a terrorist organization, beyond the pale.

6

The Diplomat and the Lawyer

Uri Savir's spiritual home was New York. The urban jungle, the bright lights and basement jazz clubs of Manhattan were music to his soul. For four years he had been Consul-General in the city where America's largest, wealthiest and most influential Jewish community lives. New York is the fount of political fund-raising, the source of well-informed thinking on the homeland, both fiercely loyal and scathingly critical. It is a place the Israeli leadership take very seriously indeed, and Uri Savir had been their vital link with the city. Yet on 1 May Savir found himself back amid the low, white, oriental architecture of Jerusalem, no skyscrapers and few, if any, all-night delicatessens. An ardent movie-goer, he missed the buzz and excitement of Manhattan, but on the day he moved into his new office in the Foreign Ministry he found an intriguing paper on his desk, and an even more intriguing trip in prospect.

Savir's own background as the son of a well-known Israeli diplomat had prepared him for a role in politics. His father had taken the family with him on his postings to London, Bonn and Helsinki, and Uri was a well-travelled child. But the family's roots remained in Israel and Uri was passionate about his country and its troubled history. His father had always been an outspoken advocate of the need to make peace with the PLO. It was an unfashionable and somewhat risky view for an Israeli in the foreign service. His opinions influenced his son and Uri Savir spent much time thinking about the real nature of the bitter relations between his countrymen and the Palestinians. Like his best friend, Yossi Beilin, Savir is an intellectual, a low-key operator, quietly spoken with a serious air. He has a deep intensity, a passion kept tightly under control.

Savir's most strongly held conviction was that there was a

growing ideological opposition to continued Israeli occupation of the territories seized in 1967. Both he and the Peres group, although loosely described as left wing, nevertheless shared Zionist ideals, and Savir believed not only that Israel should have political independence but that this independence had to be based on moral values. The Intifada, the war of stones that began in 1987 and had become an all-out conflict claiming thousands of Israeli and Palestinian lives, was a turning-point. The increasingly strong-arm tactics Israel was adopting to maintain order in the Occupied Territories were alienating a growing number of Jews, especially the young. For a country built in the aftermath of the Holocaust as a symbol of hope against terror and persecution, the television reports showing Israeli soldiers breaking the bones of West Bank youths were both disturbing and shameful.

When Savir first read the Sarpsborg Document his reaction was very positive. He noticed that the usual PLO phrases, such as 'self-determination' and the insistence on a Palestinian state, were missing. And the new concept of economic cooperation came over loud and clear. He would now be sent to test the waters.

Rabin made two conditions when authorizing Savir's trip to Oslo. The first was that the Palestinians should not use the upgrading of the Norwegian talks as an excuse to back out of the Washington negotiations. His second requirement was that secrecy must be maintained. He was still extremely sceptical about Oslo's ability to deliver and therefore did not want to risk allowing the main forum for negotiation to collapse. Exposure of the secret talks would also diminish or even destroy the main peace process. Peres and his group were pushing to invest more in the secret channel and he intended to be the brake on their enthusiasm.

The sending of a government representative of Savir's rank was a watershed. Hirschfeld and Pundak had gone as far as well-meaning, well-informed private individuals could go. The Sarpsborg Document could be tinkered with endlessly, but it would remain just an optimistic, joint-position paper unless the weight of the government was thrown behind it by someone officially qualified to negotiate. Only then could the Declaration of Principles become an instrument to create a peace accord.

The professors had been able to move in and out of Oslo without attracting any attention. It would be a very different matter for Savir. His own staff in the Israeli Foreign Ministry would need to know exactly where such a senior figure was at all times, and if he was abroad they would naturally inform the Israeli embassy in the country in question. The embassy would expect to receive him and to facilitate his trip. He could not just drop out of sight for a few days. The cover story Savir prepared for his first visit to Oslo was that he was on an official visit to Paris and would take twenty-four hours off to visit his wife, who had gone to Cannes on a business trip. He flew in to Charles de Gaulle Airport, and took an official car to his hotel. Once there he checked in, unpacked and put a 'Do Not Disturb' sign on his door. He then left the hotel, taking a taxi back to the airport. Ron Pundak was waiting for him, with tickets arranged by the Norwegians to take them on to Copenhagen and then via another airline to Oslo.

In Norway the airport VIP lounge had once again been reserved. This was becoming a regular occurrence, and the staff were irritated by the growing monopoly a junior Foreign Ministry employee seemed to have over the special room. The staff were used to royalty, presidents and prime ministers passing through, and they resented the place being occupied by a couple of scruffy Israelis in jeans and some Arabs who did not appear at all important. Their dignity was affronted and they had been conducting a silent vendetta against Mona Juul, pinning notes to the door announcing that in future she was not authorized to book the VIP lounge. They had even called the Protocol Department at the Foreign Ministry to ask what was going on. Holst had to intervene to say that Miss Juul was empowered to act on his behalf in unspecified 'emergency matters'. Mona Juul was secretly amused and, with Holst behind her, emerged the winner in the protocol battle. And so on 20 May the facility was set aside to receive yet another anonymous Israeli. The plane had been directed to use the Jetway nearest the entrance to the lounge, and Terje and Mona were waiting by the plane's door to whisk Savir and Pundak into the room with all due speed. It had been arranged that the immigration officials would not ask to look at Savir's passport.

Inside the room the Norwegians got their first look at the new member of the Oslo Channel. They saw a dark-haired man with a youthful face, offset by large square glasses which gave him a serious air. Although a young man, Savir had a noticeably reserved and formal manner and he was dressed to match in a dark blue suit and Hermès tie. Larsen and Geir Pedersen exchanged surreptitious glances of dismay. They knew that everything now depended on this man and how he would react to the particular relationship built up between the members of the secret channel. Could he adapt? Larsen was not optimistic: Savir looked too formal, too aloof and, he feared, too young.

Larsen had devoted a great deal of time to the question of how to handle the touchy subject of the first official meeting between the Israeli government and the PLO. By now he had the measure of Abu Ala and knew his pride was a factor that had to be taken into account. If they were to make progress at this crucial meeting, they had to start by creating the right atmosphere. Larsen knew the older Palestinian needed to be respected, his authority acknowledged in some tangible way. So in the back of the car on the way into Oslo, Larsen began explaining this to Savir. He intended to take the Israeli to meet Abu Ala first, in order to establish the Palestinian's stature within the channel. Larsen ran through the exact introduction he had in mind, how he would stage-manage it and what he would say. He insisted on rehearsing the meeting with Savir, as the two of them sat in the back of the car. At first Savir looked at him as if he was mad, but soon he began to enter the spirit of the thing and Larsen felt that the Israeli liked this psychological approach. In fact Savir was rather puzzled by Larsen's unorthodox approach and decided to humour him. With his sunglasses and rather rumpled elegance, Larsen looked, thought Savir, like a detective in a French movie, working out the moves and timing of some undercover operation.

Although they did not discuss it openly, both men knew that this exploratory meeting had two purposes, neither of them part of the negotiations as such. First, he had to check out Hirschfeld and Pundak's reports, to see if they were just castles in the air or had real substance. And secondly, he intended to get the measure of Abu Ala and determine if the Palestinian could deliver.

Earlier, when Abu Ala had arrrived in Oslo, Larsen had told him: 'Look, this Israeli fellow who's coming, he's here for one sole purpose as I see it: to check you out. He wants to know what you're like as a person, your credibility. He'll ask a thousand questions, it'll be just like an exam. You really have to pass.' Larsen was concerned that Abu Ala show Savir his warm,

charming and intelligent side – not spout the old-style PLO pro-
paganda, which he was quite capable of doing. Larsen wanted
Abu Ala to like Savir, and to be liked in return.

Uri Savir was clearly very nervous; he said little as they neared
the meeting-place where the Palestinians, accompanied by Yair
Hirschfeld, were waiting. This time Larsen had chosen another
typical Norwegian house, the Thomas Heftye cottage. A wealthy
merchant had built this large log cabin at the turn of the century,
as a weekend ski retreat for his family. He left it to the municipal-
ity of Oslo and today it is a guest-house for the use of Cabinet
Ministers. The views are stupendous: forests of pine trees and,
beyond, the Holmenkollen ski-jump. Skiing is not just a modern
sporting pastime in Norway, it has almost mythic associations in
Norwegian folklore and royal history. The Holmenkollen ski-
jump is more than a recreational facility, it is a kind of totem-pole
symbolizing Norway's national identity.

It was in this simple setting, in a room with wooden walls and
rough-hewn furniture, that the first official – though secret –
meeting of the Israelis and the PLO took place. Larsen seized
Abu Ala by the hand and led him forward. Grasping Savir's arm
with his other hand he said to the Director-General of Israel's
Foreign Ministry: 'Meet your public enemy number one!'

Without a moment's hesitation the Israeli and the Palestinian
shook hands and smiled. On the surface this was an outrageous
introduction, one that would have made any diplomat faint. And
Larsen boldly compounded it, taking Savir down the line to
Hassan Asfour: 'Meet your public enemy number two!' Then Savir
was introduced to Maher El Kurd – public enemy number three.

For Savir it was a strange and oddly exciting moment. He felt
keenly the historic nature of the encounter and the responsibility
placed on him, the representative of the State of Israel. Abu Ala
immediately began sizing up his opponent. Abu Mazen, the
expert on Israeli personalities and politics, had told him that
Savir was young but well qualified and a skilled negotiator. Abu
Mazen was impressed although, in common with many
Palestinians, he was somewhat suspicious of Savir's close links
with American Jewry. The powerful Israeli lobby in the United
States is often seen by the Arabs as an important part of what
they call the 'Zionist conspiracy'. The Palestinians were therefore
wary of Savir but they were prepared to respect him too. And for
both Abu Ala and Hassan Asfour, Savir's youthful appearance

was an asset. He represented the new generation of Israelis, and their best hope for peace.

The introductions over, there was a somewhat awkward hiatus, which Larsen rather hastily moved in to fill. He ushered everyone into a small room off the hall where a chequered cloth covered a large table with wooden chairs arranged around it. He urged them: 'Take your jackets off, loosen your ties, roll up your sleeves and let's get down to business.'

This was a rare miscalculation by Larsen: he was wrong to try to force the pace. The Palestinians and the Israelis were very formally dressed, and intentionally so, for this important meeting. They sat stiffly, saying nothing, and their jackets stayed firmly on their backs. Larsen realized he had been overly familiar. Uri Savir was a new member of the channel, and Larsen's *bonhomie* was not appropriate. Flushed with embarrassment Larsen quickly made his exit. Mona Juul was waiting outside the door.

'I've made a bloody fool of myself in there, I've ruined the whole thing. How could I have been so stupid?' he moaned.

Mona was her usual matter-of-fact self: 'Cool down, wait and see. I'm sure you handled it the way you thought right. Why don't we wait and see.'

The men inside the room felt relief as Larsen left. His clumsiness, though not intended, had the effect of bringing them together. They knew they all felt the same about his intervention, and that shared feeling drew them closer. So once again Larsen's handling of the situation had had positive results.

Then Uri delivered a half-hour speech in English. He began by speaking about his own personal commitment to the peace process and the determination of the Labour government to see it through. Then his speech became more blunt, for he had decided not to mince his words. He attacked the approach of the Palestinians in Washington, who were demanding the release of prisoners and other confidence-building measures before they would get down to discussing the real issues. Savir believed they should go straight to the heart of the issue, a land-for-peace deal.

'We are fed up with you asking for gestures, for so-called confidence-building measures. There's a contrast between your asking us to ease up on the situation and the basic belief, which we both have in common, that occupation and human rights are incompatible. You can't have it both ways. We are here to change the status quo. We want to make it work.'

Abu Ala gave no sign of displeasure at this tough talking. Quite the contrary. In his reply he spoke about the Palestinians' deep commitment to the peace process:

'We are very pleased that the Israeli government has sent us an official representative. It proves that it attaches importance to this channel and it convinces us that your government is finally serious in its intentions to make peace. I hope we can come quickly to an agreement on this Declaration of Principles and have our Palestinian delegation in Washington sign it.'

Uri Savir stressed that, for the Israelis, their security had to be the paramount consideration in coming to any deal. He complained that the document, as it stood, had hardly any content on this difficult area, and warned that they would need to work this issue out in greater detail. Abu Ala listened carefully and said that he understood Israel's need to guarantee its own security. Again, as he had with Hirschfeld, Abu Ala stressed that justifying both their positions on the basis of their history was fruitless: the two sides must look forward, never back. Uri Savir, like the vast majority of his countrymen, had never met anyone from the PLO. This was not the demon he expected. He was impressed with Abu Ala's straight talking and his way of doing business. The initial exchanges over, they immediately began to discuss the three specific issues Savir had been instructed to pursue: Jerusalem, Jericho and the arbitration of any disputes that might arise once interim self-government by the Palestinians had been implemented.

Outside, Terje Larsen and Mona Juul waited for an hour, and then another and another. Larsen was worried, no one came out, not even to go to the toilet. Eventually he could contain his curiosity no longer. He opened the door and went in, a tentative expression on his face. The seven men were sitting there in their shirtsleeves, their ties loosened or removed altogether. They all smiled sheepishly up at Larsen and then the whole room erupted in gales of laughter.

With a short break for dinner, the talks went on into the early hours of the morning. They had argued back and forth over the three issues. Much time was devoted to the question of whether the most difficult issue – the fate of Jerusalem – should be included in the Declaration of Principles at all. The last draft of the DOP produced at Borregaard had linked Jerusalem's fate to the West Bank and Gaza, which made it clear that the Palestinians would only accept an interim self-governing arrangement in those two places if they could have Jerusalem too. Savir wanted to set aside the question of the city so that they could move quickly towards an interim agreement.

The Israelis had captured East Jerusalem, the Arab part of the city, in the 1967 Six Day War. Jerusalem is the Holy City of the three great religions of the Middle East: Judaism, Christianity and Islam. It is a place of great beauty, rising white and dazzling from the cypress-covered hills and olive groves surrounding it. At its heart the Wailing Wall, the Temple Mount, the great silver and gold domes of ancient mosques and the Via Dolorosa bear witness to its history. For thousands of years, Jerusalem has aroused strong emotions – love and hatred on all sides.

The Israelis have sworn that this place must be the eternal and indivisible capital of their country. Since 1967 they have expanded the Jewish population of Jerusalem tenfold. From a sleepy little town, Jerusalem has grown into a sprawling metropolis of 500,000 people. The issue of whether Jerusalem should be the Israeli capital, or divided so that the Palestinians too might have it as their capital, had been one of the main causes of the impasse in the Washington talks. The Israelis were forced to accept that the problem of Jerusalem would have to be addressed in years to come, when the final status of the Occupied Territories was decided. But they argued that Jerusalem, with all its symbolism and its intractable problems, should be excluded from the interim agreement. Otherwise the two sides would never make any headway. The Palestinians had resisted this strongly for eighteen months at the official talks. But now, in Oslo, Abu Ala left the small room at the Thomas Heftye cottage and went next door to call Abu Mazen. He returned to tell Savir that the PLO would agree to negotiate this Declaration of Principles on the interim period without the inclusion of Jerusalem.

Just as, at the start, Abu Ala had argued against Gaza First, so he had been against conceding the issue of Jerusalem. But now that the official negotiator had arrived, he accepted Tunis's decision. The PLO had shown that it was prepared to make concessions and, by doing so at this important juncture, won a tactical advantage. The move had the right effect on Savir, for he saw that the PLO could be flexible. The Israelis believed they had set another test. But if Yasser Arafat and Abu Mazen had already accepted that they would have to compromise on Jerusalem, this

moment presented Abu Ala with the chance of winning the max-
imum advantage.

In the early hours of the morning Savir went home with Terje
and Mona – staying in a hotel with a register of names would
have been too risky, for then the press might be able to prove he
had been in Oslo. Mona went to bed and Terje kept Uri company
on the balcony of the apartment. They sipped white wine and
gazed at the sleeping streets below. It was a calm night, with a
myriad stars above; the smell of spring was in the air. Savir was
deeply moved by the day's events. He was openly impressed
with the leader of the Palestinian delegation, a man who could
compromise and yet who did not miss a trick. His initial feeling
of optimism about the Borregaard Declaration of Principles had
been strengthened by his first exchanges with the man with
whom he would have to engage in the negotiations. 'He knows it
all,' he said admiringly, despite his diplomat's caution. 'He has a
historical perspective and I can do business with him. I will try
and sell it.' Abu Ala had passed the exam Larsen had warned
him about, with flying colours.

As Savir stood looking out over Oslo, he could not stop thinking of the moment when he had shaken Abu Ala's hand. For the
Palestinian banker, though no terrorist himself, symbolized to
Savir the deaths, the blood, the tears which the PLO had inflicted
on Israel since their conflict had begun. And now he had held his
enemy's hand, and Abu Ala had held his. It was as if they were
assuring each other that they knew the time had come when both
their peoples should reach out the hand of peace.

The next day the Larsen household slept late. Mona and Terje
were in the open-plan kitchen when a dazed Savir wandered out
of the spare bedroom clad in jeans and T-shirt, shaking his head
and muttering: '*Where* am I? *Who* am I? And *what* am I doing here?'

Terje and Mona laughed at Savir's physical and mental disori-
entation. His sense of being in a dream increased when later that
day he took a stroll with Abu Ala, Larsen and Asfour in the
woods around the Thomas Heftye cottage. The walk was Savir's
introduction to Norwegian-style negotiations, and this urbane
Israeli had never encountered anything like it. The keen movie-
goer could only imagine he was somehow trapped in an early
Ingmar Bergman film. It was a bizarre experience but the
Palestinians, in their business suits and as much fish out of water
in this place as he was, appeared to have become quite used to

the Norwegian way of solving problems by communing with nature.

Savir was also somewhat intrigued by Larsen's conversation. The Norwegian asked many questions but not about subjects like Jerusalem or the mechanics of implementing UN resolutions. He wanted to know how the Palestinians and the Israelis felt, what emotions they had displayed the night before. 'How did you feel meeting your arch enemy?' he enquired straightforwardly. Did you ever think you would?'

Larsen, a trained social scientist and a keen amateur psychologist, asked such questions out of genuine curiosity. He believed in the sociological approach when dealing with small groups. He was convinced that, if he could encourage them to form a tight-knit group by discussing and sharing their feelings and their emotions, they would be able to build trust, and even intimacy, on a personal level. And that would have an effect on the outcome of the talks.

On their walk, as they laughed and joked, Savir began to be drawn into the heart of the group. Larsen was trying to 'socialize' him, to make him part of the specific culture which had developed within the secret channel. He knew that if they could not re-establish the atmosphere of Borregaard, with Uri as an integral part of it, the talks would fail. A tribe had been formed, with its own language, values and style of coping with problems. Larsen wanted to teach the new recruit the tribal language.

Part of that language was the ability to share a joke, to be informal, to use humour to break the impasse or to deflect personal animosity over disagreements within the talks. As the four men wandered along the dirt tracks around the ski-jump the talk was not of the Middle East or of their problems, it was the kind of talk that all men indulge in from time to time. They told dirty jokes, of a rather highbrow calibre, not just smutty or lavatorial. And the Israelis and the Palestinians, roaring with laughter in the quiet woods, saw that the same things made them laugh. Even Hassan Asfour, whose English was not as fluent as the others', had no difficulty understanding and sharing in the humour.

A certain chemistry began to develop between Abu Ala, Uri Savir and Terje Larsen. All three of them are complex characters, operating on several different levels, highly intelligent men who are also intuitive and therefore shrewd observers of human behaviour. Abu Ala and Uri Savir love to manœuvre, to manipulate and to play the arcane games of political negotiation. Larsen loves to manœuvre and to manipulate the people around him, to position them according to the rules of 'organizational sociology' and to achieve positive results.

At the outset the sympathies of Terje and Mona lay more with the Palestinian side. The Norwegians' knowledge of the history and the living conditions of people in the Occupied Territories had tilted their own feelings that way. Abu Ala knew this, and wanted to reinforce his advantage. Several times in the early days of the channel he had told Larsen: 'This thing we are doing, it's ours, yours and mine, it's *our* baby!'

He felt that it was the meeting in Tunis between himself and Larsen, and subsequently with Yasser Arafat, which had really got the channel going. Therefore the two of them had a special responsibility and a special position within the group. Larsen had to admit that, although he liked and admired Hirschfeld and Pundak, Abu Ala was the man who had really captured his imagination. But now the new Israeli arrival was changing the equation. Savir and Larsen had an immediate rapport. They both came from itinerant families, as youngsters they had travelled widely, and they were still restless, always seeking new experiences. They were both idealists and they shared a similar sense of humour. Abu Ala was older but an inveterate traveller too, happiest in well-appointed hotel rooms. He too had a multilayered personality and a well-developed sense of humour. His experience in exile and the lessons in political survival he had learnt within the PLO had given him a harder edge, a cruel streak perhaps, a cunning that the others lacked. But his great humanity and his warmth, the qualities which had captivated Larsen, began to work their spell on Savir too. From now on the twosome of the Palestinian banker and the Norwegian social scientist would, with the introduction of the Israeli diplomat, become a triangle. That triangle would lie at the heart of the secret channel.

After a short meeting on the second day Savir was anxious to leave. He had been absent from Paris for more than twenty-four hours and he knew this would arouse suspicions. There was just time for him to pay a brief courtesy visit to Holst, at his home. The two men spent ten minutes talking in the driveway before Savir left. Back in Paris he attended his prearranged meetings and then flew home. On the plane home he had much to think about. It was immediately clear to him that there was more at stake here than just a declaration of principles on Palestinian self-government in Gaza and Jericho. Israel was now talking officially, if secretly, to the PLO: it was legitimizing Yasser Arafat and so the old pattern of rejection, hatred and terror would have to alter. On that first morning, when he had woken up in Larsen's flat, Savir had even started to jot down some notes, suggestions as to how the PLO's official view of Israel would have to change if the two sides were to open a new chapter in their dealings with each other. He had not discussed this with Rabin or Peres before coming to Oslo, but it was clear to him that if these meetings continued the whole foundation of the relationship between Israel and the Palestinians would need to be demolished and something more positive built in its place.

Back in Jerusalem his advice to Peres and Beilin was clear-cut. With no hesitation he told them the secret channel had serious potential. The government should now engage in real negotiations in Oslo. For that they needed an experienced lawyer to accompany Savir to Norway: someone who could take the draft Declaration of Principles and turn it into a basis for face-to-face negotiations. Savir told Peres he was convinced that Abu Ala could deliver and that the Israelis should be prepared to negotiate with him as the representative of the PLO. Savir was not yet sure of the extent and strength of Arafat's backing but felt that, none the less, Israel should make a commitment to serious bargaining in Oslo.

Until Savir's arrival, everything that had occurred in the secret channel was, in essence, prenegotiation: exploring the areas where a deal might realistically be made. Now the talks would become real negotiations, with Savir in charge on the Israeli side. Hirschfeld and Pundak would move from the front to the back seat of the channel. The two academics could never have negotiated a deal; not only did they lack the authority, they were too far to the left of mainstream political and public opinion and they were intellectuals, not hard-nosed administrators with an eye for details. But Hirschfeld and Pundak had fulfilled a vital function. They had opened a real dialogue and they had broken down barriers by changing the Palestinians' perception of the Israeli people.

To Palestinians, cut off from everyday contact with their Jewish neighbours, Israelis had somehow acquired a superhuman status: clever, cunning, ruthless and immovable in the face of adversity. But the professors, with all their failings, were people with whom the Palestinians found they had much in common. Hassan Asfour, in particular, was much affected by this realization. The two Israeli academics were not slick politicians with the killer instinct, they were human beings and fallible ones at that – especially Hirschfeld, with his clumsy ways, his heartfelt convictions, his habit of bickering with Pundak and his prodigious appetite. The Norwegians described him to each other as a combination of Bob Dylan and Karl Marx, passionate, socially aware, idealistic in a 1960s way. To their amusement he could never pick up a glass without spilling its contents, never sit in a chair without it collapsing. He was a man whom people felt affectionate towards.

Asfour's attitudes towards the faceless enemy he had confronted for so many years were being forced to undergo a remarkable change. In conversations over dinner, or late at night, Larsen had encouraged Asfour and El Kurd or Hirschfeld and Pundak to talk about their personal aspirations, what they wanted out of life, their dreams, their secret desires. Asfour realized they shared the same goals: a happy family life, security and peace. He became aware that these men could be, indeed were fast becoming, his friends.

It was agreed in Jerusalem that Hirschfeld and Pundak would remain part of the team, attending the meetings to give continuity and maintain confidence. They would help with the increasingly complex logistics and continue to type up all the documents. For the two men there were mixed emotions. From the beginning, Hirschfeld had dreamt of the day when the secret talks would become official. When he returned to Jerusalem, after Savir had been in Oslo, Hirschfeld confided in his daughter that no one could stop the channel now. But he knew that he and Ron Pundak would have to step aside now, and that would be hard to take.

In Tunis Abu Ala and Hassan Asfour conveyed their impressions of Savir to Abu Mazen. Abu Ala thought Savir was serious about negotiating a peace settlement, not just exploring options in an open-ended way. Hassan Asfour was encouraged by Savir's youth. Just four years older than Asfour himself, Savir was from the younger generation who had not been old enough to fight in the 1967 war. Asfour told Abu Mazen it was clear that Savir was from the Peres group and shared his vision of a peaceful future. Yasser Arafat was then briefed. Abu Mazen had been convinced that Savir meant business; Arafat was not so sure. But he wanted a deal and he decided to reserve judgement for the moment.

Now, in the last week in May, the final important player entered the stage, the Israeli lawyer Joel Singer. As the secret channel had begun to develop, in February and March, Beilin shaped the Foreign Ministry team to respond, hence his desire to have Uri Savir in the top non-political post. He had also decided that the Ministry's legal adviser, a British lawyer regarded as something of a cold fish, would not be the best person for the job. He wanted someone more alive, more dynamic to work with. Then he remembered Joel Singer.

Singer had been a colonel in the Israeli army, a member of the military advocate's unit specializing in international law. As a young officer he had taken part behind the scenes in the disengagement agreement with Egypt in 1974, culminating in the Camp David accords of 1979. For twelve years he had been head of the section which wrote many of the laws for the military government in the Occupied Territories. During those years he had lived and breathed every tortuous detail of the peace process in the Middle East. He had been involved in secret peace missions on behalf of his government and he had proved a sharp and talented lawyer with a formidable reputation in the courtroom. For five years he had worked for Yitzhak Rabin, while Rabin was First Minister of Defence. The two men knew each other well and when, in 1988, Joel Singer decided to leave the army, Rabin had told him: 'Its not the end, you know, one day ... well ... just wait and see.'

In March 1993, unaware of the fate that lay in store for him, Singer was sitting in his comfortable office in the luxurious glass and steel tower that houses the prestigious law firm Sidley and Austin, in Washington, DC. For four years, Singer had been a successful international lawyer, making a new and prosperous life for himself and his wife and children in the United States. Then he received a phone call from Jerusalem, from Yossi Beilin, calling on behalf of Shimon Peres. Would he consider becoming the legal adviser to the Foreign Ministry?

'This comes as a bit of a surprise,' said Singer in his matter-of-fact way. 'I've already given up eighteen years of my life to public service. Now I've started a new career and I'm not sure I want to change again.'

'Listen,' said Beilin, 'Shimon wants you to work with him very much. And it's going to be very interesting over the next few years. It's very important that you should be there. Shimon has consulted with many other individuals and they all support his choice – namely, you.'

Singer was hesitant; he asked for time to think. He had no desire to return to Israel or to exchange his healthy salary for the lean remuneration of government employment. He was also aware that the Foreign Ministry was not where the power lay when it came to the peace negotiations, and feared he would be out of the real action. But friends back home convinced him that he could make a difference if he really wanted to, and that he had a duty to accept the post. So he agreed and was told to wait until the Foreign Ministry had gone through the usual motions of selecting several candidates to satisfy the unions.

Two weeks later he got a phone call. There was a document they wanted him to look at. Rabin and Peres had decided it was very confidential and he had to come to Israel to examine it and to attend a meeting.

'When?' asked Singer.

'Immediately, take the first plane and come,' was the reply.

Singer got leave of absence from his office and set off that afternoon on the ten-hour flight to Israel. In Jerusalem Yair Hirschfeld handed him a three-page document which he glanced at quickly before the meeting. It was the second draft of the Sarpsborg Document, produced after the March meeting. The quick look Singer gave the document told the experienced lawyer this was not a serious piece of work. In the meeting with Beilin, Savir and the two professors, he was informed that the PLO had made certain promises in talks which had 'evolved out of the fringes of the multilaterals', and that those promises were contained in the document. Singer, a tall, dark man in his forties, is very much the ex-colonel in his bearing and he has a physical restlessness about him. He fills a room with energy and purpose. His directness of manner can be quite breath-taking as he looks you in the eye and tells it like it is. He had a reputation in Israel for telling his political masters, not why he could *not* do something, but what he *could* do and what the limits of a deal were. He had attended countless high-level negotiating sessions and he knew the nub of any deal was the commitment made on paper. When he was told that the PLO, through Abu Ala, had made a number of verbal promises, he brusquely swept all explanations to one side: 'Yeah, but what they're supposedly promising isn't written in the document. On the contrary, something else is written here and it's very unpromising. In fact, it's a lousy document!'

Hirschfeld and Pundak defended their work. They had done their best in trying to get down on paper the verbal promises made by Abu Ala. It they had not been successful, then they obviously needed someone like him.

'That's why I called you,' added Yossi Beilin. 'Listen, we don't know whether this is a good or a bad document. We don't have the means to judge it. We need you. We want you to tell us. Is this serious or not? And how should we proceed from here?'

'Well, since you're asking, I think it's a bad document and I don't recommend doing anything further with it. However, based on the conversations with the PLO representative, which Yair and Ron have explained to us, well, maybe there's something there. But it's definitely not reflected in the document.'

'Well, can you write down for us what your analysis of the document is?' asked Beilin.

So Singer wrote a one-page analysis: the document was 'a half-baked cake' and there were many technical problems with the draft. He reiterated that the oral indications were perhaps something that could be pursued. What had caught his ear, if not his eye, was that if Hirschfeld and Pundak were correct the PLO was saying the opposite of what the Palestinian delegation under its control was insisting on in Washington. At the State Department, for example, the unshakeable Palestinian position was that during the transition period to Palestinian autonomy the Palestinians should have jurisdiction over the Jewish settlements in the Occupied Territories and East Jerusalem, and that a Palestinian state should be immediately declared. From Oslo the message via Hirschfeld was that the PLO was ready to compromise.

Joel Singer then met with Shimon Peres and gave him the same gloomy analysis of the Sarpsborg Document. Peres too had worked with Singer before and, though they were very different characters, he respected the straight-talking lawyer. Now the Foreign Minister filled Singer in a little on the history of the Oslo Channel and the discussions between himself and the Prime Minister. Rabin was less than gripped by the possibilities presented through the Oslo meetings. The only enthusiasm he had shown, Peres confided to Singer, was over the proposal to bring Singer to Israel to give his opinion. Now the lawyer realized he occupied a unique position: he alone was trusted by both the major players, and that might be a key factor for the success of the channel. He handed over his one-page analysis, presuming it would eventually end up on Rabin's desk. Then he left for the airport.

No sooner had he arrived back at his Sidley and Austin office in Washington than Beilin was on the line again. 'Come back, we want you to see Rabin.'

Singer immediately returned to Israel. It was the beginning of a three-month period of continuous shuttling back and forth across the Atlantic. When he arrived in Israel, Singer met with Peres and Rabin, and repeated his reservations. Rabin was critical of the document in the same way that Singer was, but the lawyer was still intrigued by the verbal promises given to Hirschfeld. He realized that Peres, a man he respected, was convinced that the PLO had changed its fundamental position but that a more sceptical Rabin was not getting this message from the document. Singer knew that, in the small circle of people who were involved in the secret channel, he was the only one whom Rabin trusted. He could therefore be a conduit between the two old rivals, the man to help them in their own negotiations over the future of the channel. He listened as Rabin told him: 'I want to hear it from your own lips if the PLO offer is a real one. You must go to Oslo.'

Until now Rabin had occupied a lonely position on the Israeli side of the secret channel, set apart from Peres and his Blazers. Now he had found an ally, an ex-soldier like himself. Both Singer and Rabin were men who confronted problems head-on. They had both taken a hard-line stance on the question of Israel's security and they had an obsessional regard for detail. Including Singer in the team was a clever calculation, another example of the Peres camp's determination not to have its operational freedom compromised by Rabin's suspicions. Singer could provide a much-needed link, but there were risks too. How would the Palestinians react to him? And would Singer come to share the Blazers' conviction that the Oslo Channel was the route to peace?

7

Strawberries at Gressheim

This time Joel Singer did not go back to the United States. He stayed in the Foreign Ministry for the entire weekend, working day and night to prepare for his trip to Oslo. He had been away from Israel for three years while the Madrid peace process had been grinding on, and now he asked to be updated on every single detail of the negotiations between Israel and the PLO during those years. He was brought boxes and boxes of material and he sat there ploughing through it. The experience was a frustrating and depressing one, for he soon realized that nothing of real substance had happened between day one and the last meeting in Washington in May – a period of two years. The paperwork did, however, give him a sense of the main points of contention and where the obstacles and the booby-traps were laid. With the experience he had gleaned from eighteen years of negotiation, mainly with Egypt, Singer started to develop a way to bypass the major problems. But Rabin had made it clear that, before there could be any real negotiations over the future of the Occupied Territories, Singer had to explore the point of view of the PLO men in the Oslo Channel and try to gauge their sincerity.

While Terje Larsen began preparing for the next secret meeting scheduled for early June, Mona Juul accompanied the new Foreign Minister, Johan Jorgen Holst, on an official visit to Israel. A month into the job, Holst wanted to explore the extent of Israeli political involvement in the Oslo Channel. The Norwegians were still in the dark as to whether Rabin knew about the talks and, more crucially, whether he backed them. Holst had taken the opportunity on 28 May, while on a trip to Washington, to brief Warren Christopher about developments. He told the US Secretary of State that there was now official participation on the Israeli side. Christopher was supportive but did not wish to know the details. He was preoccupied with his own country's role in the Washington talks and Holst reassured him that Norway would not upstage that process.

A long meeting with Shimon Peres convinced Holst that the Israeli Foreign Minister was fully behind the secret channel. But when the Norweigian asked if he should mention the subject to Rabin, when he met him later in the day, Peres advised him not to do so. That afternoon Rabin was friendly, but there were other people in the room and they could not speak openly. Holst thought he caught some oblique references signalling that the Prime Minister was aware of the Oslo Channel but at the same time did not want it mentioned. So Holst left Israel none the wiser as to the real extent of commitment on the Israeli side.

The Norwegians were often kept in the dark by both sides, and their frustration grew. They had proposed, and readily accepted, their limited role as facilitators rather than mediators. But as the months passed they inevitably became drawn into the details of the developing deal. In such a small, tight-knit group they were the ones called on to sort out all the problems – especially when the parties returned to base.

Terje Larsen was still the focal point of the Norwegian effort; he devoted all his time, his efforts and his energy to the secret channel. When away from Oslo, the two parties never telephoned each other – it was impossible at the time to telephone an Arab country from Israel. So Larsen was the middleman, charged with relaying messages between the two parties. After Uri Savir joined the channel the stakes had been raised, and everyone in the small group began to realize they carried a heavy responsibility for the future of the whole Middle East. It was a heavy burden and the strain began to tell.

Abu Ala would be most vulnerable should things go wrong. He had spearheaded the Palestinian effort from the start and had invested more than any of the others. Like all who had survived within the PLO, he was keenly attuned to the politics of any situation. But he was a financier, not a diplomat, a professional negotiator. Yet he alone was presenting the PLO view and defending its positions. Even within his own small delegation there were rifts. He had grown closer to Hassan Asfour during the Olso process: his respect for the younger man increased day by day. Asfour was now an ally, an equal, not just the assistant he had been at first. But Maher El Kurd was another matter. Abu

Ala had fallen out with him. He knew Maher's first loyalty was to Yasser Arafat and suspected he was being undermined. He determined he could not continue with Maher in the team.

The Israelis had their differences of opinion too, and there was tension between Rabin and Peres. But the Foreign Minister had a cohesive team who were deeply committed to the Oslo Channel. Abu Ala had the full support of just one man, Abu Mazen. Arafat's intentions and the extent of his support were hard to fathom. Abu Ala was taking enormous risks and the pressure on him was building daily.

While Mona Juul was away in Jerusalem, the phone calls to Larsen reached a crescendo – in the office, at the flat, on the mobile phone Larsen carried with him wherever he went. On average there were twenty calls a day. Abu Ala would often ring at 3.00 a.m. to ask peremptorily what Larsen was doing. As the Norwegian struggled out of an exhausted sleep, the Palestinian would demand he call Israel to find out what was going on. Sometimes he shouted, even screamed, that his instructions had to be obeyed. Larsen told himself that Abu Ala was under enormous pressure and must be reassured at all costs. He was close to Abu Ala, and growing closer. But there was also something akin to hatred in their relationship. Larsen was becoming a punch-bag for Abu Ala. The bullying streak in the tough banker found its target in the Norwegian, and Larsen chose to absorb it – at great personal cost.

Deep down, however, Larsen found it increasingly frustrating that both parties expected him to be the go-between on the phone, when he only partially understood the content of the messages he was relaying. It had been his aim from the start to stay at arm's length, not to become involved in the substance of the talks, but now he could see the practical difficulties. The knowledge the Norwegians had in the early days at Borregaard had now substantially increased but Larsen, Juul and Pedersen still did not participate in the meetings, nor were they informed of the exact positions each side took. Larsen therefore was not confident he fully understood what the Israelis and Palestinians were trying to achieve when they used him as their medium. Occasionally they briefed him fully, but more often they did not, and when for example Abu Ala asked him to clarify something that Savir wanted, Larsen sometimes had to guess what the missing details were. He felt that both sides unwisely handicapped him on some crucial occasions when he was unable to make meaningful interpretations for them.

The phone calls were made more complicated by the code they all adopted to try and hide the real nature of the secret talks. They assumed that several intelligence services would be interested in eavesdropping on their conversations, amongst them Mossad, the Israeli secret service, and the American CIA. As far as the Norwegians were aware, neither of these agencies knew about the channel. The players were never referred to by name. Rabin was 'the grandfather' and Arafat 'the other grandfather', Peres was 'the father' and Beilin 'the son'. Abu Mazen, the mysterious man whom none of them knew, was 'the Holy Spirit'. And Abu Ala's name was 'Puntoffle', the Yiddish word for slippers. Savir and Singer were 'number one' and 'number two'. Israel was 'the little country', America 'the big country' and the PLO 'those across the sea'. There were no secure lines, no ciphers or elaborate precautions. Perhaps this rather amateurish code was the reason that no intelligence service was alerted to the existence of the secret channel.

After three days of non-stop, nerve-racking phone calls, Larsen noticed his hands were beginning to shake when he held a coffee cup. He felt he might lose control and, with Mona Juul away and no one at home to confide in, he was scared that he would scream back at Abu Ala or Hirschfeld or Savir the next time one of them called. Such an outburst would finish him as a neutral middleman. Finally he unplugged the phone, having called his office to say that he would be unavailable for the next few days. Then he packed a bag and went away. It was the first time since the Oslo Channel was opened that he had not been at the beck and call of the Israelis and the Palestinians, and both parties were furious with him. But he did not care, he had had enough.

Ironically Larsen did not seek a complete change of scene, a quiet and reflective wander by a fiord. Instead he attended a seminar in a hotel outside Oslo where, as an expert in organizational sociology, he had been asked to speak to top management from Siemens, the industrial company. His subject was how to handle conflicts between groups within commercial organizations. Although his listeners did not know it, his lecture contained some very recently learned lessons. Despite the fact that his encounter with the world of international negotiations was proving somewhat bruising, Larsen believed it was not so different from what he had been doing for years – running a research institute full of prima donnas. The cast of characters was much the same.

When Larsen returned to Oslo, somewhat refreshed and ready for the fray, Abu Ala had already arrived and was intensely curious to know where he had been. Larsen was non-committal and Abu Ala, delighted at discovering he had a secret, decided that, with Mona absent, another woman must be involved. He told Larsen a story he had heard the week before in Greece from a government minister. The minister's friend had lost his wife after many years of marriage. The man sat alone at home, his head bowed, weeping and saying softly again and again, 'I'm all alone.' Then his tone changed, a new realization crept into the words 'I'm all alone'. The man's head lifted, his look brightened and finally he leapt up shouting with glee, 'I'm all alone! I'm all alone!', and danced around the room. This, Abu Ala suggested, was a story Larsen would appreciate. The two of them roared with laughter and determined to tell Uri the story next time they met. It was Uri's kind of joke, they decided – and they were right. From that time on, in the tensest moment of negotiations when it seemed they had reached an impasse, Abu Ala or Uri would quietly mutter 'I'm all alone' and the meeting would dissolve in laughter.

On 11 June, Yair Hirschfeld and Ron Pundak were sent on ahead to Oslo to make sure that flights, hotels and timetables were in order. Uri Savir and Joel Singer flew to Norway together and discussed their strategy on the plane. The Israelis had been booked into a small, old-fashioned hotel, the Norom, away from the city centre and in the same street as Terje and Mona's apartment. The Israelis had all been booked in under Larsen's name and Terje hoped that Savir, in particular, would be able to remain anonymous there. The Palestinians had not yet arrived, and Larsen took the four Israelis to eat in a local Spanish restaurant, the Don Quixote. Singer was, like Uri on his first visit, clearly nervous and somewhat disoriented. First he found himself in a hotel straight out of an Ibsen play: there was no hot water, an antiquated telephone and the furnishings left much to be desired. Then minutes later he was eating tortillas across the street to the sound of guitars. Over dinner Larsen, Geir Pedersen and the Israeli team tried to convince Singer that these talks would be different, that there was a special atmosphere, a small group, a kind of 'Oslo spirit'. The lawyer looked unconvinced and retorted: 'How do I know this isn't just another load of Washington bullshit negotiations?'

Larsen set off to meet the Palestinians at the airport while the others were finishing dinner. He brought the three men from Tunis back to his flat, where the talks were to begin that night. They climbed the five flights of stairs to Terje and Mona's eyrie on the top floor of an elegant nineteenth-century apartment block. The amosphere was tense, it was obvious the newcomer would not fit in easily. The subtle Savir, with his diplomatic skills and easy manner, was accompanied by someone with the unmistakable stamp of the Israeli military. Singer was not interested in pleasantries or in creating any special 'atmosphere' around the meetings. Over dinner he had given Larsen a withering look when the Norwegian tried to explain the sociological strategy that had so impressed Savir. Pedersen and Larsen sensed that the whole group was in for a rude awakening and retired to a room along the corridor, leaving the two sides alone in the open-plan living-room.

With no preamble or diplomatic niceties Singer informed the Palestinians that he had less than two days to spare and a long list of questions to get through. Abu Ala told him bluntly that he refused to answer any questions. Singer replied that the questions came from the Prime Minister of Israel. This was what the Palestinians needed to hear – at last some real indication that the top man was on board.

Abu Ala gave no sign of either excitement or consternation. He calmly countered that he too had a big list of queries. Singer abruptly replied: 'I am serious, I am ready to reply to any questions.'

Singer then launched into his questions. His style, thought the Palestinians, was that of the military interrogator: rapid-fire demands, never content with the answers, always probing, demanding clarification on every single aspect. His aim in this prenegotiating session was to find out what the PLO was ready to offer the Israelis rather than whether it could deliver. That would come later. For now he wanted to talk, not about concepts and ideas but about practical details and even timetables.

He concentrated his interrogation on the real stumbling-blocks in Washington. The future of the settlements in the Occupied

Territories was top of the list. More than 100,000 Jews live in 150 settlements ranging in size from a small camp to a town. These are dotted throughout the Occupied Territories, in Gaza and on the West Bank, or Judea and Samaria, as the settlers call them. The Jews who live there believe they are returning to 'Eretz Israel', the land of Greater Israel, the inheritance of their forefathers.

Some settlements have been established for political reasons – for example, on the spot where Palestinians have attacked Jews during the Intifada. Others have been located on strategic ground overlooking the Jordan valley or vital communications links. A network of roads connects the settlements with each other and with cities in Israel. These settlements have aroused enormous resentment amongst the local Palestinian community. They have created many land and water disputes, and their establishment is seen by many local Arabs as a deliberate ploy to make it impossible to return the land to the Palestinians. Over the years the Settlement Movement has been a potent force which politicians of all parties have handled with caution. Under the right-wing Likud government the settlements expanded enormously, helped by grants and tax breaks. Rabin committed himself to curbing them but still the Labour Party was careful to protect the rights and the security of the settlers. If the Palestinians were to have autonomy in the Occupied Territories, the settlers would have to be assured of Israeli protection. In Washington the official delegation was insisting that these areas should come under Palestinian jurisdiction. Now Singer wanted to draw out of Abu Ala what that meant in practice.

'If we hand over to you the Department of Education in the territories, do you intend to be responsible for running the schools inside the settlements?'

'No,' came the short answer from Abu Ala.

'And is your position that you wish to be responsible for running the hospitals in the settlements that the Israelis will use?'

'No.'

'So how about the welfare provision for people in the settlements – will that be your responsibility?'

'No.'

'So you're telling me you virtually don't want any responsibility inside the settlements.'

'Right,' said Abu Ala.

Although the Palestinians were not prepared to give in on the all-important question of whether the Israeli army or a Palestinian police force would be in charge of the settlers' security, the answers Abu Ala gave were radically different to any of the signals coming from Washington. Nothing so encouraging to the Israelis had ever been conceded so directly in the many months of talks.

The Israelis present at the meeting remember over 200 questions asked in quick succession, the Palestinians recall 300, and to the Norwegians it seemed like 500. Abu Ala gave measured responses. Where he could, he gave a clear answer; where he did not know the practical details of health and education policy he wrote down all the points and said he would come back with detailed answers. He appeared cool, calm and collected. The two other Palestinians said nothing. All they knew of Singer was that he was a lawyer – they were not in favour of lawyers – that he was an Israeli colonel – they were not in favour of Israeli colonels – and that he was close to Rabin – and they were not in favour of Rabin's hard-line tactics. As Singer continued his questioning, Hassan Asfour's hostility towards the Israeli became almost tangible, it filled the room. For the Communist Party member from Gaza, this man before him epitomized everything that made the Israelis the enemy. Hassan Asfour, like Singer, was the repository of every detail of the Washington negotiations and he knew what Singer was doing: nailing them down on every tiny point in preparation for the hard bargaining to come.

For hours on end Joel Singer grilled the PLO. In a short break Abu Ala whispered to Terje Larsen: 'This man Singer, he is really a caricature of a Jew. Uri, he is not like this man. But,' he added with a wry smile, 'I learn a lot from Singer; he sees things I have not yet seen.' It was a mark of Abu Ala's flexibility that he was prepared to learn from the Israeli and to admit that the endless questions had clarified his thinking.

As the evening wore on the atmosphere became acrimonious. A rueful Larsen, wandering into the living area from time to time to refresh people's drinks, watched his pristine apartment, decorated in a minimalist style, begin to resemble a pub at closing time. Half-filled glasses of wine and dirty coffee cups clustered on the wooden floors, and there were overflowing ashtrays on the black leather and chrome Bauhaus chairs.

Singer's interrogation continued until 4.00 a.m. and resumed early the next day back at the Thomas Heftye cottage on the

Holmenkollen hill. There were, however, the usual lighter moments which characterized the exploits of the Oslo Channel. The Norom Hotel, the charming but somewhat outdated old hostelry where they were staying, which lacked many modern amenities, also had some unusual ones. Inside each bedroom a rope dangled from the ceiling near the window, a rudimentary fire-escape to enable the occupant to shin down to the ground. The hotel was not Singer's idea of a suitable residence. But Yair Hirschfeld was captivated by the Norom and reassured the other Israelis that, if they failed in their task, they could always put the ropes around their necks.

On the second day Jan Egeland made his appearance at the ski cottage. He had just returned from a seven-week tour through Bosnia with Thorvald Stoltenberg. With him he brought some ominous news – a small cutting from a newspaper quoting the news agency Agence France-Presse. He had been handed the cutting that morning by the Norwegian Foreign Ministry press spokesman who, with a stiff little smile, had said: 'My goodness, Jan, whatever are you up to?'

The story reported that there was a secret back channel in Norway between the PLO and Israel engineered by Dennis Ross, the chief Middle East official at the State Department, and that in May several meetings had taken place in Oslo. The story had been printed in several Middle Eastern papers and the Norwegian press were asking for a comment. Egeland had told his spokesman to fob them off by saying Norway had brought the two sides together at the recent multilateral talks on refugees in Oslo. The first person Jan Egeland spoke to at the cottage was Yair Hirschfeld, who read the cutting and turned pale. Uri Savir was more philosophical. 'We'll see how much they make of it and how much they get hold of,' he said calmly. 'I'd advise you not to tell the Palestinians, because we're into a very constructive phase right now,' he added somewhat disingenuously, as Singer was at that very moment firing questions at Abu Ala with Hassan Asfour glowering in the corner.

It turned out, however, that the Palestinians, whose grapevine excels all others, already knew about the report. 'Don't tell the Israelis,' Abu Ala said to Egeland; 'we're into a very constructive phase and they might get nervous.' To everyone's relief the Agence France-Presse story was a one-day wonder.

By mid-afternoon on the second day Singer was still hard at it;

his list of questions seemed endless, as did Abu Ala's patience. The witness refused to buckle under the onslaught of the examination and finally Larsen had to interrupt them to tell them that the plane was leaving in fifteen minutes. In the car Joel Singer confided that he was impressed by Abu Ala. Singer's reaction, his words even, were an echo of Savir's on the last occasion: 'He's wise, he knows everything. He's totally familiar with all the ins and outs of their positions. Remarkable intelligence – and he really understands the political issues.'

Just as the Palestinians had their unflattering stereotype of a Jew, so the Israelis had their dismissive image of a high-ranking PLO official. But Abu Ala had exploded their idea of a crude, fanatical, single-minded individual, pushing outdated rhetoric and unrealistic demands.

When he arrived back in Tunis, Abu Ala gave vent to his feelings. Angry and depressed, he went with Hassan to see Abu Mazen. The good news was that Rabin seemed to be on board, the bad news was that Singer was his messenger. Abu Ala was being forced to clarify his own thoughts and, while he was pragmatic enough to agree that in the end they would have to come down to details, the process was an uncomfortable and somewhat humiliating one. But Abu Mazen was jubilant. His knowledge of the bad blood between Rabin and Peres since 1975 had made him doubt that Peres would bring Rabin in at all. Now this lawyer, with his military background and his negotiating experience, was proof that the Prime Minister was involved. He told Abu Ala not to be downhearted.

'This is the critical moment,' said Abu Mazen. 'When the Israelis hear what Singer has to say, they will either break negotiations or go on to conclude an agreement. If they come back to us after this session we will go right to the end. If not we'll just have to forget it.'

Abu Mazen and Abu Ala told Yasser Arafat of the new developments. Abu Ala went through his detailed notes with the Chairman of the PLO. Arafat now realized the Oslo Channel was more than an academic exercise, and he recognized the hand of Rabin in the demands for precise and practical explanations and timetables. He determined that he too must get involved in working through the details.

Singer flew to Vienna, where Peres was attending a conference, and gave the Foreign Minister an upbeat report of his experience in Oslo. He was impressed at the way Abu Ala had handled the questioning and he concluded that the Palestinians meant business. He reported to Peres and then to Rabin that he had deliberately put the emphasis on the issue which had proved the stumbling-block in Washington: the future of Jerusalem and the settlements. He had wanted to find out if, behind their public statements, the Palestinians had fall-back positions for the secret channel.

When he had briefed Peres and Rabin, Singer returned to Washington to prepare for the next round. Rabin had given him the green light to write an Israeli proposal to be presented at the next meeting. It would be the text of an outline agreement. He had less than a week to write it. Some of the material was already in his head, some of it he developed as he read the Washington protocols. The rest was based on the answers to the many questions he had asked Abu Ala in Oslo. He tailored his document around what the Palestinians had told him was feasible from their side. His intention was to seize the pragmatic proposals they had made in the secret channel while accommodating some of their publicly stated requirements. He appreciated that they had taken very definite stands in Washington on various issues, and that they could not realistically be expected to abandon those positions entirely, allowing themselves to be seen to surrender to Israeli wishes. But both Singer and Savir were still adamant that the Palestinians would have to give some ground on their Washington declarations. Significantly Singer decided that in order to make the document more palatable he would put the most difficult elements not in the document itself but in a subsection called the 'Agreed Minutes'.

As Singer worked in his high-rise office, just a few blocks away in the State Department the official talks were once more sliding into stalemate. The American 'full partnership' was not having the desired effect of pushing the two sides to some conclusion. The complex web established by the Madrid process was visibly unravelling. Direct talks between the two parties had been the agreed cornerstone but the Americans were now acting as intermediaries. On 30 June they put forward a so-called 'bridging document'. The Palestinians thought that it was biased towards the Israelis, and that they now faced two opponents instead of one. In the early days of secret negotiation Yossi Beilin had intended that the ideas thrown up by the Oslo Channel should be fed discreetly into the Washington talks. When Oslo produced the first draft of the Declaration of Principles, the Sarpsborg Document, both sides hoped that somehow, with the backing of Rabin and Arafat, the proposal could be given to the two official delegations and become the key to unlock the door to peace. But it was becoming clear, as Larsen had predicted to Holst in April, that Washington was going nowhere while the Oslo Channel was creating its own momentum. Now, in the first days of July, the real forum for direct and meaningful negotiations would shift decisively to Norway.

In Tunis Abu Mazen received the message he had been waiting for. The Norwegians called to say that another meeting had been proposed for the weekend of 3 July. Abu Mazen knew that this would be the real thing. The prenegotiations were over. Abu Ala would meet Savir and Singer again and this time, Abu Mazen told him, there would be hard bargaining.

In Norway Jan Egeland was supposed to be on holiday. He felt guilty about the work and the responsibility weighing down his friends, Mona and Terje. Borregaard was being refurbished and no further meetings could be held there for months. Finding the right place for the talks was a constant headache and Egeland decided that, holiday or no holiday, he would find it himself. Both the Palestinians and the Israelis were now fearful that the Norwegians would not be able to maintain the shroud of secrecy over the talks. One of the groups had bumped into Egeland at the airport as he was arriving on another plane; this showed them all how easily they could run into someone who would recognize them. Egeland wanted to move their point of entry to Bergen or Stavanger, other Norwegian towns with international air connections. But that would have meant even more tortuous routeing. For the Palestinians to come to Oslo for three days already meant a six-day round trip from Tunis. Fornebu remained the only practical airport, but both parties were adamant that they wanted a more remote location for the meetings.

Egeland began to phone round the small boarding-houses and hotels dotted about the Norwegian countryside. July was not a good month in which to find somewhere suitable; it was the height of the school holidays and there were no rooms to be had anywhere. Egeland was wrangling with his wife, who was fed up with him spending his hard-earned holiday on the phone.

Finally, on an outing to the Tivoli Gardens in Copenhagen, Egeland told her what was going on. She promised to find somewhere safe for the group to meet. She racked her brains, until she remembered a woman, Annelisa Melby, who had been sitting next to her at a recent conference: she and her husband owned a large farm and manor-house.

The Egelands left a message on the owners' answering machine, but heard nothing back. Finally, with less than two days to go, the Deputy Minister was about to ring Jerusalem and Tunis to say it would have to be an Oslo hotel or nothing, when he heard back from Mrs Melby. She was willing to have the group to stay on one condition. She asked Egeland: 'Can I put new tablecloths and curtains on the bill, as mine aren't good enough?'

'OK, you can put what you like on the bill as long as you can be ready for us in forty-eight hours!' said Egeland with relief.

Not only was the small team of Norwegians stretched to the limit finding secret places to meet, it was aware of growing concern amongst the two sides about their own physical safety. The Palestinians, in particular, were all too aware that some Arab factions regarded communicating with the enemy as an act of treachery, punishable by death. The group had discussed its security before, and Ron Pundak had voiced the general feeling that they should not break up the intimate family atmosphere developed at Borregaard. But by the end of June they all decided it was time to call in some protective cover. Jan Egeland had his doubts; the Norwegian secret police did not have an unblemished history in its dealings with the Middle East.

After the Black September outrage at the Munich Olympics, Mossad agents had roamed the world, tracking down the PLO men they believed responsible for the massacre of eleven Israeli sportsmen. One by one they killed suspected Palestinian terrorists in Europe and the Middle East. In July 1973, in Lillehammer, Norwegian home of the Winter Olympics, they gunned down a Moroccan waiter they had mistaken for a terrorist. The public outrage backfired on the Norwegian secret police. They were criticized for their lack of efficiency in allowing Mossad agents to infiltrate the country and then, after the crime had been committed, for blundering over the arrests and investigation. It was feared that some Israeli hit men had got away because Norwegian intelligence had not been sharp enough.

In 1991 another unfortunate event occurred to tarnish further the Norwegians' reputation for handling Arabs and Israelis. Just as the Socialist government maintained strong links with its Israeli Labour Party counterparts, the Norwegian secret police had good relations with Mossad. In the wake of the Gulf War, a number of leading Palestinian figures, including PLO men, asked for asylum in Norway. They were told that experts would debrief them as part of the procedure. The Norwegians then invited their Mossad friends to send an Arabic-speaking team to carry out the interviews. Worse still, they did not tell the Palestinians who these men really were, and there was no Norwegian intelligence officer in the room while the questioning was carried out. When the story broke, there was a huge political row and questions were asked in the Norwegian parliament. The Palestinians involved were furious and afraid that, having talked unwittingly to Israeli agents, they would now become targets for assassination. The head of the secret police was forced to resign and the organization suffered a further loss of public confidence.

However, by the summer of 1993, the Norwegians felt they had no choice but to call in the security forces. The group of negotiators was larger and more high-level now, and the anxieties of both sides had to be addressed or they would insist on bringing their own security men with them in future. Holst called a meeting on 1 July with the head of security in the anti-terrorist branch of the service. Holst asked him for his help but gave few details about what the visitors were doing in Norway. It was decided that a six-man team would be sufficient. A leader was assigned immediately and was sent to see Terje Larsen, who made it clear that this would be an unusual job requiring a special sort of person, the kind who could be friendly but not intrusive, sensitive to mood while at the same time alert to potential dangers. Most importantly, Larsen stressed, the security men must treat both sides equally, giving exactly the same attention to each. They were to steer the parties through the airport and to act as drivers, guards and companions.

With the negotiators expected within hours, the five other men needed to make up the team had to be recruited and briefed immediately. Through luck, more than anything, a team was pulled together. These men were to become part of the channel, minders but also companions, even friends, of those they protected.

The new security team met the Israelis at Fornebu on Saturday,

3 July. They were taken north to Gressheim, an hour's drive from Oslo. Geir Pedersen went with them. Later that day more agents waited with Larsen and Mona Juul to collect the Palestinians and to take them, too, for a summer weekend in the country. This time there was a new man in Abu Ala's team, an accountant named Mohammed Abu Koush. In his late forties, with grey hair and a moustache, he was, like the others, smartly dressed and deferred to Abu Ala. A lawyer by training, Abu Koush lives in Germany and serves on the PLO's delegation at the UN in Geneva dealing with social and economic matters. In Oslo he was clearly fulfilling the role of Abu Ala's assistant, as Maher had before him. No explanation was given for the change of team. The Israelis and the Norwegians were intensely curious, and somewhat worried, about Maher's disappearance, but they thought it wisest to say nothing. They assumed, accurately as it turned out, that there had been internal disagreements. But from that day on, none of them could discover what had really happened to Maher.

The group arrived at a beautiful old manor-house, painted the traditional white and grey. The place had been in Annelisa Melby's family for generations. It was smaller than Borregaard but much the same in atmosphere, and it was someone's home, not a company house. Annelisa Melby greeted her guests and showed them round. The five living-rooms on the ground floor were painted in the traditional colours found in country houses in Norway: green, blue and yellow. But the rooms contained grand, ornate mahogany furniture and fine paintings.

The Palestinians had been assigned bedrooms in the main house. As usual Larsen was careful to give Abu Ala the best room, Mohammed Abu Koush had the one next door, and Hassan was left with the pokiest space. He grumbled good-naturedly to Larsen: 'Anyone can see that you're not a communist; you're a real capitalist!'

The Israelis were billeted in a small cottage five minutes' drive away at the end of a dirt track. This cottage was the weekend hideaway of the high-powered woman director of one of Norway's largest banks. It had been Mona's idea to introduce the two teams to the simpler style of Scandinavian life and the harmony inspired by rustic living. Hirschfeld and Pundak were enchanted but Savir and Singer looked somewhat askance. This was not their natural habitat.

As the seven men met that warm and humid afternoon, they

knew that the real negotiations were about to begin. They all sat down to read the Israeli proposal that Singer had drawn up, the new draft of the Declaration of Principles. The Palestinians nearly fell off their chairs when they saw it. For there, in black and white, was a legalistic agreement incorporating everything that Abu Ala had, at the previous meeting, indicated that he might be prepared to concede. The new declaration differed markedly from the one that had evolved out of the Borregaard talks. It got down to the basics: the details of the withdrawal from Gaza and Jericho and the form of the autonomy arrangements, the fate of the settlements and the timetable for elections. This was no joint approach, this was the Israeli version of the Declaration of Principles and it was hard for the Palestinians to swallow. Hassan Asfour exploded with anger and marched to the centre of the room.

'You are trying to destroy what we have spent the last six months creating! This just takes us back to square one. You're living in the past and you won't look to the future. Don't you realize that if you go on like this you'll be destined to be the occupiers for evermore and we will have to continue the struggle against you!'

After his outburst there was silence. The Israelis were aware that the men opposite them were deeply depressed. After six months and numerous drafts of the Declaration of Principles it seemed as if they were indeed starting all over again. Abu Ala went for a walk with Larsen and expressed his more measured opinion.

'Why, why do they do this? We have a Declaration of Principles already, which we drew up with Hirschfeld and Pundak. They should just sign it! They don't want to, so they clearly aren't serious about peace. This is all Rabin's idea, he's the one behind it.'

When they reconvened Joel Singer suggested they go through the document word by word. Next to every point the Palestinians disagreed with, they should put, in brackets, their own position. This proposal was accepted and the men worked through the night until dawn, by which time they had completed a draft that incorporated all the Palestinian reservations. Suddenly, it seemed, there was progress; the Israelis even felt privately that they might do a deal by the end of the weekend. After a few hours' break everyone was back around the table, ploughing on until late afternoon. Then Uri Savir, Abu Ala, Larsen and Hassan Asfour went down to a nearby lake for a stroll. Mona Juul went jogging. It was warm and sultry, a shower was imminent. The mood lightened, there was laughing and joking.

When everyone gathered together for dinner that evening, they found that Jan Egeland had arrived to give Norwegian political authority to the proceedings. The owners of Gressheim had been told that their visitors were academics writing a book. But the raised voices and angry exchanges, and the six hefty minders ranged around the house, made that an unlikely scenario. So Larsen confided in them that these were Israelis and Palestinians connected to the recent Oslo multilateral talks on refugees. That explanation was plausible but did not give the game away.

The host and hostess were most gracious, acting as waitress and butler to serve the dinner. They had hired a chef, who produced a gourmet meal of Norwegian salmon, trout and other fish baked in lemon, wine and cream. Hirschfeld made great play of asking for a salad – he was on a diet, he claimed, to much hilarity. Salad was, as usual, not available and so, his conscience free, Hirschfeld ate an enormous meal. Hassan Asfour, who did not eat fish, was served chicken, which caused the same old jokes the group had made before at his expense: his name means 'bird' in Arabic, and everyone laughed at the idea of fowl eating fowl. For dessert there were strawberries – baskets and baskets of them. Strawberries were in season and the guests greedily devoured 18lb. of them. Hirschfeld, they claimed, ate 12lb. of them himself.

While most of the negotiators were still sitting at the table, enjoying their coffee and dessert, Joel Singer stood up abruptly and turned on his heel. 'I've got work to do,' he announced, and went back to the meeting room to shuffle through papers. The others exchanged glances; the new recruit had not yet relaxed into their sociable ways.

As the night wore on, the Norwegians, sprawling in the living-room furthest away from the meeting, felt there was a positive mood in the air. Egeland was staying the night; he, Geir, Mona and Terje had booked rooms in the nearby village but, although tired, they were loath to leave. There was a feeling of anticipation abroad; something significant was about to happen, and they decided to remain at the manor-house.

Inside the meeting room the stand-off had miraculously been reduced to five points on the agenda, but five significant points, not easily resolvable: the inclusion of UN Resolutions 242 and 338, which called for Israeli withdrawal from the Occupied Territories; the permanent status negotiations for the future; the Gaza/Jericho First approach; the elections to be held in Jerusalem; and the fate of Palestinians displaced by the 1967 war. At 2.00 a.m., and again at 4.00 a.m., the group broke for coffee. Things were proving more difficult than the Israelis had imagined. They went back for one more try at 4.30 a.m. By six it was daylight. Larsen, exhausted, was asleep on the sofa with Jan Egeland dozing beside him. The group had been at Gressheim for forty-four hours and the Israelis and Palestinians had spent thirty-five of those hours in intense negotiation. Then suddenly the door burst open; there was shouting, running and sounds of hurried packing all at once. 'It's impossible, we can't do it! Can we leave right away?' said voices on both sides. They all just wanted to get away as quickly as they could.

The minders revved up the cars and in fifteen minutes everyone had left. The owners came down to prepare breakfast for sixteen people and found the place empty. Egeland, who had had his own Golf VW parked at the manor, had driven off with Abu Ala. Halfway to the airport the Palestinian swapped places with Uri Savir, who had been in a security man's car. So each delegation leader had his private moment alone with the Deputy Foreign Minister. Egeland took a dejected Savir to the airport and waited there until Savir's plane left for Copenhagen, from where it would fly on to Moscow, where Savir was due that same day.

The Israelis had been too confident, and they had been disappointed. Savir and Singer carried authority from Rabin to sign if the agreement was right, and they made that clear to the opposite side. If they could keep up the momentum, and carry the Palestinians with them, it was technically possible to conclude a deal that night. The agreement could then be passed on through Washington for public consumption and the Oslo Channel would have fulfilled its promise. But Abu Ala knew this was the Israelis' plan, and he was not going to make things easy. The PLO wanted a deal but the game of negotiation was just beginning and Abu Ala would go back to Tunis for further instructions and guidance on how best to play the next round.

It was part of the pattern of the Oslo Channel that before leaving Norway the two parties would visit the Foreign Minster, Johan Jorgen Holst, at his house to brief him secretly on the progress they had made. This was partly courtesy and partly a way of maximizing Norwegian political involvement at a significant level. Holst's status as Foreign Minister, and the distance he deliberately kept from the talks, gave him a more detached view.

Sometimes the visitors would stay for drinks or dinner with Holst's family. At the end of that weekend at Gressheim they sat on the porch in the warm dusk, sipping wine and chatting sociably after the business had been dealt with. Marianne Heiberg was there and Edvard, their blond four-year-old son, played happily on the floor with his toys. Yair Hirschfeld could not resist picking up the boy's water pistol and having a shooting match with him.

8

A Trip to Tunis and Jerusalem

Within a week, on 10 July, the political bosses in Jerusalem and Tunis had sent their teams back to Oslo. They wanted to keep up the momentum of the actual negotiations, which had started so promisingly at Gressheim. On their return the Israelis and the Palestinians met first with Johan Jorgen Holst and Mona Juul, who were setting off the next day on a prearranged official visit to Tunisia. Again Larsen had had some trouble finding a venue for the talks. Both the Palestinians and the Israelis had wanted to return to Borregaard, but the house was still being refurbished. Larsen's union contacts came to the rescue, suggesting a small seminar and conference centre outside Oslo. The Halvorsbole Hotel and Conference Centre, owned by the Seamen's Union, is situated beside the country's third largest waterway, the Randsfjorden. It is a spectacular setting: towering mountains, pine forests and the intense ultramarine of the deep-water inlet. The hotel itself was built in the 1960s, and is a Bauhaus-style single-storey block with a bar, conference room and bedrooms. Panoramic windows overlook the stunning scenery. The group arrived during the summer holidays and Larsen's contacts had persuaded the hotel's manager to find rooms in local guest-houses for the few academic guests who were already booked into the hotel.

It was Larsen's turn to drive with Abu Ala. The other Palestinians followed behind with their secret police driver, who told them stories about the places they were passing through, their history and their folklore. Hassan Asfour was overawed by the beauty of the countryside, so different from Gaza, and exclaimed: 'It's so blue – and green! Look at all this fresh water! If only we could have water like this in my country. Here it's too much, it's too green, and too wet!'

The mood when they all met up in the afternoon was jovial. The Palestinians and Norwegians went out to meet the Israelis, who arrived after them. They all stood together in front of the hotel sign board shaking their heads and trying to outdo each other in the pronunciation of the very Norwegian 'Halvorsbole'. The secret police were the referees but were laughing so much they could not decide who had won the competition. Uri Savir announced: 'We can't make an international agreement at this place. There's no way we can come up with something here. "The Halvorsbole Agreement"? It's impossible! No one would be able to pronounce it!'

Little did he know how prophetic his words were to prove. However, it was not the name of the location but the complex games of negotiation that would prove a stumbling-block to the agreement.

As the group met for drinks and dinner everyone was optimistic. The Norwegians felt they had been so close to a deal at Gressheim the week before that perhaps an agreement would be reached that very evening. Moreover, Joel Singer and Terje Larsen agreed that what they called 'the structural forces' in the Middle East were now so strong that a breakthrough was imminent. Larsen even made a bet with the security men that this would be the last meeting. He told them that they should prepare video equipment and have a stills photographer on stand-by, in case the parties actually reached the point of signing the Declaration of Principles that night. On his mobile phone he alerted Johan Jorgen Holst in Oslo that he should be prepared to come to Halvorsbole at a moment's notice, to witness such an event. After dinner, as the parties adjourned to the conference room and closed the door behind them, there was an air of expectancy, of controlled excitement, amongst the Norwegians left outside.

But suddenly the mood was shattered. This time the Palestinians turned the tables on the Israelis. Savir and Singer had come prepared to work on the five sticking points that remained from Gressheim. Rabin had asked them to add three more demands on various aspects of security: the security of the settlements, the borders of the areas where there would be withdrawal, and the security of Israelis travelling through those parts. But when they saw the new draft of the Declaration of Principles presented by the Palestinians that day the Israelis were aghast. Abu Ala had introduced twenty-five new points and, when the Israelis remonstrated, he replied with a smile: 'They're just cosmetic changes.'

Among those changes were four or five which the Israelis considered fundamental. For the first time, 'Palestine Liberation Organization' was written in where the word 'Palestinian' had been before, so placing the PLO squarely in the frame as the political body who would assume control in the West Bank and Gaza after an accord was reached. The document stipulated that the Palestinians should have control over the passage between Gaza and Jericho, 150 kilometres apart. And it proposed that this passage should take the form of a wide linking road which would be Palestinian territory. Such a road would effectively cut Israel in two.

To the two Israeli negotiators, the hand of Arafat was clear in the new document. Just as Rabin had been the force behind some of the tougher proposals they had introduced at Gressheim, so the leader of the PLO was behind these new 'cosmetic' changes. Indeed Abu Ala had spent long hours with Arafat and Abu Mazen before he returned to Norway. The Chairman had told them that the Singer document was 'not acceptable', and the three Palestinians had reworked it, introducing more demands than would be accepted. This was partly a question of tactics: when forced to compromise they would still be left with a reasonable gain. It was also a signal that the talks were becoming deadly serious. What had started as an academic paper, which Arafat had skimmed through, now looked as if it could become reality on the ground. Each party had to identify all its requirements and flag them clearly before it was too late. In Tunis the Palestinians had asked a lawyer, Taher Shash, to help them with the drafting. Shash, an Egyptian, was the legal adviser to the Palestinian delegation in Washington. Joel Singer had worked with him before, on the Camp David accords, and recognized his hand in the new draft the Palestinians brought to Halvorsbole.

The Israelis, looking grim, requested an hour's break and left the room. As the Norwegians stood in the corridor outside, they could see that things were bad. Singer looked thunderous and Savir was shaking his head in disgust and repeating to himself: 'It's a catastrophe, this thing just won't fly.'

The two Israelis then retired with Hirschfeld and Pundak to consider their response. They decided they would not even negotiate the proposal made by Abu Ala. Uri Savir was angry with the PLO, but he was also disillusioned and impatient with himself for having believed that Abu Ala was somehow different from the rest, that he represented a new, more pragmatic, spirit in the Tunis leadership. 'To hell with them,' he muttered to Singer; 'that's the real PLO for you!'

Singer was not surprised at the Palestinian tactics. He had had much experience at negotiating with Arabs, Europeans and Americans. The Arab way of conducting talks, he had found, was very different from that in the West. In negotiating a contract in America there would usually be a few opening positions, then the parties would gauge the gap between them and try to bridge it. Finally a compromise would be found. In the Middle East, he maintained, each side also had a starting-point. But then one side would move towards the other, which would then promptly move back a step. The first party would move towards the other again, and the latter would retreat once more. Rather than the gap narrowing, one party would chase the progressively changing position of the other. This had been Singer's experience in Lebanon and Egypt, and he felt, quite realistically, that negotiating with Arabs was neither better nor worse than negotiating in the West – the difference was simply a cultural one. It reminded him of bartering in the bazaar in Cairo. He had even warned his Israeli colleagues that this would happen.

Nevertheless, both Singer and Savir saw that this new development cast a potentially fatal shadow over the whole channel. If they returned home with the Palestinians' proposal, they knew that Rabin, and perhaps Peres too, would dismiss the entire venture. So they returned to the conference room and Savir made a short but tough speech very different in tone from anything he had said thus far.

'We will not even negotiate this new draft – this will not fly, it hasn't a chance. We will not even present this back home. It would just be rejected out of hand. You are crossing the red lines of what is acceptable. You should reconsider whether you wish to make this document a formal proposal. You would be better to take it back – withdraw it. Otherwise it will be the end of the channel.'

'Well, we had a document with Hirschfeld,' said Abu Ala pointedly, 'and then suddenly you came with a new proposal. We felt the same then as you are feeling now. We have the right to do to you what you did to us.'

Abu Ala then produced a handwritten letter from Yasser Arafat in which the Chairman said how important he considered the Oslo talks to be. The PLO wanted to convince the Israelis that the will and the high-level backing were there, and that they should be prepared to tackle the new draft. But Savir was adamant; he would not negotiate their document. Abu Ala left the room and called Arafat in Tunis. 'Tell the Israelis I am sincere about peace,' was the message he brought back.

They broke up that night with nothing resolved. The next day, over breakfast, the atmosphere was strained and grim. Everyone sat together – that was one of the ground rules of the channel, and on numerous occasions it had fostered a relaxed and jokey mood. But this Sunday morning the Norwegians felt uncomfortable and Larsen did not even try to crack his usual jokes. He knew it would just seem artificial and insensitive. The Palestinians adopted a rather superior, moralizing attitude, saying that they were only giving the Israelis a taste of their own medicine.

After breakfast the negotiators held a short meeting in which the Israelis tried to persuade Abu Ala to take back his proposal and return to the unresolved Gressheim draft. The Palestinians argued that the earlier draft was an Israeli document, and that they should have the right to present theirs too. Savir pointed out that it may have started as an Israeli draft, but that they had spent a total of thirty-five hours at Gressheim converting it into a joint proposal, with five outstanding points; there was no reason to reject it. At this point both sides realized they had no option but to return to base and seek advice. Although nothing had been resolved, Savir and Singer felt they had done their best to persuade the other side to redefine the Israeli paper as just ideas, not an official proposal. They hoped the Palestinians would be able to convince Arafat to take this line, but they were not optimistic.

The cars were brought round to the front of the hotel and groups split up. As the Israelis left they suspected that this might well be the last time the two sides would meet. But the security men felt that Abu Ala seemed quite sanguine, despite his refusal to give way in the negotiations and the sense of crisis this had provoked. A few miles from the gates of Halversbole he suddenly requested that they make a detour – he had some shopping he wanted to do. The security men were mystified.

What could he want, indeed what could he find, in the middle of the Norwegian countryside? The driver was instructed to pull up in front of a large and famous factory, Hadelands Glassverk. Abu Ala revealed yet another side to his character, that of the avid collector of handmade and antique glass – in his house in Tunis, a large vitrine holds his prize possessions. Hadelands is a Mecca for an enthusiast and Abu Ala had long wanted to see its wares. He bought numerous specimens of the Norwegian glass and asked the assistant to pack them carefully in lots of tissue paper and stout boxes. Hassan Asfour sighed as the back of the car was stacked with Abu Ala's purchases. Then they resumed their journey to Oslo.

By now the Norwegian Foreign Minister was ensconced in Tunis with his entourage. The visit had been planned by Thorvald Stoltenberg before he went to Bosnia; a trip to see Habib Ben Yahia, the Foreign Minister of Tunisia, followed by a few days' holiday on the coast. Holst was accompanied by his wife, Marianne Heiberg, their son Edvard and Nicholas, Marianne's fourteen-year-old son from a former marriage. Mona Juul was there as Holst's aide, and there were other Norwegians in the delegation too. Larsen flew out to join them after the abortive meeting at Halvorsbole. The Tunisia trip was the perfect opportunity to sound out Arafat in person, in the PLO headquarters in Tunis. Arranging a special trip to see him would have aroused too many suspicious, but a single meeting in the context of the Ben Yahia visit would not be remarked upon.

And so, on 13 July, the Norwegians visited Arafat in the prosperous suburbs of Tunis where the Palestinians have their enclave. When he was Defence Minister, Holst had had experience of the PLO chief. In 1979, in Lebanon, a thousand PLO fighters had been deployed in the same area as Norwegians serving with the UN. The two men had had prolonged discussions on how their forces could coexist, and Holst had found that when Arafat made a deal with him it had stuck. Therefore he was optimistic that he could read Arafat and that he would be told the truth.

When the Norwegians were ushered into the Chairman's office on the ground floor of the spacious villa at 58 Yagorta Street, they found Arafat sitting at his desk, positioned at one end of the room. In front of the desk there was a long conference table at which Abu Ala was sitting, discreetly going through some papers. Arafat asked Abu Ala to come over and sit beside him. He then took hold of Abu Ala's hand and drew him close. Abu Ala was smiling broadly, as if to say: You see, he trusts me, we are in close contact and he knows and approves of what I am doing.

Arafat gave his usual declamatory performance to the people gathered in the room. It was short on substance but designed to please the crowd. When Arafat was stuck for a word in English he would turn to Abu Ala, who would prompt him. Larsen noticed how Abu Ala used his acute social sense to read the reaction of the Norwegians to certain phrases used by Arafat. When the Chairman had finished, Abu Ala tactfully suggested that perhaps he, Abu Ala, could clarify some of the points that had been made, and proceeded to give a less extreme formulation, yet doing so in such a way as not to antagonize Arafat. It was clear that Abu Ala knew how best to handle the suspicious and irascible leader of the PLO.

The Chairman of the PLO was clearly irritated at the recent developments in Washington. He showed Holst a copy of the latest American bridging proposal, produced on 30 June, two weeks before. He had marked up the text and concluded that more than three-quarters of it was from the original Israeli draft presented in Washington, and less than one-quarter from the Palestinian one. 'This is not even-handedness,' he angrily exclaimed. 'There are three parties now around the table – and two of them are pro-Israeli!'

Arafat's view was that he would find it difficult to sell an American-brokered agreement to his people; to have legitimacy it would have to be a direct deal between the two antagonists. Norway had no intention of mediating directly, and Holst got the impression that this approach was more acceptable to the leader of the PLO.

Then Holst asked for a few minutes' private conversation with Arafat. The two men, accompanied by Mona Juul and Terje Larsen, went upstairs to a small, sparsely furnished room. In an instant Yasser Arafat's manner changed completely. The rhetoric went, he seemed relaxed and at the same time alert and in command. He began at once to talk about the Oslo Channel and made it clear that he had complete confidence in the way they were handling the situation.

The Norwegians were pleasantly surprised by Arafat's

Holst with Jan Egeland, Norway's Deputy Foreign Minister, who got the secret channel under way.

Mona Juul and Terje Larsen in Jerusalem for the signing of the mutual recognition letter.

Uri Savir, the urbane Director-General of the Israeli Foreign Ministry who led the Israeli team.

Joel Singer, a tough lawyer and former colonel in the Israeli army, was Rabin's man.

Hassan Asfour, a PLO firebrand from Gaza who was transformed by the Oslo spirit.

Abu Ala, the wily and charming banker who led the Palestinian team.

Shimon Peres, the Israeli Foreign Minister, who drove the Oslo Channel to its successful conclusion.

Abu Mazen, the veteran PLO official who was the Palestinian force behind the secret talks.

Yair Hirschfeld, a jolly academic from Haifa University, who had long championed the cause of peace.

Yossi Beilin, leader of the Blazers and Deputy Foreign Minister of Israel.

Borregaard Mansion at Sarpsborg, the favourite meeting-place of the secret channel.

Norway's Foreign Minister, Johan Jorgen Holst, with his son Edvard, the 'diplomatic ice-breaker'.

This is the picture that caused such friction in the Norwegian team. Left to right: Marianne Heiberg, Johan Jorgen Holst, Terje Larsen and Mona Juul.

Arafat signing the letter recognizing the State of Israel as Holst looks on; Tunis, 9 September 1993. Back row, left to right: Mona Juul, Yasser Abed-Rabbo, Terje Larsen, Abu Mazen, Abu Ala and Hassan Asfour.

Yitzhak Rabin, flanked by Holst and Peres, recognizes the PLO with a stroke of his famous pen.

Done at Washington, D.C., this ____ day of _____, 1993.

For the Government of Israel   **For the Palestinian Delegation**

_____   _____

                                   Witnessed By:

The United States of America   **The Russian Federation**

-23-

All the Israelis and Palestinians involved in the secret talks signed each other's copies of the Declaration of Principles as a memento of the times they had spent together. Only Ron Pundak's name is missing, as he was absent at that time.

A victorious trio: Uri Savir, Joel Singer and Abu Ala after the Washington signing.

Arafat and Warren Christopher in a euphoric mood as Abu Mazen signs the Declaration of Principles to Bill Clinton's obvious approval.

familiarity with all the details of the agreement they were trying to hammer out in the secret channel. He got out some maps and began to show them what his concerns were about the practicalities of implementing the Gaza/Jericho First option, particularly the question of how the PLO and he himself would travel between the two areas across the Israeli territory in between.

'I want kissing points,' Arafat said emphatically.

Holst looked at Larsen and Mona Juul, uncomprehending.

'Kissing points! Are they on the plan?' repeated the Chairman irritatedly.

'You mean checkpoints?' ventured Holst.

'No, no! Kissing points – like this ...' Arafat made the appropriate noises with his lips. There was no doubt about what he had in mind, but what exactly did it mean? Finally the Norwegians worked out that the PLO wanted contact points between the Jericho territory on the West Bank and the Gaza Strip – literally a point where the territory on both sides would briefly touch or 'kiss'. Holst suggested that they incorporate the term 'safe passage' into the agreement. Arafat seemed satisfied with this. However, there were other, even more gnomic, utterances from the Chairman:

'I am not Nelson Mandela, I am not Mandela,' he kept saying. No one dared to ask what he meant by this; the Norwegians were pressed for time and it had taken them long enough to get to the bottom of the 'kissing points'.

Holst praised Abu Ala in order to test Arafat's attitude to the most important Palestinian in the channel. The leader of the PLO is notoriously suspicious of able men around him who might become powerful enough to jeopardize his own position.

'Abu Ala is a very skilful negotiator, and he makes good use of humour – for tactical purposes, of course. He can break the tension in a situation with a joke. And he can manufacture a crisis – not a real one – to underline a point,' explained Holst.

Arafat seemed to appreciate Holst's opinion of Abu Ala's abilities. He clearly liked the notion of a Palestinian outwitting the clever, self-confident Israelis. Then Holst steered the conversation round to the all-important question of how Arafat would handle the strategic problem of persuading the many factions within the PLO to accept an agreement with Israel. Arafat assured Holst that he had spent many years creating a consensus in the PLO. 'Consensus' is not the word that many observers would use in connection with the Palestine Liberation Organization, and Holst tried to impress upon the Chairman that there were hard choices to be made; there would be strong opposition within the PLO ranks.

Arafat defended himself by saying that he, above all others, understood the nature of the opposition forces within his own organization, and that he had always been able to deal with them in the past and would do so again if an agreement could be reached. Holst pressed him on the point – it was the Israelis' main reservation that Arafat would, in the end, wriggle out of any deal.

The Norwegians' fifteen-minute conversation with Arafat convinced all three of them that he was familiar with all the details of the various proposals that had been worked on in the Oslo Channel. This was reassuring, for before this moment they had not known whether Abu Ala and Abu Mazen had been keeping the Chairman informed of developments. At least he knew what was going on, even if there was still the old, old problem that no one knew what Arafat really intended to do, or how committed he was to negotiations of any kind. The Norwegians believed that Arafat had accepted there were certain 'red lines', as the Israelis called them, which Rabin and Peres would not cross, and that he would agree to return to the former proposal as a basis for negotiations.

When the Norwegians got back to their hotel there were urgent messages waiting for them. Uri Savir had been frantically calling Oslo, to tell Egeland and Geir Pedersen that the channel was in trouble. Rabin did not believe that Abu Ala had the necessary backing. Savir wanted the Norwegians to come to Israel for discussions; he would not say with whom, just that it was imperative they come at once.

There was disagreement in the Norwegian camp over what to do. By now the official part of the Tunisia trip was over and the Holst family, with Larsen and Mona Juul, had moved to a large resort hotel on the beach at Sousse, for the few days' holiday they had planned. Holst felt that, as the Foreign Minister, he had his own schedule and his own priorities. At this moment he wanted to take a break with his family, not to rush off to Jerusalem, perhaps for nothing more than a meeting with a lowly official. Egeland and Pedersen were calling constantly to explain how important it was for them to go and Larsen felt they had no choice. Mona Juul was in a difficult position: Holst was her boss but she agreed with Terje that they were needed in Israel. After two days of discussions Holst finally agreed to let the other two go alone. He sent them with a letter he had written to Peres, which contained a full account of his assessment of Arafat's views.

When Terje and Mona arrived in Jerusalem they were shown into a room where the full Israeli contingent, barring Rabin, was waiting. Peres was there, with Beilin and Savir and their aides, and the two professors. For two hours the Norwegians briefed them on every detail of their meeting with Arafat. It was clear to Terje and Mona that their assessment of Arafat would be the decisive factor in whether or not to close the channel.

The next morning Peres met with Rabin, to pass on the information and to decide what should be their next move. The two men attended a Cabinet meeting and then Peres returned for a two-hour conference with his people and Larsen and Mona Juul. It was endless: the questions, the analysis of every word Arafat had said, the dissection of his statements on the various issues, his attitude to Abu Ala. There was also the psychological assessment: the Israelis wanted to know about Arafat's mental state. In April 1992 he had miraculously survived a plane crash and there had been speculation that, despite the official denials, he had suffered brain damage as a result. The Israelis made it clear that they were not the only ones who had reason to suspect Arafat's sincerity. King Hussein of Jordan, like Shimon Peres, had been betrayed in the abortive 1987 peace deal with the PLO. He maintained that every one of his many agreements with Arafat, both oral and written, had been broken by the Palestinian. And the message from the Americans, too, was not to trust the man – he was a liar, a deceiver and a traitor, impossible to do business with.

Although the specific problem faced by the Israelis was the new draft of the Declaration of Principles presented by the PLO, they saw it as part of the same old general question. Would Arafat ultimately deliver? Was it worth attempting to persevere with tougher negotiations when he might draw back at the last minute? Only by being reasonably sure of his commitment to the process, and to Abu Ala's game plan, could the Peres group feel confident of progressing further. Singer's presence meant that Rabin was being drawn closely into the details of the agreement, but the Prime Minister was not nearly as committed as the Peres group. His scepticism overshadowed the whole process on the Israeli side. Although the Norwegians were not, at this stage, clear as to the extent of Rabin's involvement, they were made aware in this second meeting with Peres that if their interpretation of Arafat's intentions was incorrect, and the Oslo Channel ended in disaster, Peres would be personally caught in the crossfire, his political future on the line. Mona Juul tried to be as encouraging as possible without reading too much, either positive or negative, into Arafat's words. She told Peres:

'Arafat seems reasonable; he is open to discussion on the issue of Jericho. He would, of course, like to have safe passage, and he wants it under Palestinian control in some way, but accepts there must be some joint way of handling the aspect of control.'

However, she and Larsen also stressed that they could not guarantee that Arafat would stand by what he had said. They acknowledged that the term 'safe passage' was very vague. Did it mean a road linking Gaza and Jericho? Or did it merely mean that Arafat and PLO officials would have to be guaranteed safe passage, however they travelled between the two areas – by plane or helicopter or on the ground?

The two Norwegians left the next day to rejoin Holst, who was still holidaying in Tunisia. It had been agreed in Jerusalem that they would have another meeting with Arafat, to see if they could satisfy the sceptical Israelis. This time Holst tried to clarify Arafat's intentions on the vexed question of safe passage. But the Chairman replied to his queries about a road, or passage by air or other means, with an impatient wave of the hand and a string of affirmatives: 'Yes, yes, yes.' He would not settle on one definition alone. Holst showed Arafat a letter, written by Peres to the Norwegian, in which he asked him to pass on the message that Israel was sincere and that there must be more clarification of the details.

Perhaps because the Israelis had aroused their suspicions, Larsen and Mona Juul came away from this second encounter feeling less confidence in Arafat. Holst disagreed; he was sure Arafat was prepared to compromise and to pledge himself at last to peace. Above all, he believed that Arafat had understood that there were 'red lines'. The road from Gaza to Jericho, for example, was not acceptable. Therefore the Palestinians would have to go back to negotiating on the basis of the Gressheim draft, not the one they had presented at Halvorsbole. Larsen pointed out that there was a chance that Arafat, with the traditional Arab regard for rank, was merely paying lip-service to Holst, saying what he thought the Norwegian Foreign Minister wanted to hear. Larsen gave Holst his appraisal: 'Look, there are two different scenarios, two possible interpretations of what Arafat said. One is based on the assumption that he was not lying – the "honesty scenario", let's call it. The other, the "lip-service scenario", is based on the assumption that we can't guarantee that he was not lying!'

On their way back to Oslo the Norwegians stopped in Paris to meet Ron Pundak, sent from Jerusalem to be updated on the latest encounter with the Chairman. The Israelis did not want such sensitive matters discussed on the phone. The Holst family, with Larsen and Juul, arrived in Paris for an overnight stay. They decided to use a flat there belonging to a Norwegian diplomat. The flat was being used by Holst's elder daughter, who was living in Paris. It was easy for her family to stay there without arousing any suspicions. The Norwegians were afraid that the French secret service, with its reputation for efficient monitoring of the airports, might notice the Foreign Minister arriving unannounced in their country and set surveillance on him to find out what he was doing.

Ron Pundak listened and took notes while Holst repeated his view that Arafat was sincere. Larsen was more sceptical and warned Pundak that they had spent only a short time with Arafat and did not have enough information to be able to confirm that the Palestinian leader would deliver. Larsen wanted Pundak to make this clear in his report to Peres, for he wished the Israelis to be the ones to decide whether or not to continue with the channel. But Larsen was not confident that Pundak would pass on all the pros and cons, for both Pundak and Hirschfeld were passionately committed to the Oslo process and always took the most optimistic view in discussions with their superiors.

In the end, the letter that Holst had written to Peres, after his first meeting with Arafat, persuaded Rabin to continue the negotiations. And so, four days after the Paris meeting, Savir and Singer and the two professors were allowed to return to Norway. They believed that their message had got through, and that the Palestinians now understood that the proposal they had presented at Halvorsbole would be replaced with the version negotiated at Gressheim earlier in the month.

On 24 July the two groups made their way back to Halvorsbøle. Yet as they drove along the quiet roads, past prosperous farmhouses and fields yellow with corn, towards the still waters of the fiord, the radio brought news of death and destruction. An all-out war threatened in the scorching summer heat in the Middle East. That morning Israel had launched its fiercest onslaught in more than a decade against Arab guerrillas in southern Lebanon. This was Rabin's response to Hezbollah attacks on Israeli troops deployed in the self-styled security zone north of the Israeli border. 'We want to make it unequivocally clear that, if there is no quiet here, there will be no quiet for the residents of southern Lebanon,' warned the Israeli Prime Minister.

For a week the Israeli army pounded the area with a massive air, artillery and sea bombardment. Two hundred thousand refugees streamed north towards Beirut, hundreds of people were wounded and at least fifty killed. Hezbollah fired back Katyusha rockets at settlements in northern Israel, killing civilians there. The world condemned the Israeli action, and the UN gave a warning, but Rabin seemed determined to wipe out the Hezbollah gunmen who inhabited the nine-mile-wide area of southern Lebanon occupied by Israeli forces.

The Israelis expected their government's action to have a negative effect on the talks in Norway. But Abu Ala and the others hardly even mentioned it, and there were no recriminations or questions about what it meant for the Oslo Channel. It seemed as if the members of the channel had become so absorbed in the task before them that the outside world could not be allowed to intrude. They were there to battle it out around the negotiating table, and the war between the Israeli tanks and the Hezbollah rocket launchers was almost irrelevant.

9

Crisis by the Fiord

In the conference room, with its peaceful and majestic views, the Palestinians produced their new draft of the DOP. It was a bitter disappointment to the Israelis, for it was more or less the same as the previous one. Abu Ala had not gone back to the Gressheim version. There were some changes – the road had gone and East Jerusalem was left out of the interim arrangements once more. But this was not enough to satisfy Savir and Singer.

The group took a break – a 'cooling-off period', they called it. Savir made it clear to Larsen, in his slightly mocking way, that the latter had been fooled by the Palestinians, sweet-talked into believing they would make compromises. Larsen was stung by this, for he felt he had tried to qualify the assessment of Arafat, although Holst had shown fewer doubts about the leader of the PLO. Now the head of the Israeli delegation had accused him of naivety and made it clear that he was questioning his judgement.

However, despite the difficulties, neither the Israelis nor the Palestinians were prepared to walk away. Both sides had invested too much at this point. Singer and Savir told themselves that the new document was just tactics on Abu Ala's part and that if they could keep the bargaining session going, by the second day they might succeed in changing their opponent's position. They reconvened and both sides agreed to take the text produced at Gressheim on 3 July and the disputed one from the last Halvorsbole meeting, and try to combine them by going through them word by word in order to find compromises.

All three groups – the Israelis, the Palestinians and their Norwegian hosts – were now investing every ounce of will and effort into keeping the channel going. The positions were being dictated by Peres and Rabin, on the one hand, and by Abu Mazen and Arafat on the other. Everyone at Halvorsbole was personally committed to making a workable agreement, yet each side had to play the games of bluff and strategy to maximize its own advantage. However, they all knew this could not go on indefinitely. The existence of the Oslo Channel was bound to leak before long, and then the whole thing would be blown. Now close to fifty people in total – in Israel, Tunis and Norway – knew or suspected something of what was going on. The press were hot on the trail of rumours that had begun to surface in the summer. They had unearthed other clandestine contacts: the Israeli Environment Minister, Yossi Sarid, had met with Arafat's Cairo aide, Nabil Sha'ath; Haim Ramon, the Israeli Health Minister, had been talking to Dr Ahmed Tibi, an Arab doctor from Jerusalem who was close to the PLO. The group at Halvorsbole reassured each other that theirs was the only channel that really meant anything, but the discovey of these contacts was unsettling; it indicated that both Rabin and Arafat were losing faith in Oslo's ability to deliver.

Furthermore it was becoming harder for Savir to find excuses for disappearing for days on end. His secretary, Rachel Shabi, suspected that her boss was engaged in secret negotiations, although he never mentioned them to her. At the start he had asked her to find a reliable travel agent, outside the Foreign Ministry network, to make bookings at short notice and plan circuitous routes. Together with the travel agent, Rachel used all her skills of organization to get Savir on planes at a moment's notice. On one occasion she even managed to hold an aircraft for half an hour at the gate at Ben-Gurion Airport while the Director-General was driven at top speed from Jerusalem to catch the flight, supposedly so that he could visit a sick relative somewhere in Europe.

Rachel, who works fourteen-hour days and is devoted to Savir, found ways of warning him of possible danger without ever openly confronting him with what she knew. In early July she had slipped a small newspaper cutting into an envelope marked 'Private' and left it on his desk. The article said that a highly placed official from the Israeli Foreign Ministry was secretly meeting someone from the PLO.

'How can you think this is me?' Savir scolded Rachel when he found the envelope. 'If you think it's me, then I'm angry with you – and if it isn't me, then who do you think it is?'

'OK, only time will tell,' retorted Rachel with a smile. 'I thought you should see the article anyway.'

In Tunis, Abu Ala's assistant had made a similar calculation. Salah Elayan had worked for the boss of Samed for five years and was loyal and discreet. There was an unspoken understanding between the two Palestinians about what was going on and Elayan was pleased and proud at what his boss was doing for the Palestinian people.

The small team at Halvorsbole knew that they had to make a breakthrough soon. The negotiators were now a tight-knit group, but the old suspicions still existed and, in the intensity of the bargaining, were apt to flare up for the slightest of reasons. The Israelis constantly suspected that they were being lied to, and they accused the Palestinians of creating disinformation. And from the start the Israelis had known that the Palestinians harboured many conspiracy theories about their true intent. Abu Ala accused them of plotting to undermine the PLO by ferreting out their fall-back position in this intimate, secret forum, with the intention of exposing them to gain advantage publicly. He voiced the fear that the Israelis would use this knowledge to enable their official negotiators in Washington to get the better of the Palestinian delegation there. Sometimes the Israelis would be accused of conspiring with the Americans in this secret channel. Or the hapless Norwegians would be suspected of siding with the Israelis against the PLO. Larsen bore the brunt of this, and again at Halvorsbole he was singled out as a target for Abu Ala's frustrations.

The next morning the Israelis and Norwegians met for breakfast at the agreed time of nine o'clock, but the Palestinians did not show up until ten. Abu Ala hit the roof and accused Larsen of deliberately misleading him so that the Norwegians and Israelis could spend time together discussing the negotiations. Larsen sought to ignore this outburst and asked Geir Pedersen to take a walk with him. In his usual way, he wanted to try out his theories of what was going on, at this fraught moment, in the minds of the negotiators. But he did not manage to avoid another confrontation. On his way back from his walk he met Abu Ala and Hassan Asfour, and again Abu Ala brought up the subject of why the Norwegians and the Israelis had come down early for breakfast. He wanted to know why he had been lied to.

'This crazy man,' he said, indicating Larsen, 'told me I should have breakfast at ten – but it was at nine o'clock. He is obviously an Israeli agent!'

There was a mocking smile on his face, an edge to his voice. His contempt and suspicion were clear. Again Larsen let it pass. He realized that in his frustration Abu Ala had really marked him out for vindictive treatment. The Palestinian would blame the impasse not on Savir, but on Larsen, who did not really know what the substantive problems were.

'This is all your doing,' Abu Ala accused Larsen. 'I know it's you behind it. It's not Uri, it's you who are manipulating the Israelis to do this.'

Larsen tried to soothe him, knowing that it was Abu Ala's way of letting off steam which could prove dangerous if vented on the leader of the Israeli delegation.

Yet there were lighter moments at Halvorsbole too, as there were every time the group convened. On this second day, an irate German family suddenly turned up in the reception area of the hotel, demanding to know why it could no longer have the rooms it had booked. The receptionist tried to explain that the hotel was full, that there was a private function. The Germans pointed to the rows of keys hanging neatly behind the front desk, a silent testimony to many vacant rooms. They angrily demanded to see the manager. Since the manager was not present that day, Larsen, who was in charge, quickly found the leader of the security team and told him to put on a jacket and tie. He then explained to him that he had a different job to do, another role to play in order to keep the talks a secret. The tall and rather distinguished-looking security officer strode confidently into the reception area, and tried to pacify the Germans. It took him an hour to persuade them to leave. As the door swung shut behind them, the whole group erupted in laughter, relieved and somewhat guilty at the plight of the German family.

Sophisticated computer equipment from FAFO was lugged to each meeting by the Norwegians so that new drafts of the DOP could be produced in an instant. Ron Pundak was in charge of this part of the operation, and it was a constant source of anguish for him. The printer always seemed obstinately to refuse to spew forth the text locked in the computer. At Halvorsbole it was the same story once again, and the small, despairing figure of Pundak could be seen pacing through the hotel calling for help from the security men. One of them was a computer buff and would calm Ron down and make the recalcitrant machine behave.

As the day wore on, the Israelis found that Abu Ala and Hassan Asfour were proving extremely resistant to any compromise. They struggled on through the two texts but finally, at three o'clock in the afternoon, progress ground to a halt. Only a third of the twenty-five matters at issue had been resolved. Sixteen points remained. Both sides declared they could go no further. The only way out now, they both knew, was to employ high-risk tactics of brinkmanship. Abu Ala and Uri Savir, the two main figures in this high-stakes game of political poker, faced each other across the table.

'We are stuck,' said Savir. 'We are going home now – the plane leaves shortly – and we may never come back. This is totally unacceptable. Unless you take it back, we'll terminate the channel and we'll go back to the official talks in Washington. Maybe we'll meet you again in twenty years' time, when this whole thing is sorted out. But for now, that's it.'

Abu Ala, not to be outdone, immediately retorted with a short but forceful speech. In a measured way, but more in sorrow than in anger, he said that he had a personal statement to make, and then he announced his resignation. He was careful not to declare the secret talks over but said that, as far as he was concerned, there was nothing more to be done. He ended by thanking everyone, saying that it had been nice to meet them. All that he could do now was to wish luck to his successor, whoever he might be:

'I will help whoever succeeds me, whoever Abu Ammar decides to appoint in my position. I will give him all the documents. But as for me, I am an old man. I cannot go on any longer.'

Uri Savir was determined not to be upstaged by this masterly manœuvre, which had concentrated everybody's mind on the disastrous repercussions of losing the chief Palestinian negotiator. His counterblast was very different from his usual, measured, diplomatic style.

'Everyone in the world knows the PLO will never seize the opportunity to make a real peace. The minute before they have to make the final decision, Arafat always draws back. When the history books about this period are written, no one will believe that because of just sixteen words the Palestinians were forced to continue living as they live today. You care more about yourselves than about the Palestinian people!'

When he had finished there was silence. Hirschfeld was on the verge of tears and Abu Ala seemed to be fighting his emotions too. Then the normally genial professor stood up. For weeks he had willingly remained in the back seat as the ideas and discussions, which he could claim to have begun, turned into serious negotiations. He had held his tongue on many occasions when he felt he could have handled things better. Now all his pent-up frustrations merged with his fears that the months of work, the striving for peace in which they had all participated, would come to nothing. He felt an enormous sense of betrayal.

'It's a black day for both our peoples. We have all let them down,' he said. Then, turning to the Palestinians, he continued in a trembling voice: 'For heaven's sake, I delivered everything I promised you – those meetings we had at Borregaard, which moved into real, substantial negotiations. Now we've almost got what we wanted, and you are throwing it away. By doing this you will create a terrible reality on the ground. We will go home, all of us, and we will have our fine lives, but out there, people are going to die and live in misery! If you wanted to show that we could bridge the gap just by coming here, and then by standing up and walking away, then that's your business. But we will have to tell our leadership that the gap can never be bridged, and that no one can speak to the PLO – because they really do not want peace. You are slamming the door on the generations to come. If that's your aim, then go ahead. It will show us that you misled us all the way, when we did not mislead you.'

When he finished speaking no one said a word. They all merely filed out of the room. The Norwegians hovered in the corridor, sensing the catastrophe. Abu Ala hobbled away, leaning on a cane. The day before he had hurt his foot jumping off a hillock in an exuberant moment while walking with the security men. Now the Norwegians watched his retreating back and heard the dismal tapping of the stick echoing down the passage. It sent shivers down Larsen's spine, reminding him of a Count Dracula movie – the hunched, dark-suited, wild-eyed figure of Abu Ala and the awful silence from the others left behind. Then the Israelis and the other Palestinians shut themselves away in two seminar rooms. As soon as the door closed behind him, Joel Singer addressed his three colleagues: 'Well,' he said matter-of-factly, 'we will have an agreement.'

Based on his experience of high-level negotiations, Singer believed that before every breakthrough there had to be at least one crisis. He acknowledged that this one was serious, but he was sure it had been manufactured by Abu Ala and that even now the Palestinian was waiting for them to reappear with a fall-back proposal that would give the Palestinians part of what they wanted. He even saw the crisis as a hopeful sign, a sign that the leaders on both sides were now deeply commited, and that the positions of both teams had hardened as a consequence.

In his room upstairs, Abu Ala called Abu Mazen in Tunis. 'Everything is destroyed,' he said. 'It's finished, over. There's no way to carry on, no way.' Then he went back downstairs, calling imperiously for Larsen. 'Fetch the cars! Change the airline tickets! We are going – and we're never coming back.'

But instead of packing or heading for the door, Abu Ala went into a small sitting-room next to the bar and sat there in solitary splendour. Uri Savir and Joel Singer stayed in the salon next door; they suspected Abu Ala's resignation was part of his game plan. Yair Hirschfeld and Ron Pundak nervously paced the corridor with Larsen. Pedersen and the security men stayed in the background. Hassan Asfour and Mohammed Abu Koush were talking quietly to Mona Juul. Everyone was waiting for the next move in the game.

Yet Larsen felt that this time he could not just wait to see what would happen next. He was distraught, believing that the channel was about to be destroyed for ever. He had to do something, so he went to Abu Ala in the bar. The Palestinian was sitting there, staring straight ahead, leaning on his silver-topped cane. He reminded Larsen of a proud Spanish don with his mournful, aristocratic look.

'I just want to talk to you,' Larsen began gently.

'What do you want to talk about?' Abu Ala's voice was cold. 'Why don't you go to your friends, the Israelis?'

'Please go and talk to Uri alone, it's the only way.'

The Palestinian refused; he was bitter and his anger was directed at Larsen. The Norwegian let him rail, for he wanted him to wind down somehow. Then he asked him again:

'Please go to Uri, do it for me.' This was the first time that Larsen had come off the sidelines and become personally involved, the first time he had pleaded with one of the parties to do something for his sake.

'Don't do that. You can't ask me for such a thing,' warned the Palestinian.

For the third time Larsen asked Abu Ala to do it for him. Finally the Palestinian conceded.

Meanwhile, in the room next door, Savir had found a way to move ahead. He suggested to Singer that the negotiators split the sixteen points of contention into two groups of eight. Then he would propose to Abu Ala that the Israelis take the eight they felt they could most easily concede and the Palestinians should take the eight they could be most flexible on. Each group would return home to convince its leaders to agree to compromise on all the eight issues. What Savir was suggesting was a combination of a package deal and a swap arrangement.

The points of contention could be divided roughly into those relating to security, and those pertaining to the Gaza/Jericho First deal. For the Israelis the first group was the key. From the start Rabin had emphasized security. He had personally decreed that the army should continue to protect the settlers, and that it should control the borders between the Jericho area and Jordan, and between the Gaza Strip and Egypt. Israeli troops should have freedom of movement in Gaza and Jericho. Savir now suggested to Singer that the Palestinians should try to get Arafat and Abu Mazen to give way on these points, for there was little chance the Israeli side would compromise on them.

The other group of problems centred on the nature of the Gaza/Jericho First agreement: the powers and responsibilities of the new Palestinian council, where that council should be located, how authority would be handed over, and the question of the passage between Gaza and Jericho. Savir's idea was that he and Singer should try to persuade their political masters back in Jerusalem to find ways of compromising on these issues, for he knew these were the areas where Arafat would not give way.

Then Savir told Singer that he intended to play the Israeli trump card, the offer of formal recognition of the PLO. The night before, the two men had worked on a long document they hoped would change for ever the nature of the relationship between the two enemies. It was an agreement on mutual recognition: Israel would recognize the PLO as the official representative of the Palestinian people, and in return Yasser Arafat's organization would recognize Israel's right to exist and renounce violence. Such an agreement would indeed be historic, even more so than the Declaration of Principles they were now struggling to establish. Overnight Yair Hirschfeld had translated the mutual recognition paper from Hebrew into English, and now Savir quickly reduced it to seven main points on a single sheet of paper. These were the points that the Israelis wanted Arafat to make in black and white in whatever recognition agreement the PLO exchanged with Israel. These seven points covered not only a declaration of Israel's right to exist and the renunciation of violence and terrorism, but also a pledge that the Charter of the PLO, the foundation-stone of the organization, would be altered.

Larsen now came from his pleading with Abu Ala, to appeal to the Israelis.

'Uri, Abu Ala is really depressed. This time it's for real. I'm asking you to see him now.'

'OK,' said Savir. 'Go back and try to persuade him to agree that we should talk together. Say that I have something I want to speak with him about. Certain points.'

Savir was the one who now physically made the move, in deference to the older man. Larsen took him to Abu Ala and left the two men alone. For two hours they stayed in the room. Both men were honest with each other, and talked about the personal and political difficulties they faced, back home, in trying to sell the deal. That such admissions could now be made without being interpreted as signs of weakness showed the closeness of the two men's relationship, the sense of kinship between them. Then Savir put forward his two proposals. He could see immediately that the mutual recognition deal was something Abu Ala wanted, for the Palestinian brightened up considerably. But Savir warned him that the 'swap deal', as he called it, could not be made selectively.

'We'll take half home and you take half home. But it must be yes or no, to all the eight points on the DOP and to the mutual recognition deal as well. We don't accept you conceding part of this alone. And I must tell you that I am doing this on my own initiative; it hasn't been officially approved. I must check back that we can follow through on this.'

Savir had spoken firmly but both sides knew they had to be flexible. The Palestinians had played tough at Halvorsbole, but the Israelis, despite their insistence that they had reached the end, had come back with something new. They were no more prepared to walk away from the channel than the Palestinians. That is why Savir proposed the swap deal and why, most importantly, he had dangled the prospect of mutual recognition before the PLO. It was something that Arafat, shut out of the Washington process, longed for. By accepting the PLO's right to represent the Palestinian people, Israel would also be implicitly accepting the PLO's political agenda – the Palestinians' right to self-determination and their own state. If the swap deal was the stick that Savir had proffered, mutual recognition was the carrot.

As soon as Savir had talked through the two proposals with Abu Ala, he said that he had to leave. There was barely time for him to catch his flight. Joel Singer then came in and sat with the Palestinians, and they began to go through the points in detail while Mona Juul took Uri Savir to the airport. On the way he told her what had happened and said that Terje Larsen would now need to transmit complicated messages about the swap deal between the parties in Tunis and Jerusalem.

There were still a number of general points to be decided, such as the agenda for the permanent status negotiations and how UN resolutions could be incorporated into the DOP. But from now on, the real hard bargaining would revolve around the two centres of disagreement: security and the framework of the Gaza/Jericho First agreement.

Halvorsbole was the turning-point, the crisis that had to happen. This crisis had been building for some time: first with the Israeli proposal at Gressheim; then at the first meeting by the fiord, where the Palestinians had made their counter-proposal; and on through the Norwegians' trips to Tunis and Jerusalem; culminating back at Halvorsbole when it became clear that both sides were determined to hold their ground. The deliberate creation of crises, to kick-start stymied proceedings, is a well-known feature of any political negotiation. But the question was whether Abu Ala had, by his resignation, deliberately provoked a crisis, in the interests of brinksmanship – or had that crisis been genuine?

10

Ménage à Trois

Amongst the many observers at Halvorsbole, opinions were divided about Abu Ala's motives. The Israelis were in no doubt that his action was a deliberate ploy, although they admired the way in which he had carried it out. The Palestinians, including Abu Ala, later insisted that he had really reached his lowest ebb and that matters were very serious at that point in time. The secret police, who were watching every move, although only at a distance, told each other that it was another example of Abu Ala's clever tricks. They had often seen him deliberately set out to alarm Terje Larsen and then turn and wink at them conspiratorially. Mon Juul could not decide whether it was tactics, though she had evidence that Abu Ala was quite capable of pulling off such a pretence. At the Gressheim meeting, she had been for a walk with Abu Ala and Hassan Asfour, and they had told her that they were going to play a trick on Larsen. When they met him coming the other way, Abu Ala threw his hands up in despair and began exclaiming that everything was over, it had all collapsed. Larsen was taken in completely and, watching Abu Ala's face, Mona had marvelled at his superb acting skills. Now, at Halvorsbole, she did not know whether this was just another performance by the Palestinian.

Larsen, however, believed that Abu Ala's distress and his offer of resignation had been genuine. The Norwegian had been in the room alone with him immediately afterwards, and had seen his despair. Abu Ala had again vented his anger on him, and there must have been a reason. And yet, while Savir and Abu Ala had their private meeting together, Larsen and Hassan Asfour had gone for a walk together and Larsen had been amazed that all the Palestinian wanted to talk about was the protocol of any signing ceremony that might be the outcome of the secret channel.

'Abu Mazen must come from Tunis to sign along with Abu Ala. On the other side there will be Uri Savir but there should also be Shimon Peres,' said Asfour. This was not the sort of conversation to be having in the middle of a crisis, and Larsen wondered if, after all, Abu Ala could have been fooling him.

For days after he returned to Tunis, Abu Ala continued to berate Larsen on the phone for his interference at Halvorsbole, for the way he had pushed Savir and the Palestinian together for a private meeting. 'What you did at Halvorsbole, it was a major mistake,' he grumbled.

Larsen now suspected that Abu Ala had intended to hold out for longer before rejoining the bargaining session, or even to go back to Tunis, leaving the Israelis to sweat awhile. The Norwegian had upset his game plan and that was why he was being blamed.

The crisis illuminated another dimension to the Oslo Channel: the interaction between the characters. The bonds already created had been strengthened; there were new understandings and some honest talking in the fraught atmosphere at Halvorsbole. Increasingly the personal relationships were what gave the secret negotiations their momentum. There was a shared will to succeed even when the outlook was at its most bleak. Abu Ala had provoked the crisis by the fiord, but no one had called his bluff by walking away, to see if he really would have abandoned the Oslo process. Although the priority for each side was still to win the best deal for its people, there was also a group dynamic at work, a sense of the seven against the outside world. Sometimes that outside world included the leaders back home. The seven men all worked together in Norway to reach a compromise which had a chance of overcoming the obstacles that Rabin and Arafat had put in the way.

At the heart of the many friendships that developed within the secret channel lay the relationship between three men: Abu Ala, Uri Savir and Terje Larsen. The most complex character was the chief Palestinian negotiator, Abu Ala. The oldest and the most experienced of the group, he had been hardened by exile and the cutthroat nature of the internal politics of the PLO. He was by nature a man with a split personality, one minute charming and seductive, the next menacing and cruel. Sometimes he genuinely frightened Larsen, but he fascinated the Norwegian too. Yet it was Abu Ala's ability to display a Jekyll and Hyde nature which made him such a skilful negotiator. 'If you were a merchant in Cairo,' Larsen would often tell him, 'you'd be a millionaire many times over!'

Larsen had no choice but to bear the brunt of the Palestinian's stormy moods. He realized that Abu Ala occupied a lonely and exposed position both in Norway and, at times, in Tunis, and he felt that he had to be a buffer for Abu Ala's emotions in the way a spouse or child might be. Larsen knew the Israelis were often impatient at his own passive stance, but he recognized that the only way to prevent the channel from fracturing was to absorb Abu Ala's fury.

But underneath Abu Ala's hostility there was an undertow of warmth and generosity. Each time he came to Oslo he would bring a token gift for his Norwegian friend: an expensive tie or a traditional Palestinian cushion embroidered by refugee women. This gesture seemed to be Abu Ala's way of reassuring Larsen that he was always in his thoughts. He could display tender affection, as if to one of his own sons. Sometimes, after Larsen had received a verbal lashing from Abu Ala, the Norwegian would remonstrate with him in private:

'Come on, Abu Ala, you cannot carry on in this way.'

'But you are not only my friend, you are to me more than a friend,' Abu Ala would reply in astonishment, as if that explained everything.

Many of the participants in the channel believed that the Palestinian, who prided himself on his pre-eminent position in the group and his ability to manipulate, was put out by Larsen because the latter had assumed the role of stage-manager of the talks. Although not part of the actual negotiations, Larsen loved to place people in the right setting, to steer the conversation, to create an ambience around the talks. 'Silent poetry' was the way Uri Savir described what Larsen had created. In doing this, Larsen could at times be at loggerheads with Abu Ala, and the intensity of their personal relationship often made the situation worse.

Late one night, after an angry scene with Larsen, Abu Ala suddenly tried to explain how the art of negotiating was an almost physical obsession with him. His description had a visceral, almost an erotic, quality. 'When I negotiate, I negotiate with my eyes, with my ears, with my nose, with my sense of smell, with my mouth. I use my whole body – everything!'

Uri Savir was not in love with the game of negotiation in the same way as Abu Ala. But in many respects he too was obsessive about the process. He spent much time dissecting the behaviour of his opponent, in an attempt to understand it and to predict how it would affect the outcome of the talks. A man of emotional contradictions and deep passion, both of which are kept well under control, Savir saw a mirror of himself and the Jewish people in the more demonstrative Palestinian. It was a twisted reflection, for there were important differences. But underneath, many characteristics were the same: the lack of self-confidence, sometimes hidden beneath bluster, that comes from being a persecuted people; the tendency to complain and to be overly suspicious. Savir could, like Abu Ala, be utterly cynical. But, also like the Palestinian, he had great warmth. And the two men shared a fascination with the human condition, for death and life and existence. The driving force for both men was the search for peace. They had children of the same age and saw how meaningless the future would be for the Israelis and the Palestinians without that peace.

Larsen spent hundreds of hours watching the two men. His job was to know them better than they knew themselves, and to use that knowledge to oil the workings of the secret channel. He found himself fascinated by, and attracted to, both the Palestinian and the Israeli. He had many traits in common with them: passion, warmth and an intellectual quality. Moreover his professional training in sociology allowed him to recognize and to admit that there was a special relationship – a *ménage à trois* or magic triangle – developing at the heart of the secret channel.

Mona Juul watched her husband being drawn into the central triangle of the channel. She did not attempt to prevent this from happening, for she knew it was a vital part of the dynamics of the process. The role she chose to play herself was less emotional. Like Larsen, she was a close observer of the scene before her, but she concentrated on making political and social analyses of the characters, not on dissecting their emotions. On occasion she restrained Larsen from making judgements before the time was ripe, cautioning him to wait and see how things developed. Sometimes her presence put a necessary brake on the proceedings when emotions were running high and tempers flared. She had the civilizing effect a woman can often have on a group of men. Larsen needed her expertise in the politics and history of the Middle East, and she earned a special respect amongst the group. When Mona pronounced upon a factual detail the others generally accepted it. 'Terje, you are nothing without Mona,' Abu Ala would say, smiling.

But the cool diplomat always remained something of an enigma to the group. There was also something mysterious, they all decided, about the Norwegian couple's motives. Sometimes the Israelis and Palestinians could not really understand what made Terje and Mona give up their personal life and even, some felt, jeopardize their marriage on the physical and emotional roller-coaster of the channel. It was not something the two Norwegians had consciously entered into at the end of 1992. By now, seven months later, there was no room or time in their lives for anything else. They felt a heavy responsibility for the secret talks, and the toll was heavy too. But it was nevertheless an exhilarating and unique experience, and Larsen knew enough about himself to realize that it was something he had to see through to the end. For he shared a certain obsessional trait with Savir and Abu Ala.

There were others in the group, too, who came to know themselves better for their experience in Oslo. Joel Singer, once the prickly outsider, had now been absorbed fully into the group. His introverted character had become more forthcoming and his attitude had relaxed. He was now more interested in understanding the psychology behind the talks. The Palestinians had come to value his directness, his refusal to camouflage his meaning. Savir was a formidable opponent, subtle and sophisticated, with an intellectual approach. Singer's style was abrupt and interrogatory, but with him there was no game-playing, no ulterior motive. As the Palestinians described it, Singer would deliberately bounce straight at the walls that both sides had constructed around the negotiations, whereas Savir would bounce over them, evading the obstacles as if they did not exist.

Yet the most significant transformation to occur at Halvorsbole was that undergone by Hassan Asfour. Everyone saw how this thoughtful and committed Palestinian, with deeply held convictions, openly and courageously allowed those convictions to be challenged by the Oslo process. In long conversations with all the Norwegians, he revealed that his views of the conflict and of his opponents had been radically altered by the Israelis he had met in Norway. Even in the midst of hostile exchanges with Joel

Singer, who most conformed to his image of the enemy, he had learnt that Singer too was a person with a family and a longing for a peaceful, prosperous life. Now the Communist from the Gaza Strip realized he had much in common with the Israeli ex-colonel, despite the gulf of experience that separated them. They were both men of integrity, who spoke the truth even when it was the most unpalatable option.

In the middle of the first negotiating session at Halvorsbole, at 3.00 a.m., Joel Singer and Hassan Asfour had taken a long walk by the dark shore of the fiord. Singer was angry and disillusioned. He appealed directly to Asfour to tell him what the Palestinians were trying to achieve by their demands. Asfour reassured him that it would all work out in the end.

'It's necessary for the negotiations that I regard you as my enemy,' Asfour said honestly. 'But in another situation we would be friends. We will always have our differences but now I know our struggle in the future will be a struggle undertaken together. What we are doing is for our families, our own people – the Palestinians. And in the end it is for peace itself.'

As a student of Marxist theory living in Moscow, Asfour was someone whose views of the Palestinian conflict had been shaped by cold war ideology. Now he realized that, just as the Berlin Wall had crumbled as a result of economic and political realities in Eastern Europe, so his own beliefs had been dismantled by the experience of living, working and arguing alongside four Israelis.

Joel Singer and Hassan Asfour, the two men at the furthest ends of the political and personal spectrum of the channel, walked back to the hotel as dawn began to break. The Oslo spirit had worked its magic on them and their lives would never be the same.

As the group had become closer over the weeks, a common vocabulary had developed in the channel. There were buzz-words and phrases like 'this will fly', indicating that a new draft or a new section of the DOP could be made to work. 'As you wish' was a throw-away line the Israelis or Palestinians would use to indicate they had conceded a point. And 'I'm all alone' remained the key to unlock the tension when there was an impasse. For all three groups – the Palestinians, Israelis and Norwegians – the private language of the Oslo Channel had a special meaning. None of the participants was speaking in his native tongue: they all spoke and wrote, argued and redrafted, in English. Some were completely fluent but others had more difficulty expressing themselves. Savir was never at a loss for words, the ready quip, the mocking epithet. Abu Ala spoke volumes in short, emphatic sentences. Singer was direct. Hirschfeld and Pundak were voluble, forever arguing as Pundak played devil's advocate with Hirschfeld's theories. Mohammed Abu Koush was quiet and rarely expressed his own opinions in the meetings. Hassan Asfour was most acute but his English was the most limited. However, he took it in good part, joking that the agreement had to be simple because he could only understand the main points.

The bombardment of southern Lebanon was continuing as the members of the Oslo Channel reached home on 26 July. Now another intensive round of telephone calls began. Larsen was again the conduit, this time for hard bargaining over the swap deal. His conversations with Abu Ala, in Tunis, always began in cheery style: 'Hi, it's me, Larsen the terrorist.' Only Larsen could get away with using such sensitive terminology with a member of the PLO.

Larsen would then convey Savir's latest message. The Israelis were standing firm on the swap deal.

'This is what he says, this is the message: it's a package deal. It's yes or no. OK? You get eight, he gets eight. It's yes or no. It's not, you get ten and he gets six. It's eight each, and this is what he's offering you, nothing more. It's yes or no.' Larsen could almost hear Abu Ala tearing his hair out.

'I don't accept this "yes or no"! This is negotiation we are in. But this is not the way to negotiate.'

In the decision-making process Israel too had its own crisis. Rabin was furious at what he saw as the PLO intransigence revealed at Halvorsbole. He had always been highly sceptical of the whole process and, despite Singer's presence, the group had difficulties persuading him that the secret channel could deliver anything. He had not yet accepted, as had Peres and his Blazers, that the PLO and its old-style leaders were the only ones with whom Israel could do a deal. And Halvorsbole had confirmed his scepticism.

Savir was refusing to return to Oslo until he had a pledge from the PLO to accept the swap deal. The Palestinians had decided that they would accept the seven-point plan he had put forward on mutual recognition. But they wanted it to become part of the Declaration of Principles they were negotiating. The Israelis rejected this 'linkage', as they called it. Peres had decided that they should conclude one deal before embarking on the other. And so the Israelis continued to press for a commitment to resolve the two remaining sets of problems on the DOP.

By now Larsen was finding it difficult to give the necessary details about the outstanding issues over the telephone. The information was complicated and almost impossible to convey in code. And so an unofficial meeting was set up in Paris. Abu Ala met Yair Hirschfeld, with Mona and Terje in attendance, to sort out exactly where each party stood on each of the sixteen points. They worked together again in the flat that Holst's daughter had borrowed. This time the atmosphere was more relaxed and constructive. Abu Ala had brought one of his three sons, Isam, who had just finished his university education in the United States. Hirschfeld told them he had come as a typist, with his computer ready, to write down exactly what the Palestinian positions were on the elements of the package deal. With Isam's help, Abu Ala and Hirschfeld sat there refining the language of the latest draft, settling all the details of the requirements for the Gaza plan so that negotiations could be restarted. Afterwards they felt that they had made real progress in Paris. There was a kind of pattern emerging: crisis and brinkmanship at Halvorsbole, followed by a period of constructive work as Abu Ala showed he could put things back together.

And now, in the first days of August, there were a number of significant developments in the public sphere of the Middle East negotiations. Warren Christopher began a major round of shuttle diplomacy in the region with a clear warning to all the parties: 'Decision time is rapidly approaching,' he said, reminding them that there had once been hopes they could achieve something by the year's end.

Ironically his statement reflected what the members of the Oslo Channel were telling both themselves and their leaders. But Christopher was not talking about the secret PLO Israeli initiative; he was focused on mending relations between Israel and Syria. The Clinton Administration knew that the talks in Washington were almost moribund, for the 'full partnership' initiative had not solved anything. The Americans were growing impatient with the Palestinian delegation who, they felt, would not make decisions, either because they did not have the power themselves or because they could not get Yasser Arafat to address the issues. As Christopher shuttled between Damascus and Jerusalem, it became clear that he felt this track of the negotiations was the only one that would prove fruitful. In Jerusalem, anxious Palestinian representatives, including Hanan Ashrawi, wanted to know if America was bypassing them.

The Palestinians were 'concerned about whether there were any special arrangements with Syria', Christopher conceded to the press. In other words, the Palestinians feared that Prime Minister Rabin and President Assad of Syria would make a separate deal to return the Israeli-occupied Golan Heights to Syria. Arafat was in a dilemma. He had not wanted the Washington talks, which excluded him, to deliver anything, but now the PLO was in danger of being left out altogether.

On 3 August the US Secretary of State met with Yitzhak Rabin. Their talk centred on the Syrian situation, and Rabin seemed to agree that this avenue looked the most promising. His principle seemed to be that he would make progress where he could. Although he knew that Arafat both wanted and needed peace, Rabin felt that the PLO leader would simply not commit himself. Rabin and Christopher also talked briefly about the Norwegian initiative, and the Israeli Prime Minister admitted that in theory they were getting close to some kind of deal on Gaza and Jericho. But he was still very sceptical and said that he doubted the PLO could ever agree to anything of real substance in negotiations over the interim period of autonomy. The Israeli Prime Minister added that the issue of mutual recognition had been raised, but he doubted whether the PLO would agree to it. The Americans had not been briefed on the secret channel since Holst had spoken to Christopher in May, and Christopher understood from his conversation with Rabin in August that the initiative was, as the Americans had thought all along, going nowhere.

Although his intention was to focus attention on the Syrian front, Christopher's Middle East tour was proving the catalyst to crystallize discontent amongst the Palestinians, who were threatening to break ranks. This was to have a vital bearing on Rabin's decision-making and, consequently, on the Oslo Channel.

It emerged that when Christopher arrived in Cairo at the beginning of his tour, Abu Mazen had, on behalf of Arafat and

using Egyptian intermediaries, discussed new Palestinian proposals with the US Secretary of State, without consulting the
local West Bank delegation. When the angry local Palestinians
examined those proposals they found Arafat had made significant concessions, in particular over Jerusalem. Instead of
insisting, as they had always been told to do in Washington, that
the status of the city had to be decided now, as part of the interim
agreement, Arafat was in fact prepared to postpone any discussion of the issue until the final stages of the negotiations, in years
to come. Moreover, the new proposals made Jericho the focus,
not Jerusalem. Hanan Ashrawi, Faisal Husseini and Saeb Erekat,
the leading members of the local delegation, tendered their resignations in protest.

In typical style Arafat refused to accept the resignations and
somehow managed to paper over the cracks. But the PLO was
floundering and the Chairman was under increasing pressure.
The financial woes of the organization were now an open secret.
The PLO had tried to suppress the news but there had been riots
in Amman and Libya when the widows and families of
Palestinian fighters did not receive their monthly stipend. The
bureaucracy in Tunis was grinding to a halt as salaries were
frozen and telephones disconnected because of unpaid bills.
Welfare payments to 50,000 families in the Occupied Territories
were ended and hard questions were being asked about the lack
of accountability and democracy at the very top of the PLO.

To some in Israel, both the internal wrangling of the
Palestinians and their financial crisis were a sign that this was a
moment that should be seized before it slipped away. Yossi Beilin
said on Israel Radio: 'If it turns out that we have nobody to talk
to among Palestinian residents of the territories here, we will
have to rethink this matter very seriously, perhaps breaking
taboos that have already been eroded.' Beilin saw that now the
issue of direct talks with the PLO could not be avoided, and that
this revelation might serve to drive the Oslo Channel to its natural conclusion.

In the other Israeli camp the same thought was occurring.
Yitzhak Rabin had been loath to abandon hope of some accommodation with the Palestinian people through local leaders in
the Occupied Territories. He had also been reluctant to concede
that the Washington talks were leading nowhere. But the recent
furore in the Palestinian ranks had proved two things: first, the

new leadership was proving just as intractable as the old over the Jerusalem issue; and secondly, the local Palestinian leaders were not the ones who wielded the power. The truth was unpalatable but unavoidable: Arafat and the PLO were the only ones who could deliver a peace deal.

11

A Night in Stockholm

Deliberate, direct, some might say lugubrious, Yitzhak Rabin is not known for his enthusiasm on any subject. But he is a realist and he now saw the reality of the situation. Washington was no longer the main avenue to peace; the back road via Oslo had turned out to be the most direct route. Now Rabin became almost forthcoming on the subject of the secret talks. In particular, he felt that the offer of mutual recognition might clinch the deal. And so just days after Warren Christopher returned to America, as the Palestinians sat nursing their self-inflicted wounds, Rabin authorized the Israeli team to return to Norway. Savir and Singer were hopeful that this might be the last round of negotiations, but they realized that it might take some time to finalize the Declaration of Principles.

Again Larsen and the other Norwegians had to search high and low for a place to meet. Once more, by popular demand, the first choice was Borregaard. The house had brought them luck before, and now they hoped that it would again prove a place of good omen. But although the refurbishment of the old manor was now complete, it was already booked. Larsen appealed to the proprietor, Heyerdahl, who was a friend, and the latter agreed that they could return to Borregaard, although they would have to vacate the main house, and move to the annexe, for part of the weekend. On Friday, 13 August, the two groups of negotiators arrived in Oslo and were driven down to Sarpsborg.

It was now high summer, and the pine trees around the house were dark and fragrant, no longer loaded down with snow. The trees in the garden were laden with fruit and the old tennis-court gate stood open. Uri Savir, Joel Singer and Mohammed Abu Koush had heard much about the place and they were curious to see it. Geir Pedersen had spent his childhood in Sarpsborg but had only ever gazed at the big house through the old iron railings surrounding it. Now he chauffeured Hassan Asfour up the drive. The old hands among the negotiators displayed a rather proprietorial air as they walked around the house.

On the first evening everyone assembled for dinner in convivial mood. Palme Ericsen, the housekeeper, maintained her kitchen's reputation for good cuisine by serving them the food she remembered had been their favourite before. They ate smoked fish canapés followed by roast fillet of lamb with a Norwegian speciality, potatoes baked in cream. For dessert they had ice-cream. After dinner, as they relaxed on the red velvet sofas under the portrait of the seventeenth-century notable who had built Borregaard, they decided it had been such a pleasant evening that they would hold only a short preparatory meeting, and leave the substance of the negotiations for the morning.

The following morning the two teams began early, and the Israelis were encouraged when they found that the new Palestinian draft incorporated some of the eight points they had taken back to Tunis as their part of the swap deal. In return Savir and Singer made three concessions. On the question of mutual recognition Abu Ala announced that the Palestinians agreed to the seven points put forward at Halvorsbole. But then he handed over their paper on the subject, which proposed that, before the PLO would recognize the Jewish state, Israel too should renounce violence and terror. Savir rejected this immediately:

'If you want mutual recognition at all, it has to be sharp and clear and signed by Arafat, and in return we will recognize the PLO. You are just making things worse. Let's stop the whole mutual recognition thing, and continue for the moment with the DOP.'

Shimon Peres was not prepared to jeopardize the Declaration of Principles which they had worked on for so many months. He was concerned that if the mutual recognition agreement ran into difficulties it would drag down the DOP. So now Savir and Singer persuaded Abu Ala to shelve the recognition issue until the open questions on the main accord were settled. But the Israelis hoped that the incentive they had dangled before the Palestinians would spur them on to agree to the DOP.

The transfer of powers from the Israeli military government to the Palestinians in Gaza and Jericho was still causing problems. So was the definition of Jericho; did the name refer simply to the town itself or to the whole district? The seat of the proposed Palestinian council was another sticking point, as was the timetable for withdrawal. Yet again the major point of contention was whether the Israeli army should retain responsibility for the security of the settlers in Gaza and Jericho after its withdrawal.

In the afternoon the group had to leave the main house, adjourning to the nearby annexe to continue talks. Mona Juul and Geir Pedersen shepherded them over. Terje Larsen had left to attend a party back in Oslo that night. Before the secret channel had taken over his life, he had promised to be the toastmaster at a close friend's sixtieth-birthday celebrations, and he felt he could not let him down. Mona took on Larsen's role as stage-manager and decided that the Norwegians should not have dinner with the two groups this time, for it was clear that they were deep in discussion and she did not want to break the mood. She arranged for their dinner of cold veal and calf's liver, followed by fruit salad, to be served for them in a small room in the annexe. Just before midnight the two teams walked back to the house under a clear sky studded with stars. Mona felt there was a real impetus to the talks; everyone seemed to want to finish them that night, however long it might take.

By now the two teams had reached agreement on several long-standing problems. The Palestinians had managed to get the Israelis to accept that the agenda of the final status negotiations would be set down in the DOP, even though the document was mainly concerned with the interim period. And the Israelis had also conceded that the final talks would lead to the 'implementation' of UN Resolution 242, which calls for complete Israeli withdrawal from all the Occupied Territories. But the two teams were still stymied over aspects of the Gaza/Jericho First approach: the timetable for withdrawal and the security of Israelis in those areas.

At around midnight Abu Ala indicated to the Israelis that he could clear the last hurdles. He would just need to call Tunis to get final approval from Abu Mazen and Arafat. Savir and Singer felt that he genuinely believed this, and so did Mona, who was observing closely as people came and went from the main sitting-room. Terje was not yet back. He had gone off with one of the secret service men as chauffeur, and had a full communications set-up in the car. Mona had arranged that she would call him by mobile phone if he was urgently needed.

Uri Savir and Joel Singer sat chatting with Mona on the sofa while the Palestinians made telephone calls upstairs. The two Israelis appeared relaxed, although they knew that if Abu Ala came back with authority to agree the remaining few points, the secret channel would indeed have cause to celebrate. They were not as eager, as pushy, as they had seemed at previous meetings, for example at Gressheim. They appeared to be indicating that, although they would not strike the actual deal that night, they would get final decisions on all outstanding issues. 'Now everything is ready,' Savir told Mona; 'we'll just wait now for Arafat's answer.'

Two hours later, at 2.00 a.m., Abu Ala came downstairs and they all jumped to their feet. With sinking heart Mona saw him shaking his head, a grim look on his face. The seven men trooped back into the sitting-room and closed the door. Mona immediately called the security man waiting for Larsen outside the birthday party and told him to get Terje out at once.

Fifty miles from Borregaard the celebrations were in full swing. The host was a distinguished member of Norway's Labour Party élite and a popular figure, and the somewhat preoccupied toastmaster found that there was a veritable queue of people wanting to make fulsome speeches. Each one required a witty introduction and it was impossible to get away. Just as he was about to slip out, a large woman launched into a long, emotional song. Finally Larsen escaped and tried to speak to Mona over the mobile phone as he roared along the road to Borregaard. Something was clearly wrong but she didn't want to go into details on the mobile. The Israelis were becoming intensely afraid of leaks, and had asked the Norwegians not to use this risky means of communication. So, in the early hours of the morning, Larsen and his escort had to search for a public phone booth. Mona's voice was tired and dispirited as she told him what had happened.

An hour after Abu Ala had returned, and they had gone back into the sitting-room, Mona was still waiting downstairs. She noticed that it was deathly quiet above and so she walked hesitantly up to the first-floor room. The door was flung wide open, the lights were blazing and papers were scattered on the table. But there was no one there. Then Yair Hirschfeld and Ron Pundak came slowly down from the Israelis' quarters on the top floor. Hirschfeld, always a ready emotional barometer, was fighting back the tears. 'It's over,' they told her dramatically. 'Arafat's turned his team down.'

They said that Abu Ala and Hassan Asfour were angry and upset. The Palestinians felt they had given their word to the Israelis that this time Tunis would back their judgement. But now the final agreement had been withheld and they were bitterly disappointed.

Mona went quietly to Abu Ala's room. He had never just disappeared before, without saying good night to her. She knocked softly on the door and he told her to come in. It was a warm and comfortable bedroom, decorated in shades of yellow, glowing in the dim light from the bedside lamp. Wearing the slippers that had become his trademark in the channel, Abu Ala sat on one of the twin beds. Mona sat down facing him on the other. The Palestinian confided in her that he was upset and surprised that they had not got the answer they were confident would be given. He felt that he had misled Savir, that he had told him it would be easy to sell the final points. At the nadir of his spirits, he seemed to find talking to one of his Norwegian friends helpful. He had a soft spot for Mona – his own youngest daughter shared her name. 'You are Mona, you are my daughter,' he would say.

Mona was moved by the whole night's events. First the emotional outburst from the two Israeli professors, and now the calm air of defeat that hung over the Palestinian chief. Terje arrived back to find there was little he could do except talk to his wife. Savir had gone to sleep and Abu Ala was in no mood for talk. At 5.00 a.m. Mona and Terje went to bed exhausted.

The next day, at breakfast, nothing seemed as bad as it had in the dark hours of the night. Mona felt that Hirschfeld and Pundak appeared rather sheepish, as if they had overplayed their hand the night before. Perhaps Savir or Singer had sent them down to make sure the Palestinians got the message, via the Norwegians, that they were not prepared to hang around indefinitely for Arafat to make up his mind. 'Don't worry, Mona,' Ron Pundak told her anxiously. 'There are ways, we will make it work, you'll see.'

Since Halvorsbole, Terje and Mona had determined to be very careful in their handling of the parties. In the early days, and even as late as July, they had not known much about the substance of the talks. They were well aware that in their role as go-betweens, with only partial knowledge, they could be used –

and probably had been – by both sides. They knew it would be tempting for the Israelis and the Palestinians to plant disinformation via the Norwegians, in order to reinforce their bluffing and their game-playing. Everyone on the Oslo side took it for granted that this had already happened during the last nine months, but they did not want to be exploited at this critical juncture, as the negotiations headed towards a peace deal.

Abu Ala wanted the Israelis to stay on at Borregaard. He insisted that he could get the last points agreed with Tunis if only he was given time. But Savir left immediately. He was determined to increase the pressure on the Palestinians. When Savir arrived back in Israel that night, Larsen called him to say that two more small changes had been conceded and that the gap had narrowed to three or four open questions.

The Oslo Channel was now up against a natural deadline and everybody who was involved knew it. Shimon Peres was due to make an official visit to Scandinavia on 17 August, in two days' time, and Norway was naturally on his itinerary. Although his official delegation was not informed of the fact, the Israeli Foreign Minister had, in consultation with Yitzhak Rabin, decided that the deal should be finalized and sealed during this visit.

Early on the morning of 17 August, Johan Jorgen Holst was asleep in Iceland where he was on an official engagement. A call from Shimon Peres, in Sweden on the first leg of his tour, roused him. 'Can you meet me secretly in Stockholm tonight?' Peres asked. 'It's make or break time now.'

Holst agreed at once and asked Terje and Mona to make the arrangements. Larsen, accompanied by the leader of the secret service team, immediately took a flight to Stockholm. They had to work out how the Norwegian Foreign Minister could travel discreetly to a neighbouring country for a meeting with a visiting foreign dignitary whom he was already due to meet shortly in Norway. It would arouse suspicions. They would have to tell the Swedes something that was neither a lie nor the whole truth. The Norwegian secret service man had phoned ahead to the Swedish intelligence agency and the two men were met at the airport by a woman officer driving a van with blacked-out windows. She drove them to the Foreign Ministry, where Larsen had requested a private meeting with a Swedish official. He told the man that Norway had some outstanding points to settle with the

Israeli government, and that it would prefer to do this before Peres landed on Norwegian soil, as there were rather delicate issues involved. It had to do with some orders for heavy water, the nuclear material, which Norway had agreed to supply to Israel. And he added, with a hint of the truth, that there were also some issues to be resolved regarding Norway's involvement in the multilateral part of the Middle East peace process. Larsen requested that as few people as possible be informed, and the official promised he would tell only the Swedish Foreign Minister. Then Larsen and his security escort left immediately for the Haga Palace, where the Israeli delegation headed by Peres would be staying.

The official hostess at the residence, a beautiful nineteenth-century Swedish palace set in an enormous park, was somewhat bewildered to learn that another VIP, this time from neighbouring Norway, would be jetting in at ten that night, too late for the state banquet but requiring a meeting room instead. She offered Larsen the use of a big salon with tall windows overlooking the gardens. Then the two men returned to the airport to meet the Norwegian government jet carrying Holst and Mona Juul. Their Swedish secret service woman took the van with blacked-out windows right to the foot of the aeroplane steps, and Holst and Mona sprinted down into the vehicle, without being identified by anyone. They were then taken back to the Haga Palace, where they waited in the salon for Peres's official dinner to finish. At ten o'clock the double doors were flung wide open and a smiling Peres, his aide Avi Gill, and Joel Singer entered. It had been decided that Uri Savir should not attend; he was too well known and his presence in Stockholm would have been remarked upon, not least by the Israeli embassy officials accompanying Peres.

Peres explained that he wanted to finish the negotiations that night, and then he and Singer ran through the outstanding points with Holst, to put him fully in the picture. Uri Savir stayed by the phone in Jerusalem and Rabin maintained contact with Peres in the Haga Palace.

'I want to get Arafat himself on the phone,' Peres instructed. 'I don't want to speak to him myself. I would like you, Johan, to be my mouthpiece. I would like you to indicate to Arafat that I am here and will stay here throughout the negotiations – as I am needed. He can discuss things with me through you.'

Larsen dialled Arafat's office in Tunis. The Chairman came on the line immediately and Terje handed him over to the

Norwegian Foreign Minister. Arafat listened as Holst outlined what was going on and told him that they wished now to settle all the issues with him personally. 'That will be difficult,' replied the Chairman.' I do not like to speak in English on the telephone.'

Arafat was obviously unwilling to have detailed, legalistic discussions in his rather broken English. It was agreed that he would bring Abu Ala to the phone. But Abu Ala could not be found. Eventually, an hour later, a breathless Abu Ala came on the line. It was clear to those listening in Stockholm there were several others in the room besides Arafat, whose high-pitched voice could be heard issuing a stream of instructions in quick-fire Arabic.

In fact, at the Tunis end there were six men sitting in the Chairman's office: Arafat himself, Abu Ala, Abu Mazen, Hassan Asfour and two others. These other two were Yasser Abed-Rabbo, the smooth-talking PLO official who was increasingly acting as Arafat's spokesman, and a Lebanese politician, Muhsen Ibrahim. Abed-Rabbo had discovered about the secret channel inadvertently. He is one of Arafat's key advisers and he had been present one day when the Chairman was discussing the Oslo connection with Abu Mazen. Abed-Rabbo, a former leader of the Marxist Democratic Front, now heads the Feda faction of the PLO. He is a well-known moderate, handsome, media-friendly and a favourite of foreign reporters. He had been let into the secret somewhat reluctantly, under strict instructions to tell no one. Muhsen Ibrahim, a close confidant of Arafat's, is a lawyer whose advice and good sense are highly regarded by the PLO. He had been aware of the Oslo Channel for some time and was asked to be present for this session.

The five men sat ranged around the long table in front of Arafat at his desk. Behind the Chairman hung a vast panoramic picture of the famous Dome of the Rock in Jerusalem. The other walls were decorated with mementoes of Arafat's long and bloody struggle against the Israeli occupation; the room was a shrine to enmity and sorrow. Among the artefacts on display were a picture of a prowed galley – composed of tiny mosaic pieces in the Palestinian national colours of green, red and black – sent to Arafat by Palestinian prisoners; and in a glass case, a single sharp-edged stone, a poignant symbol of the Intifada, a present from the boys of a West Bank refugee camp; and on the wall facing Arafat, a large square frame surrounding a stark set of photographs showing the leader of the PLO with two close associates, Abu Iyad and Abu Jihad, both victims of the assassin's bullet.

By now it was midnight, and the atmosphere inside the room was electric with anticipation. The first of endless cups of coffee were handed round. Cigarette smoke began to fill the air. Outside, the armed guards, who were forbidden to enter the room, whispered to each other: 'The Norwegian Foreign Minister is on the phone. No one can go in or out and no other phone calls are to be put through. Something must be going on!'

And so the negotiating started. Holst conveyed proposals, waited while Abu Ala conferred with Arafat, and then communicated the response back to Peres who would discuss them with Singer. After an hour Peres, who had had a long flight that morning from Tel Aviv, decided that he would take a nap and asked Gill to wake him if he was needed. As the night wore on, everyone grew hungry and thirsty and Avi Gill asked the official hostess if they could have some sandwiches. Somewhat pointedly, she told him that no one had given her adequate notice of this unusual all-night meeting and that there were none available. Moreover she intended to complain to the authorities in the morning. So the Norwegian security men went down to the kitchens of the palace, to raid the fridges and bring back whatever they could find. That night the team finished up the cold leftovers from the banquet in honour of Shimon Peres.

For eight hours, the negotiations swung back and forth. Singer was running the negotiations for the Israelis, and, on the other end, Arafat kept up a running background commentary as Abu Ala's voice grew hoarse with smoke and tension. If there had ever been any doubts, there were none now: Arafat ran the show in Tunis and he was letting everybody know it. Three times Avi Gill woke Peres, who came back and made the big decisions. He was tough and his timing was perfect. At a particularly sticky moment he exploited Arafat's worst fear. 'Tell them we'll go with Syria,' he said, and went back to bed.

It was doubtful whether, at this time, there was any real likelihood that the Israelis had a Syrian option. Deep down the Palestinians probably knew that. But they could not afford to risk the chance that Israel would do a deal over the Golan Heights, the territory seized from Syria, without the Palestinian claim being settled.

Holst, too, played a difficult game with skill and diplomacy. He grasped the intricacies of the points at issue and formulated the words to everyone's satisfaction. It was the climax of the Oslo Channel, the hour of triumph for the Norwegian method of facilitation, not mediation, for Holst still stuck firmly to the principle of non-interference. He assisted, he put forward various options, but he did not suggest which ones should be adopted. Watching him, Terje Larsen was openly admiring but he gave the impression that he felt a certain sadness and even a twinge of envy. He had been the main orchestrator of the channel until now, the bellwether of mood and progress, but as the negotiations moved towards their conclusion, so the official Norwegian presence, in the shape of the Foreign Minister, moved centre stage. The whole emphasis of the secret talks was changing, as the close-knit team at the centre gave way to the politicians, who now had to accept the public responsibility for what their teams had done.

That long night they argued over three main points. The first was settled at 3.00 a.m., when Israel won concessions on security. In the Agreed Minutes of the DOP it would be stated that 'the withdrawal of the military government will not prevent Israel exercising powers and responsibilities not transferred to the council'. The protection of the settlers, it had already been agreed, would remain a matter for Israel, and would not be transferred to the Palestinian council. Now Israel could interpret the 'powers and responsibilities' clause to mean that units of the army could remain after the withdrawal from Gaza and Jericho was completed, in order to assure the security of Israelis living there.

The last two points at issue were contained in Annexe 2 of the DOP – the annexe that dealt with the details of the Gaza/Jericho First agreement. At 4.00 a.m. the word 'responsibilities' was changed to 'matters', a subtle nuance giving more room for legal manœuvre in the paragraph dealing with the security, foreign affairs and settlements issues, which lay outside the control of the interim Palestinian council.

The final point, which was agreed at 5.00 a.m., was, perhaps fittingly, a compromise for both sides. It concerned the location of the new Palestinian council. The PLO wanted it to have offices in 'Gaza, the Jericho area and other places on the West Bank'. The last phrase left the way open to bring Jerusalem back into the frame, before the final status negotiations in five years' time. The

Israelis wanted the council to be limited to Gaza and the Jericho area. But they eventually agreed to add the phrase 'pending the inauguration of the Council', which left more flexibility for movement later.

So in the end each side held out for its most crucial concerns – the Israelis for the security of their people, the PLO for the powers it would get from the Gaza/Jericho First agreement as a first step along the road to self-government in the Occupied Territories. The main elements of the agreement were that the military withdrawal would begin from Gaza and the Jericho area by December 1993, and be completed by April 1994. By mid-July of that year a Palestinian council would be elected. At that time authority would be transferred from the Israeli military government and civil administration to the council in the spheres of education and culture, health, social welfare, direct taxation and tourism. Israeli military forces already withdrawn from Gaza and Jericho would then deploy outside populated areas in the rest of the West Bank. They would retain responsibility for the security of Israeli settlers. By December 1995 negotiations would begin on the permanent status of the Occupied Territories, and by the end of 1998 that final settlement would take effect.

Dawn was breaking over the parkland of the Haga Palace. After eight hours of intense debate, the deal had finally been agreed. Holst asked to speak to Arafat. 'You did it! Congratulations!' were his words.

Peres was woken up and, when he entered the room, he looked perfectly refreshed. He smiled and joked and slapped everyone on the back. On the phone Abu Ala talked on, followed by Yasser Arafat. They could only keep repeating one thing to Holst and to Larsen: 'Thank you, thank you, thank you ... on behalf of the Palestinian people.'

At the Tunis end, Abu Ala offered his congratulations to Yasser Arafat. The six men in the room stood up and solemnly kissed each other three times in the traditional way. And then the tears came as they cried with relief and happiness. They summoned the official PLO photographer and had their pictures taken together as a record of this great moment. Then Arafat made a short and heartfelt speech to his five PLO colleagues:

'Now we must take our responsibilities seriously, and implement this peace plan. Only we, in this room tonight, know what has been achieved. Now we must convey the news to our colleagues on the Executive Committee, one by one, and per-suade them that this is right.'

Arafat's eyes strayed to the chart upon the wall outlining the top echelons of the PLO, with names and faces, the hierarchy of the revolutionary organization he had created. He knew it would be the hardest task of his long and difficult career to persuade them to accept the agreement. There would be outrage, threats and danger in the days ahead.

When the gathering broke up, Abu Mazen was driven home in the cool Tunisian dawn. When he reached his house he was too excited to sleep. He woke his wife and told her what had hap-pened. 'We have made a historical breakthrough today,' he said emotionally. It was the first time he had breathed a word of the Oslo Channel outside the handful of PLO people who knew the secret. For Abu Mazen, the Palestinians' Israel-watcher, had been particularly sensitive to Israeli accusations that the PLO leaked like a sieve, that it could not be trusted to guard important secrets. Many times Abu Mazen had been confronted with rumours about a secret channel, in Vienna or in Paris. Once, an Israeli official had told a Palestinian delegate in Washington that there were talks going on in Oslo. Abu Mazen had ridiculed the suggestion, saying that the Israeli must be getting confused with advances made via Egypt. Abu Mazen had staunchly backed Abu Ala and the Oslo Channel. He had even refused a request from Arafat that summer for him to meet secretly with another Israeli public figure. He argued with the Chairman that they already had a back channel in Norway, and that they should be investing all their efforts in that direction.

In Stockholm Avi Gill was still trying to placate the irate host-ess, who had returned early in the morning. He was afraid that if she made a fuss about the meeting, people might try to find out what exactly had been going on. 'We're very sorry for inconve-niencing you,' he soothed her. 'Just send the phone bill to the Israeli embassy in Stockholm.' Only then did he realize that the embassy staff would be most intrigued to be sent a bill run up by Peres consisting of dozens of phone calls to Yasser Arafat's office in Tunis.

After two hours' sleep the Norwegians flew back to Oslo. The very next day Holst was due to receive Peres and the Israeli delegation officially, on their planned visit to Norway. The real purpose of the trip was still a secret. It was to see both sides initial the agreement reached in Stockholm that night. While the Norwegians were flying home from Sweden, the Israeli and Palestinian teams were already making their way back to Oslo.

12

The Oslo Spirit

On 19 August the negotiators arrived once more at Fornebu
Airport. This time they were not bound for a country retreat. The
Norwegians realized that with Peres in Oslo the capital was the
place where the document could be most discreetly signed.
Mona Juul, Terje Larsen, Geir Pedersen and Even Aas immediately set about arranging the details. They booked the two
groups into the Oslo Plaza Hotel, a glitzy downtown tower of
steel and glass. The building is something of a local aberration, in
terms of style and architecture; neither Norwegian nor
restrained, it would seem more suited to Dallas or New York.

Security was now of paramount importance, partly to keep the
operation under wraps and partly to protect the participants now
that the peace proposal would become a formal agreement. After
consulting with the secret service team, Larsen decided to take
over the entire thirty-second floor of the hotel. It had a separate lift
system that could only be accessed with a special computerized
card-key, so it could be kept effectively secure. On the thirty-second floor there were two magnificent complexes of rooms that
suited the group's requirements. The Palestinian delegation was
assigned the Investa Suite, which consisted of three large
bedrooms, a living-room and a meeting room. Decked out in pan-
elled walnut, with a spectacular midnight-blue ceiling studded
with gold stars, the apartment was opulent, to say the least. It
dripped with gold and crystal from every available surface, and
superb stereo systems filled the air with music. The Norwegians
found the suite rather ostentatious, but Abu Ala was in his element. It was spacious and luxurious, a far cry from the interesting
but rather Spartan furnishing to which he had become accus-
tomed during his nine-month adventure in Norway.

Along the corridor another sumptuous suite awaited the

Israelis. The Polar Suite was more Norwegian but almost an intergalactic interpretation of Nordic style. Furnished in steel and glass and decked out in shades of icy blue, the main room was dominated by an extraordinary stuffed polar bear who attracted a number of ribald nicknames. The centrepiece of the principal bedroom, assigned to Savir, was an outsize bed shaped like an iceberg, with sharp and jagged edges. Abu Ala, who had stayed at the hotel before, had had experience of this bed, and he had told Larsen he would not sleep there again, as his shins had ended up black and blue. So Savir was nominated to negotiate the perils of the iceberg bed.

As the unacknowledged Israeli and Palestinian guests settled into their locked-off quarters at the Plaza, some members of the usual security team were at the airport to await the arrival of Peres and his official delegation. Joel Singer was with the Israeli Foreign Minister and, as Holst formally welcomed Peres to Norway, Singer winked at the security men, then slipped away to join them so that they could drive him quickly to the Plaza Hotel.

Shortly after his arrival, Shimon Peres requested a brief tête-à-tête with Holst. Before the official business started he wanted to discuss the details of the secret signing ceremony. Avi Gill and Mona Juul accompanied them, leaving the other Norwegian and Israeli officials to kick their heels outside for nearly an hour. As press reports throughout the summer had continued to speculate about secret talks in Europe, Peres and Holst felt that it could not be long before there were leaks. It was therefore imperative that they have a plan on when and how to inform the US Administration. Once the signing had taken place, the Israeli Cabinet would have to be informed, and they would want to know what the American reaction had been. Both Israel and Norway had agreed all along that they would carefully coordinate their approaches to Warren Christopher, if and when the time came to formalize the Declaration of Principles. Now they began to plan a trip across the Atlantic, as soon as possible after the ceremony to sign the DOP, which they concluded should happen that very night in Oslo.

When the meeting between Peres and Holst was over, the Israeli Foreign Minister said: 'Well, now we have to go outside and play the game and conduct the formal meeting, where I brief you on the current state of the Middle East peace process.' Avi and Mona watched as Holst and Peres, with completely straight faces, engaged in an earnest discussion with their officials on the slow and halting peace initiative in Washington.

Back at the Plaza, Uri Savir was anticipating a last-minute attempt by Abu Ala to change the DOP. He warned the Norwegians: 'I know this man, he'll always claim he misunderstood this and that. He'll try to negotiate up to the last minute.' And he was right. Abu Ala was in an erratic mood when he arrived, and immediately asked Larsen if he could provide a secretary to do some typing. Larsen agreed that his own assistant from FAFO, Torild Svendsen, would bring her computer to the hotel and work as long as was needed. It turned out that, as Savir had predicted, Abu Ala had just one more 'cosmetic change' to make. The two teams set about negotiating the point in question: the timetable for the future negotiations on the permanent status of the Occupied Territories. But the Norwegians sensed that there was no air of urgency in the discussions; indeed, it appeared inevitable that the problem would be ironed out. It almost seemed to be a matter of pride: both sides wanted to keep up the pressure until the very end. But Larsen did notice that Abu Ala seemed distracted, uninterested in the negotiations themselves. Svendsen was busy typing what Larsen thought was the amended document. He glanced over her shoulder and saw that in fact it was Abu Ala's speech for that night's ceremony. He chuckled to himself as he realized that, despite the last-minute bargaining session, the deal was indeed a foregone conclusion.

Larsen and Mona went down to the Norwegian official guest-house, an eighteenth-century mansion on Parkveien Street, in the suburbs of Oslo. Peres was staying there, and an official dinner was to be held there that evening. Larsen wanted to work out how to stage the signing ceremony at the guest-house late that night, after everyone was asleep. They met with Miss Astrop, the charming but very firm official hostess, to tell her that they needed the facilities after the banquet. They did not specify what they would be doing, just informed her that there would be security men and some people from the Middle East present. They examined the three interconnecting entertaining salons on the first floor, and then worked out how long it would take people coming up secretly, through the kitchens and via the backstairs, to reach the main rooms. The security men were told to get video equipment and provide a stills photographer. Again and again

Larsen and Mona walked the ceremony through, to time and position it to perfection.

For the actual signing, Holst had remembered that there was a desk with a special history in the house. It was the one on which Christian Michelsen had signed the agreement by which Norway seceded from Sweden in 1905 after nearly a century under Swedish rule. Holst and Larsen felt it would be appropriate to use this desk to sign the agreement by which the Occupied Territories would begin to be returned to Palestinian control. It was a rather sensitive suggestion, and one that needed Israeli endorsement, but Peres agreed that the desk could be used. However, the Israeli Foreign Minister warned that both he and Rabin wanted a low-key ceremony. That day nine Israeli soldiers had been killed in two Hezbollah attacks. 'Blood and champagne do not mix,' Peres solemnly told the Norwegians.

Back at the Plaza, Geir Pedersen, Larsen's cordial Norwegian colleague, relayed the news that Savir too was writing his speech, but that the negotiations were still going on. And now the protocol of the actual signing was causing problems. Peres had declined to put his name to the document on Israel's behalf, nominating Savir and Singer in his place. The question of recognition of the PLO was still to be resolved, and it would therefore not be appropriate for the Foreign Minister to sign. Furthermore, no decision had yet been taken on how the agreement should be made public, and Washington's reaction was still unknown. So the Oslo ceremony was not to be the full-blown thing. The nominated representatives from both sides would just sign their initials at the bottom of the each page of the agreement. Since Abu Mazen had not come to Oslo, the Palestinians proposed that Abu Ala should sign with Savir and, if Singer was to sign, then Hassan Asfour would too. But this upset Mohammed Abu Koush. If two of the three in the Palestinian delegation were to sign, then he alone would be excluded. However, if he signed too, then there would be more Palestinian than Israeli names on the agreement. So the Norwegians proposed that Yair Hirschfeld and Ron Pundak sign as well, so that all seven people who had taken part in the secret talks would be included. But the Israelis pointed out that the two professors had no official position – the accusation that had plagued the two men from the start. Their unofficial status had meant they could start the channel but, now that it had come to the signing, that status excluded them.

Eventually it was agreed that only Abu Ala, Savir, Asfour and Singer would sign. Those left out swallowed their pride, although there were some bruised egos as a consequence.

Early in the evening, the official dinner guests arrived. In the glittering main salon, its yellow walls swathed in long gold damask curtains, the chandeliers glowed as the diplomatic reception got under way. Johan Jorgen Holst and his deputy, Jan Egeland, moved amongst the guests. Marianne Heiberg was there in a black cocktail dress and silver brooch, and Mona Juul wore a simple, elegant white suit. Terje Larsen found himself standing next to a friend, the Israeli ambassador to Norway.

'Terje, you must come over. I want you to meet our Foreign Minister, Shimon Peres.' Before he could make an excuse, Larsen was being propelled in Peres's direction. 'This is Mr Larsen, the director of FAFO . . . ' the ambassador began.

'I know Terje very well,' Peres interrupted, in his gravelly voice; 'and this is a great day for us,' he added meaningfully, with a broad wink at Larsen.

The ambassador was astounded at this obvious camaraderie. Larsen felt himself flushing red. Peres was obviously enjoying everyone's discomfort and bewilderment. Later, after the banquet, he sent his secretary over with gifts for Mona and Terje: a silver necklace with a carved blue stone and a silver paper-knife in an olive wood box.

Then Larsen's mobile phone brought a hysterical message from the normally unflappable Geir Pedersen, at the Plaza. The negotiators had still not resolved their differences and the deadline was approaching. Yet, strangely, the two teams still seemed to feel no sense of urgency. They had a leisurely dinner, while Pedersen chafed silently in the corner. Eventually Savir and Abu Ala agreed that the timetable for the negotiations would, as the Palestinians wanted, be 'not exceeding' five years. Abu Ala was triumphant. He had got what he was after. Savir did not seem too concerned. In fact the point had already been conceded in an earlier draft and the words 'not exceeding' had been left out by mistake, a typing error by Yair Hirschfeld. But both sides were satisfied. Now the ceremony could begin. There had been twenty-five drafts of the Declaration of Principles since that first academic exercise at Borregaard. Geir Pedersen, who was to be the chief of protocol, took the final text and bound copies of the agreement in the special red covers used for official Norwegian documents. The covers were secured with red, white and blue striped ribbon, the Norwegian national colours. Two Waterman fountain-pens were laid out in readiness for the signing.

Everyone then dressed for the occasion, in formal suits and conservative ties, and assembled in the Investa Suite at midnight. Yair Hirschfeld alone sported a more dashing pink and white striped tie. They were all very nervous as they took pictures of each other with Ron Pundak's camera – the first time anyone had dared to make a record of the group.

Then the security men came to collect them. A meticulously planned cloak-and-dagger operation had been arranged to get the two teams to the signing. They were smuggled down in a special lift to the back quarters of the hotel, through the dark and empty kitchens and down the stairs into a basement car park. The place was ringed with police in the first full-scale security operation of the negotiations. The Palestinians were bundled quickly into a transit van with blacked-out windows, the Israelis into one behind. There was much joking and laughing with the six security men, who by now had become firm friends with all their charges. Then, at top speed, they were driven through the empty streets of Oslo to Parkveien, where the official Israeli delegation were asleep. Only Peres and Gill had waited up. Gill had arranged that the Israeli security men accompanying Peres would leave the Norwegians to provide cover that night. When the contingent from the Plaza arrived at the guest-house, they tried to creep upstairs without waking anybody. Although the house was old and the floorboards creaked and groaned, they succeeded in reaching their destination undetected. The Israelis waited in a small receiving room to the right of the salon, the Palestinians in a similar one to the left. The security men lugged the Christian Michelsen desk up from its usual place on the ground floor. The lights were on, the cameras ready. The documents and pens were carefully laid out by Pedersen. It was 2.00 a.m. and the show was ready to begin.

Apart from the video cameraman and stills photographer chosen from the secret service ranks, there were the Israelis and Palestinian secret delegations, Holst and his wife, Egeland, Peres and Gill, and Pedersen, Larsen and Mona Juul there that night. Even the Norwegian security men were ordered to remain outside the salon. It was an intensely private, even intimate, moment and secrecy was still of paramount importance.

Larsen was the master of ceremonies. For him this occasion was the culmination of nine months of staging encounters, creating ambience and fostering friendships, which had done so much to shape the Oslo Channel. But although he and Mona had rehearsed the proceedings many times, and the participants were all close friends, everyone in the room was intensely nervous and, at the same time, overawed by the significance of what was about to happen. This moment had enormous historical significance and great meaning for the future lives of millions in the Middle East.

Larsen took a deep breath and stepped out of his place in the official receiving line alongside Holst, Peres, Jan Egeland and Mona Juul. Although it had been decided beforehand that Abu Ala and the Palestinians should be the first to be received, Larsen's nervousness overcame him and he turned to the right, towards the Israelis. Behind him he heard Mona's steady voice: 'Terje, you're too nervous! It's the wrong room.'

Larsen halted, returned to the line and then set off again, this time in the right direction. Suddenly he realized that Marianne Heiberg was walking alongside him, as the video recorded the unfolding ceremony. This had not been planned. She halted by the door and Larsen went on alone into the adjoining room where the Palestinians waited. Inside the room Abu Ala stood formally, dignified but shaking slightly. Larsen took his arm and said: 'OK, Abu Ala, here we go.'

Larsen then escorted him, followed by Asfour and Abu Koush, to the head of the receiving line. As Abu Ala reached Peres, the two men exchanged a steady look and firmly clasped hands. It was a short but strong and deliberate handshake, the first to be exchanged between an Israeli Foreign Minister and a high-ranking official of the PLO. Peres murmured 'It's my pleasure' as Abu Ala let go of his hand and moved on down the line, followed by his Palestinian colleagues. Larsen went to fetch the Israeli delegation from the other room.

'Now it's your turn, Uri,' Larsen said, and then added: ' You're not up to this?' Savir was pale but grinning – not his usual ironic smile, but a rather fixed expression. It was the first time Larsen had not heard him shoot back a sardonic reply.

When the gathering was complete, they moved in silence towards the square walnut desk. Peres, accompanied by Avi Gill, remained sitting at the edge of the room, and Marianne Heiberg came to sit beside them. The others stood behind the desk, with Holst seated in the middle, Savir sitting to his left and Abu Ala to his right. Pedersen placed the red-bound documents upon the green leather surface of the desk, and the Palestinian and Israeli chief negotiators opened them immediately and began to sign their initials at the bottom right-hand corner of each page.

The text was entitled 'Declaration of Principles on Interim Self-Government Arrangements'. It consisted of twenty-three pages in total, the agreement itself being nine pages, followed by four annexes and the Agreed Minutes to the Declaration.

When the last page had been completed, Savir and Abu Ala looked at each other in silence. There was a moment's hesitation as they wondered if they should wait for everyone else to sign. But then Abu Ala reached across Holst and grabbed Savir's hand and forearm. The two men stood and hugged each other affectionately and Abu Ala kissed Savir in traditional Arab style. Everyone was moved, the two men themselves perhaps most of all. Still no word had been spoken as Joel Singer and Hassan Asfour sat down and opened the other two copies of the text. Singer flicked rapidly and efficiently through the pages, almost automatically scribbling his initials; Asfour was slower, more deliberate. Then Holst added his initials, as witness to the agreement. Singer and Asfour beamed as they shook hands, and then the whole group had their picture taken.

The deed had been done, and there was a tangible release of tension – tears and smiles all around. But everyone was still very subdued; there was no exultation, just relief. For Ron Pundak the moment had a very special meaning. Twenty years before, his brother had been killed in the 1973 Yom Kippur War. Now he felt that he had completed the circle which had begun with violence and tragedy for his own family. He had helped to create a peace accord which he hoped would allow his own daughter to live a different life. They all moved back to sit on the red brocade Empire sofas and Holst took the floor for an impromptu speech:

'In order to create history you have to have a sense of history,' he told them, 'and having a sense of history means making possible that which is necessary. This is what you have done here tonight. You have lived through years of confrontation. Now you are entering a new era of cooperation.'

Then Abu Ala came forward; the tears were still in his eyes

and he told his friends it was the second time he had cried. The first time had been two nights before, in Tunis, when the deal had been finalized. Abu Ala began by welcoming the Israeli Foreign Minister. On behalf of his delegation and Yasser Arafat, he wished to congratulate Peres on his seventieth birthday, which was that day, 20 August. Peres was greatly affected by these good wishes, and his lips formed a silent thank-you. And he seemed on the verge of tears, as Abu Ala went on to wish him success in the great battle for peace.

Abu Ala's speech quickly turned to practical matters, in the banker's usual style. He emphasized the importance of quickly improving the lot of both their peoples, and went on to outline speedy steps to get the economy on its feet in the Occupied Territories:

'We do not want the victims of war to become the orphans of peace, and we regard signing this Declaration of Principles as a new chapter of hope for them, and as a new, important page of our history. Our world is like a little village and our size in it is well known. We can become bigger through cooperation, mutual respect and recognition of rights and success in the fields of reconstruction development and scientific innovation. Both our people and your people have enough potential and efficient human resources if real peace takes place, and cooperation and stabilization materialize. And they should!'

Then Savir stood up to speak. His words were more reflective; they sought to probe the relationship between Israelis and Palestinians, and to assess the changes the two sides had wrought in the special environment of Norway.

'Without Norway, this historical declaration would not have been reached today. The Oslo spirit – this special harmony you conveyed to us, between man, nature and conduct – was contagious in creating a new Middle East spirit. You are peacemakers in the true sense of the word, facilitating peace for the sake of peace itself. You have the quiet yet intense passion that helped channel our passions in a constructive direction.'

Savir then spoke of the sense of a moral crusade that had driven him throughout the negotiations:

'We Israelis have no desire to dominate the lives and fate of the Palestinians. Therefore with this agreement we are fulfilling not only a political interest, but also a moral predicament of our people. We would like our meeting ground to be a moral high ground – an encounter of peace, democracy and economic prosperity.'

Then Larsen made a simple, heartfelt speech. He recalled the beginnings of the whole extraordinary story, that lunch with Yossi Beilin in Tel Aviv. And he spoke of how Beilin had sent to him 'an unruly bear' of a man – Yair Hirschfeld. His voice nearly breaking with emotion, he told them that the unlikely friendships forged in the Oslo Channel were only just the beginning.

'There has been an element of luck,' said Larsen, 'and I think the Palestinians and the Israelis are lucky because this process was carried through by personalities, individuals who have vision, courage, creativity and – most important of all – a capacity for friendship. This is the most important thing – the friendship that has developed in the channel.'

Finally the doors were opened and the security men came in to serve drinks. Peres and Abu Ala had a private meeting. They discussed the challenges ahead, and the difficulties that both the PLO and Israel would face in pushing this agreement through at home. Abu Ala was anxious that confidence-building measures should be taken as soon as possible: the release of prisoners and the return of the remaining deportees. Then Peres and Avi Gill retired to bed, and Holst and Marianne Heiberg went home. The others returned to the Investa Suite at the Plaza, where the celebrations and the reminiscences continued until dawn. They watched a replay of the video and, in an emotional moment, the two chief negotiators inscribed the copies of their speeches with messages for each other's daughters and then exchanged them.

When they saw each other's inscriptions they realized that both had expressed similar sentiments, exhorting the girls to be proud of their fathers and hoping they would one day meet. They declared that what they had done was for their children, that they might grow up in an atmosphere of peace.

Hassan Asfour embraced Terje Larsen and held his hand, a sign of Arab brotherhood. Everyone expressed great pride in what they had achieved. They knew it would change the Middle East, perhaps even the world, for ever. Whatever happened now, however the peace deal was received in public, for them this would be the night that crowned their success.

The negotiations were finally over, and everyone let down

their guard. They began to remember the highlights of their time together, recalling the funny moments and the angry scenes. They revealed the way in which they had interpreted each other's tactics. Abu Ala gave a good imitation of Joel Singer's manner at Halvorsbole, when the great crisis had occurred: 'It's finished, it's finished,' he cried melodramatically, flinging his arms wide.

'You are the mother of all negotiators,' acknowledged Singer magnanimously.

'And we are all crooks together,' concluded Abu Ala, the highest compliment the streetwise banker could have paid his Israeli counterparts.

13

A Surprise for the Superpower

The next morning Norway's press corps attended a news conference held by Shimon Peres. Mona Juul was there and, to her alarm, Peres almost seemed to be giving the game away. He told the reporters that Norway was playing a very important role in bringing the parties together in the conflict in the Middle East: 'I am very optimistic about the situation. The two parties are much closer than you imagine. I think there will be agreement between Israel and the Palestinians very soon, and Norway has been very instrumental in this.'

Most of the questions from the press centred on the recent battle in southern Lebanon. Only one reporter enquired if Peres's fulsome words meant that Norway was setting up secret meetings between the two sides. 'If this is the case,' said Peres, choosing his words carefully, 'then I would not tell you, because then they would not be secret meetings any more.'

The reporter did not pursue his line of enquiry. The press conference ended, and on the way out an Israeli journalist drew Avi Gill aside and asked him if there was any foundation to the rumour that Peres had met a PLO man in Sweden. 'No,' said Gill truthfully, for no such meetings had taken place in Sweden. They had been in Norway.

Later that morning Shimon Peres and Avi Gill left for Iceland in euphoric mood. On the scheduled flight an exhausted Gill put on the headphones, lay back and closed his eyes. He was lost in the music, reliving the previous night's drama and oblivious of the outside world, when the steward tapped him on the arm.

'Excuse me, sir, could you be quiet, you're singing at the top of your voice and disturbing all the passengers,' the steward said. Horrified, Gill turned round to see a planeload of Scandinavians solemnly staring at him. He had been regaling them with a tuneless rendering of *Great Hits of the 1960s,* available on the in-flight entertainment system.

That weekend Mona and Terje went to Bergen to attend a cousin's wedding. On their way back to the airport to return to Oslo their mobile phone rang. It was Peres requesting them to come and join him again, this time in Helsinki. The next day Larsen, with his secret service friend, went on ahead to make arrangements for Holst's arrival in Finland. Peres wanted to discuss the next stage in the process: a trip to America, to inform the sponsors of the Washington peace talks before the news leaked out. And then the group resolved to tackle the next big hurdle, mutual recognition, which had been put aside while the Declaration of Principles was being finalized and signed.

Peres had to return home for consultations with Rabin. The matter of not bringing in the Americans until after the deal was effectively agreed would need to be handled carefully. Mona Juul, with the assistance of Avi Gill, was given the complicated task of arranging for Shimon Peres and Johan Jorgen Holst to make a secret trip to California, where Warren Christopher was on vacation.

On 26 August a small Norwegian government jet left Oslo for an undeclared destination. Holst, Larsen, Juul and two of their secret service men flew to Geneva, where another, long-distance, jet had been chartered for the transatlantic trip. The Norwegians disembarked and their jet, with the security escort on board, flew on to Tel Aviv. At 3.00 a.m., under cover of darkness, Shimon Peres, Joel Singer, Avi Gill and two Israeli security men boarded the plane, which returned to Geneva. Then, at daybreak, the whole team transferred to a Falcon 900 executive jet and took off for America. Peres and Holst were charmed by the attractive Swiss stewardess on board, who took good care of the whole party. They slept for a while and then began to prepare intensively for the crucial meeting ahead.

Meanwhile, in Tunis, Arafat called a meeting of the PLO's Executive Committee to break the news of the Gaza/Jericho First agreement and to seek approval for his controversial move. There were already many rumours that the Chairman was on the brink of accepting a peace deal which made humiliating concessions to the Israelis. Arafat and Abu Mazen braced themselves for anger and dissent: the armed guard around both of them was significantly tightened.

Aboard the Israeli jet, on their twenty-hour flight to California, Shimon Peres and Johan Jorgen Holst were somewhat apprehensive. While Rabin had always had close links with the Americans, Peres had made no bones about his more pro-European stance and his scepticism about the American ability to broker peace in the Arab–Israeli conflict. He knew that US officials viewed him as the idealist, the dreamer, and Rabin as the tough and practical man of action. Yet he also knew that the attitude of Israel's chief ally, and the main sponsor of the Madrid process, would be crucial for public acceptance of the Oslo deal.

Although the Clinton Administration had received some information about what had been going on in Norway, this information had been deliberately patchy. Since May, neither the Norwegians nor the Israelis had conveyed the substantive details of the deal they were negotiating. Only two weeks before, in Jerusalem, Rabin had expressed his scepticism regarding the Oslo talks to Warren Christopher. Over two years, Washington had invested millions of dollars and inestimable amounts of power and prestige in a high-profile peace initiative that had achieved almost nothing. Now the Israeli Foreign Minister, who had never courted American favour, and the Foreign Minister of a little-known player on the international stage were on their way to break a political bombshell to the most powerful government on earth. No wonder they felt a little nervous.

After a brief refuelling stop at Goose Bay, in the wilds of Canada, the jet finally touched down at Point Mugu Naval Air Station near Santa Barbara in California. Peres was clearly nervous as he entered the room where Warren Christopher and Dennis Ross, the State Department's top Middle East official, were waiting to receive him. Itmar Rabinovitz, the Israeli ambassador to Washington, was also present. At the back of the room stood a Norwegian flag, flanked by Israel's blue Star of David and the Stars and Stripes. Peres began with an apology for disturbing Christopher's holiday. 'This is the sort of event it's worth interrupting a vacation for,' replied Christopher.

Then Peres delivered an eloquent speech, all traces of uncertainty disappearing as he warmed to his theme. Even those who knew him well, and had heard him speak many times before, believed this was one of his most persuasive efforts. Peres said: 'There are two ways in which to end the conflict with the PLO. With the power of power or with the power of wisdom. Wisdom is better than power. If we all act wisely, the PLO will become a partner in peace instead of an obstacle to it.'

After Peres had broken the news that a peace deal had been concluded with the PLO, the Norwegian Foreign Minister was anxious to make it clear that Norway had kept America informed about the Oslo Channel. He reminded Christopher that Thorvald Stoltenberg and Jan Egeland had submitted general reports on the secret talks. In January Egeland had invited the Americans to participate, and Holst himself had given Christopher an early draft of the Declaration of Principles.

Then Joel Singer took the floor to give a fifteen-minute, concise but detailed, briefing of the content of the agreement reached in Oslo. The Norwegians watched as amazement spread over the faces of the American team, who were clearly not prepared for this at all. But Christopher and Ross quickly gave the agreement their unqualified approval.

The presentation had impressed the Americans, but they knew that the real test was in the text. So they withdrew for a few minutes to assess the document in private. Once alone, they quickly scanned the pages – Christopher with the keen eye of an attorney and the sixth sense of a politician, Ross with the experience of long and weary years studying the minutiae of Middle East peace proposals. They found the level of detail, the scope of understanding and the annexes on economic cooperation astounding.

'What do you think?' asked Christopher.

'I think we've got a major breakthrough; they've handled the key jurisdictional issues,' admitted Ross.

'Looks really good, doesn't it?'

'Yes, it's not just a conceptual but a psychological breakthrough.'

They then returned to the other room and the Secretary of State, a laconic man not generally given to effusive statements, was beaming. He told the Israelis and Norwegians: 'It seems to me you've done a fabulous job, touching on every aspect of a wide range of topics. My first reaction is very positive.'

The big question, though it was tactfully not raised that day, was why the Americans had not taken a greater interest in the proceedings in Oslo. The Israelis and the Norwegians had been careful not to hide events from Washington. However, they had also consciously told the Americans neither about the details nor, crucially, about the final few weeks, when events had moved very quickly. Dan Kurtzer, who had been the original contact for Beilin and Hirschfeld, and Egeland too, had not taken the initiative seriously. His reaction to the early draft had been much the same as Singer's: the whole thing was vague and exploratory. But unlike Singer, Kurtzer had decided that the positions taken – by the Palestinians in particular, but also by the Israelis – were so far removed from their public stance in Washington that there could be no future in the channel. The Americans knew Rabin was involved but they were not sure to what extent. He had not even been cautiously optimistic about the outcome, and the Americans had had a tendency to shrug off Peres's enthusiastic views. During May and June, when the Clinton Administration was vigorously pursuing its own 'equal partnership' policy at the Washington talks, the Oslo Channel had faded even further from their thoughts.

Now the group assembled at Point Mugu had to decide how to reveal to the rest of the world the secret deal reached not in Washington but in Oslo. The question of the mutual recognition pact was central to their plans. Peres explained that he had not wanted to link recognition to the signing of the DOP, in case it delayed or even sabotaged the main agreement. But now the Israelis had a problem. How were they to present their Declaration of Principles on Interim Self-Government for the Palestinians, which top-level Israeli officials had negotiated directly with the PLO, when neither side officially recognized the other? The intention had always been somehow to transfer the deal from Oslo to the Washington forum. However, events in the past few months had made it clear that the two official delegations in Washington were hardly likely to take on board this revolutionary new proposal without making any objections.

But the Israelis were still sensitive, both to the issue of recognizing the PLO and to the possibility of appearing to have bypassed the Americans in this matter. On the plane coming over, Peres had talked with Holst about other ways of presenting the achievements of the Oslo Channel. And now Peres suggested that the interim self-government agreement, which after all was what they had been groping towards over long months in Washington, might be presented to the world as a US-brokered document. The Norwegians, who had worked so hard, were understandably loath to forgo the credit and to forfeit their well-earned place in history. But Holst had recognized the *realpolitik* of the situation and had acquiesced to the plan. Another scenario they discussed was that Egypt and America might share the role as sponsor of the Oslo deal. It was an awkward moment, especially for the Norwegians, but Christopher forcefully rejected the idea as flawed and fraught with danger for Bill Clinton, both internationally and domestically. 'No, we can't do that because the truth is bound to surface and that would damage everything,' was his frank response.

With the Washington option rejected, everyone in the room realized that the vital question was now the issue of mutual recognition. If the Oslo deal was to be presented for what it was, an agreement between Israel and the PLO, then both sides would have to recognize each other formally. The Americans also faced a problem, for they too had broken off relations with Arafat's organization, in June 1990, after an abortive attack on an Israeli beach by gunmen belonging to a splinter group of the PLO. If the US was to throw its full support behind the Oslo deal, it too would have to recognize the PLO again. So Christopher and Ross went through the seven-point plan that Savir had put forward at Halvorsbole as the basis of the recognition pact. Ross, with his experience, suggested that the wording should make clear the PLO's responsibility for preventing any violent acts by its constituent organizations, to prevent the kind of raid which had caused Congress to sever links in 1990.

The final item on the agenda was the public presentation of the secret channel. All sides acknowledged that only America had the political power to sell the deal in the Middle East. There would undoubtedly be recriminations from the powerful states excluded by the unilateral Palestinian action of seeking peace with Israel. Syria, Jordan and Lebanon could, and almost certainly would, make trouble. The idea of a grand signing ceremony began to take shape, as a way of binding all sides together to support the agreement. It would be a public declaration of their intent to pursue the goals of peace, coexistence and cooperation. The group at Santa Barbara agreed upon a joint press statement to make the deal public in the next few days. But they agreed that the Washington ceremony could only go ahead if the two sides publicly recognized each other. And so it was decided that the inner core of Israelis and Palestinians would, with Norway's help, continue their secret meetings in order to settle the mutual recognition pact.

Then the commander of Point Mugu invited them all to lunch in the dining-room overlooking the Pacific Ocean. The day was hot and sunny, and everyone relaxed and ate an excellent meal of fish served with chilled white wine. Afterwards the Israelis and Mona Juul went to get some sleep, in rooms provided at the base, while Holst and Larsen went shopping in a nearby mall. Later that evening, before their plane was due to leave, the group went out to a bar and restaurant on the beach and sat beside the swimming pool. They had intended to celebrate, but the calls on the mobile telephone came thick and fast from Jerusalem. The news was out: that morning the main newspapers had carried stories of a meeting between Peres and the PLO in Norway. A Tunis official had confirmed that senior PLO and Israeli figures had reached an accord: Peres and Rabin's spokespeople would not deny it. The secret channel was about to be exposed. As Avi Gill fielded the calls, an American woman dining at a nearby table came up to them, breathless with excitement. 'Are you Shimon Peres?' she enquired. 'I'd love to have your autograph.'

Peres courteously acknowledged that he was indeed the Israeli Foreign Minister, and signed his name for her. Then they went back to Point Mugu to pick up their bags and board the Falcon 900 to return to Oslo, this time to the military section of an airport outside Oslo, for fear of the waiting press. Once home, the Norwegians disembarked with Singer, and Peres and Gill transferred back to the Norwegian government jet, which took them on to Israel.

Peres and Gill had planned to wake at 6.00 a.m., an hour before the plane landed at Tel Aviv, to write up the report on the meeting with Christopher for Rabin. But they slept on exhausted, and when they awoke they were on the ground in Israel and the sun was shining in through the windows of the jet. They rushed to Peres's house, where Gill prepared the report while the Foreign Minister shaved. Then they went on to Rabin's residence with the good news: the Americans had reacted well and would back the Oslo deal.

The Israeli Prime Minister called a Cabinet meeting that morning and informed his colleagues in the government that there was now a peace agreement with the PLO, a first step towards autonomy for the Occupied Territories.

In Tunis Arafat emerged from a stormy two-day meeting of his Executive Committee, the first of many yet to come, and began to spread the word of the PLO accord. The representatives of other Arab states were briefed in Beirut, and on the West Bank and in Gaza local Palestinians began to learn about their future.

That Sunday morning, 29 August, the Palestinian delegates to the Washington talks were already in their hotel in the American capital, waiting for the official negotiations to resume the next day. They were all breakfasting in the hotel coffee-shop when an Israeli journalist, Ori Nir from the newspaper *Haaretz*, came in carrying a Hebrew text of the peace agreement. The Palestinians were flabbergasted and crowded round him, asking him to translate the clauses. Some, like Hanan Ashrawi, said that they had seen the text a week before, but to the Israeli journalist it seemed that the deal had come like a bolt from the blue for the Palestinians.

Back in Israel a furious Eliyakim Rubenstein, the leader of the official Israeli delegation, was similarly shocked. Shimon Peres spent three hours with him trying to calm him down, but Rubenstein refused to return to Washington and said that he would resign.

Late that night, once the Americans had officially confirmed the rumours of the Gaza/Jericho accord, Johan Jorgen Holst, accompanied by Jan Egeland, held a news conference in Oslo. For the first time the world heard about the fourteen meetings hosted in Norway and the involvement of a research institute called FAFO. As the flashbulbs went off and the microphones were thrust before the Norwegian team, back at the Oslo Plaza Hotel the secret negotiations resumed behind closed doors, as Abu Ala, Hassan Asfour and Mohammed Abu Koush once more faced Uri Savir, Joel Singer, Yair Hirschfeld and Ron Pundak in the Investa Suite.

But as the Israelis and the Palestinians began a new and vital phase of the negotiations, their Norwegian friends at the Foreign Ministry were already feeling the strain of the media attention from which they had so assiduously shielded the two teams of negotiators. At the news conference, Holst asked Jan Egeland and Terje Larsen to come up to the table and address the journalists, but Mona Juul was not included. And suddenly Marianne Heiberg was assigned a very different role. She had not been part of the team who had organized and facilitated the secret talks, although as Holst's wife and a FAFO researcher she had known about the negotiations. Now Holst told the press that his wife too had been part of the team. The suggestion was that negotiations had taken place in their house, although in fact only briefings and social get-togethers had been held there. And little Edvard assumed a fascinating role as a diplomatic ice-breaker, although he had never been present when the diplomacy was taking place. Indeed some members of the Israeli and Palestinian teams could not remember having even met the child. Now the media were clamouring for a picture of the two married couples, posing together, to represent the story of the Oslo Channel as some homely Norwegian saga of two families who had brought the warring sides together. There was talk of a Nobel Peace Prize for the Foreign Minister, and there were many front-page interviews with the Holst family, with pictures of Edvard sitting on his father's knee. One newspaper that interviewed Marianne Heiberg reported that she had claimed to be a central cog in the machinery of the channel. The interview went on to quote her as saying that America was envious of what Norway had achieved, and that the superpower had found it hard to take.

When the papers hit the streets the next morning, there was disbelief, anger and embarrassment amongst everyone who really knew what had been going on in the Oslo Channel. Even the security men were taken aback. Already it seemed that history was being rewritten and that individual egos were replacing the teamwork which had been the trademark of the channel's success. The group's unease increased during the day as it became clear that the Foreign Minister intended to take a more direct role in the negotiations.

Johan Jorgen Holst is an avid stamp-collector who likes to have everything well defined and in its proper place. His approach to the negotiations was to identify the problems and then to work them through systematically. He believed that formulation was the key; it was a question of finding the right words and phrases to bridge the gap. Larsen's approach was more intuitive, based on understanding the motivation of individuals and using humour and persuasion to bypass the difficulties.

That day Holst shuttled busily between the two groups on the thirty-second floor of the Plaza. The ground rules of non-active participation by the Norwegians were being changed. For the first time in nine months Larsen abruptly left in the middle of the negotiations and went to bed, without his usual cheery farewell to the security men.

This change of tone on the Norwegian side was mirrored by a change in strategy by the Israelis. In negotiating the DOP both sides had come with their positions on different issues and had sought to narrow the gap between them. Now the Israelis decided to take a stand over the mutual recognition issue. In some ways they were making a tactical mistake by not giving the PLO much room for manœuvre. The Palestinians were being asked to give a great deal of ground, indeed to relinquish beliefs and ideology which underpinned the PLO. They had already accepted that the letter from Rabin to Arafat would be a straightforward statement of recognition; Israel would not have to pledge to renounce terror or violence. But the letter from the PLO leader to the Prime Minister of Israel was the core of the problem. Savir and Singer came with the text they wished the Palestinians to adopt word for word.

Rabin himself had emphasized to his negotiators that the crucial point was to get the PLO to call on its people to stop all violence and terror. Not only would the PLO itself be required to renounce violence, it should persuade the Palestinians on the West Bank and in Gaza to renounce violence too. The second requirement was that Arafat should set down, in black and white, that Israel had the right to exist in peace and security. Thirdly, the PLO Charter should be changed accordingly.

Abu Ala resented and felt insulted by the inflexible approach adopted by the Israelis. He was also in a difficult position. He had done his job of negotiating the Declaration of Principles, and done it well. But the question of mutual recognition was very much a matter for the leader of the PLO. Yasser Arafat's crusade against Israel had, after all, been almost a personal one. It had made him the figurehead of the PLO, a national icon for the Palestinians, the man who had single-handedly decided policy towards Israel since 1969. At this turning-point in the history of the two peoples, he and he alone would have to decide upon the actual words that would seal acceptance of the notion of coexistence. This was dangerous territory, watched over closely by the ideologues of the Palestinian struggle, in places like Damascus and Lebanon, dangerous men who would not treat lightly anyone who made concessions they disapproved of. For all these reasons Abu Ala was somewhat reluctant to become Arafat's mouthpiece. But Arafat had instructed him to come to Oslo and to make the deal. He had no choice, although the Israelis emphasized that the decision would ultimately be Arafat's alone. 'Arafat has to sit in front of the mirror and decide if he will change his basic ideological positions. It is he who has to make the change,' said Savir during one of the meetings.

The two days at the Oslo Plaza were difficult. There were obvious tensions in the Norwegian ranks. Holst's approach, unlike Larsen's, involved spending time with each side alone and then sitting in with Savir and Abu Ala as they negotiated. Holst even gave a letter to the Palestinian suggesting it was time to give way on certain points. This aroused anger and suspicion that Holst was siding with the Israelis. Yet Holst was clearly anxious to get things moving; the Americans were talking of a signing ceremony within two weeks. But the negotiation was a delicate process, and both sides had come to realize that the mutual recognition agreement meant more in fundamental terms than even the Declaration of Principles. For mutual recognition, in the terms the Israelis wanted, would change for ever the nature of the relationship between two bitter enemies.

The backlash in the Middle East was evidence, if it were needed, of the passions that had been aroused even by the interim peace agreement, with its carefully formulated timetable. There were stormy scenes in the Israeli Knesset, as Rabin and Peres defended their initiative. While opinion polls declared the public in favour of the peace deal, the right-wing Likud Party accused the government of selling out, of giving away Israel's birthright, the lands of Judea and Samaria. Outside, thousands of Jewish settlers held a rowdy protest and some of their number definitely established a new camp on the West Bank between Bethlehem and Hebron.

In Gaza Palestinian youths joyfully waved flags and pictures of Yasser Arafat. But Hamas vowed to do whatever was necessary to block the deal. It immediately announced a strike and threatened to kill anyone who moved in or out of the Gaza Strip that day. Beirut Radio carried a grim warning, the first of many, from a hard-line Palestinian faction threatening to kill Yasser Arafat. And within Arafat's own camp, the veteran head of the PLO's political department, Farouk Kadoumi, gave a warning that Arafat would not find it easy to get the PLO's ruling body to fall in line with the agreement he had negotiated without their authority.

In Oslo, Holst's shuttling between Savir and Abu Ala was yielding little. And the press suspected that the secret talks might be continuing in Oslo, but they had no confirmation. So there were cat-and-mouse games as journalists followed Holst wherever he went. Marianne Heiberg was also followed, for journalists believed that she too was a central figure in the negotiations. She led them to the Plaza one day, although they could not reach the thirty-second floor, which was locked off. On the Wednesday the whole group of negotiators decided they would leave since nothing was being achieved. Now the Norwegian security men had to get the Israelis and the Palestinians out of the hotel without their being recognized and pursued by cameras. The Israelis left at dawn, through the basement car park, fast vehicles driving them out of the city. To avoid detection, they changed cars on the way to the airport. The meeting at the Plaza was to prove the last to be attended by Yair Hirschfeld and Ron Pundak, and it was a suitably dramatic ending to their Norwegian odyssey.

When the Israelis had been safely delivered to the airport, the secret service team went back for the Palestinians. By now journalists surrounded the hotel. The leader of the team borrowed a laundry van and drove it into the basement car park, where he and Larsen put on white overalls. Then they hid Abu Ala, Hassan Asfour and Mohammed Abu Koush in the back, amongst the towels and sheets, and sat up front to drive them, under the noses of the journalists, out of the hotel and to the airport.

I myself, working for the BBC's *Panorama* programme, was one amongst many hundreds of journalists trying to get the inside story of this remarkable breakthrough. The signing of the agreement, it was now rumoured, was to be on the 13 September, which was a Monday, the day the weekly programme is aired on BBC 1. It was the best possible date for us, but gave us only ten days in which to make the programme, a very short time for a forty-minute documentary filmed around the world. I was anxious to try, and Glenwyn Benson, the editor of *Panorama*, gave me her full support. Fortunately I had many good contacts on both the Israeli and the Palestinian sides, having covered the Middle East for many years. In the summer of 1992 I had made a programme on the fruitless Washington peace process, and had predicted both that the Israeli Labour Party would win the election and that Yitzhak Rabin and Shimon Peres would make peace within the year their goal. Peres had told me as much in a long and thoughtful interview for *Panorama*, and Rabin had confirmed that it was his top priority when our cameras caught up with him at a rowdy campaign meeting in the suburbs of Tel Aviv.

I had decided to tell the story of the Norwegian involvement, and now I began my own negotiations for exclusive access to the team in Oslo. At the same time I was pursuing other members of the channel in Jerusalem and Tunis. For three days, from London, I tried to track everybody down. But Holst, Juul and Larsen were once more at a secret location, and I had to bide my time.

On the weekend of 3 and 4 September Peres asked the Norwegians to meet him in Paris at the Crillon Hotel in the Place de la Concorde. The Crillon is the French capital's finest and most expensive hotel, with mirrored halls, fine Louis XVI furniture and a famous restaurant awarded two toques by the arbiter of gourmet taste, the *Michelin Guide*. These rarefied surroundings were to be the venue for another marathon phone session with Tunis. But unlike the session in Stockholm, this one did not go well. The Israelis were in no mood to come to any speedy conclusion, and Peres's attitude was to let the Palestinians roast awhile. So when the Norwegians arrived, on the Friday, they had a short meeting and then the Israeli Foreign Minister invited them out for dinner. Holst was anxious to hit the phones, to get the deal done. The White House signing was now set for ten days' time. It would be a grand affair, the signing of a historic treaty, and the Norwegians hoped that their part would be given due prominence on the world stage. But Peres and Uri Savir did not seem in any hurry. The group went to a restaurant behind the Champs-Élysées. They had a convivial evening, and while they ate their dinner a gypsy band played at their table, first East European melodies with Yiddish lyrics and later the typical chansons of Paris nights.

The next day there were long phone calls with Tunis, Arafat and Peres communicating through Holst. In Tunis Arafat was under pressure, for Kadoumi was making trouble. There had been many long sessions with the Executive Committee and harsh words had been spoken about Arafat's willingness to compromise with Israel. For two days in Paris, in Holst's luxurious suite, the two sides argued back and forth. Still the Israelis seemed in no hurry to conclude the proceedings. Peres was playing hardball with the Palestinians, and meanwhile the hotel bill was steadily mounting. This was not the sort of place that the Norwegian people expect their public servants to stay, and Holst was fretting at this expensive hiatus in the negotiations. The Middle Eastern way of negotiating – the brinkmanship, the all-or-nothing approach – was somewhat unnerving for this Scandinavian politician used to consensus bargaining. He felt that he had to keep both parties talking although they were going around in circles. For nearly three days at the Crillon they only managed to reach agreement on two more points: the American-inspired requirement that the PLO accept responsibility for its own factions, and the phrasing of the recognition of the Jewish state. Arafat had wanted the statement to read 'We recognize the right of Israel to live in secure and recognized boundaries', but now agreed to change the phrase 'live in secure and recognized boundaries' to 'exist in peace and security'. The difference between the two expressions is very significant; the former suggests the right of Jews to live in the area simply because they are already there, the word 'exist' in the latter confirms the legitimacy of the Israeli state.

By Sunday night the mutual recognition text was still a long way from completion. Peres and his team returned to Israel and the Norwegians went back to Oslo. Together with the Palestinians, they now agreed to help me tell the full story of the secret channel; the condition was that I would not be allowed to reveal the details of the ongoing negotiations until after those negotiations had been completed. With exactly a week to go before the Washington signing, the *Panorama* team set to work in Norway, Israel and America, and back in London.

The Norwegian Foreign Minister was determined not to allow the Declaration of Principles to go unsigned simply because the mutual recognition element had not been agreed upon. That Monday, at home in Oslo, he spent all night on the telephone to Yasser Arafat who was sitting in the office of the President of Egypt, Hosni Mubarak, in Cairo. Yasser Abed-Rabbo was the go-between this time; Abu Ala had remained in Tunis, unwilling to get involved. The PLO leader was busy shuttling to and fro between the Arab capitals. With Egypt's help he was trying to gather regional support for the peace deal. King Hussein of Jordan had come out in favour of the deal, although he made it clear that the Jordanians were not happy at having been kept in the dark. The Syrians agreed that the PLO should be the one to decide the future of the Palestinians; their support was crucial because Damascus harbours so many extreme Palestinian factions. But President Assad was not exactly wholehearted in his approval. Arafat was under pressure; he complained that it would be political suicide to declare the PLO Charter 'non-valid', as Israel was demanding. Throughout the night Holst argued that Abu Ala should come to Europe, a face-to-face meeting was the only way to resolve things now. But Abu Ala would not come; he refused to take orders from Abed-Rabbo or even to listen to Abu Mazen's pleas. At one point during that long night Holst looked up wearily to see Larsen, head down, fast asleep at the dining-room table.

The next day the Israelis returned to Paris and asked the Norwegians to join them there as soon as possible. They all believed that Abu Ala would show up. There were now only five days to go before the signing. This time the venue was the luxurious and discreet Bristol Hotel in the exclusive shopping street the Rue Saint-Honoré. Savir had chosen it on the basis that the hotel was so famous that the press would never think of looking there. Larsen booked in the party of Norwegians. Holst had brought Marianne Heiberg, and the others present were Terje himself and Mona Juul, the secret service men and four other people, all called Larsen. There was Ulf Larsen, alias Uri Savir – the name was taken from a Jack London novel featuring a strong and silent sea captain called Ulf Larsen. Then there was Jan Larsen, also known as Joel Singer. The two other Larsens were holding rooms for the Palestinians. That night they dined together in the Bristol's elegant restaurant. The head waiter came up to the table. 'A phone call for Mr Larsen,' he said. To his astonishment three men leapt up and hastened to the phone.

At noon the next day a message arrived stating that Abu Ala was on his way to Paris. When he arrived with Mohammed Abu Koush the Norwegians could see that Abu Ala was resentful. It was clear that he had been put under a great deal of pressure in Tunis to come. Moreover, the Palestinian also suspected that Holst was interfering. It took the Norwegian Foreign Minister an hour to calm him down and convince him that there was no bias towards the Israelis. Then Abu Ala consented to meet his old adversaries, Savir and Singer, and once more the negotiations got under way, with Holst, Larsen, Juul and Heiberg in the room. Marianne Heiberg had brought along a computer and lots of dictionaries, in case they got stuck for the appropriate word. Both the Israelis and the Palestinians looked somewhat askance at this, for they knew that they had entered the endgame. The words were all there, and it was now simply a question of inching towards accepting them or finally rejecting them.

In the two days prior to this Paris meeting I had completed my interviews in Oslo, and been to Jerusalem to speak to Yossi Beilin and Yair Hirschfeld. Passing through Frankfurt on my way back to London, I discovered the location of the secret talks and immediately caught a different plane, to Charles de Gaulle Airport, instead. Late that night, on Wednesday, 8 September, I quietly booked in at the Bristol and arranged for a BBC cameraman and soundman from Paris to join me in my room, their equipment dismantled and stowed in bags so as not to attract attention. Little did the well-dressed American couples who tend to frequent the Bristol know, as they returned from their good French dinners to the hushed lobby that night, that in Suite 119 the final chapter in the saga of the Oslo Channel was getting under way. Not even the management of the Bristol knew what was happening in their hotel.

I prowled the hotel corridors looking for the action. It was after midnight and I tried to look nonchalant, as if I just happened to be staying in this £400-a-night hotel by chance. A Norwegian security man was posted outside a suite on the first floor. In his normal calm and courteous manner, he promised to pass on a discreet message to Uri Savir that I was there. Savir was the person in my sights. I wanted to interview him but, at the same time, did not want to alarm him by my presence at this crucial moment. An hour later Savir came to find me. In shirt-sleeves, his hair tousled, he looked tired and fraught. Everything still hung in the balance, he said, but he was optimistic. 'I will talk to you later if things go well, but you must promise not to reveal our whereabouts to anyone, even your own people at the BBC,' he said. I agreed, and got the crew to rig the lights, microphones and camera in my room. I warned them that it would be a long night.

14

The Handshake

Throughout that night there were endless meetings in smoke-filled rooms. In Tunis, Arafat was consulting the PLO's Executive Committee on whether they should agree to change the Charter and what wording could be used so as to preserve their rights and still satisfy the Israelis. And in Suite 119 of the Bristol Hotel, Abu Ala's chain-smoking filled the air as the negotiators battled over the text of the letter in between watching television together for the first time. On CNN the screen was filled with chanting settlers and masked Hamas supporters, all vowing to destroy the peace plan. Every half-hour, as these stories were repeated, either Savir and Singer or Abu Ala and Abu Koush would sigh and say, pointing to the screen: 'You see how difficult things are for us back home!'

Abu Ala and Arafat consulted with one another on the telephone. In Tunis the Chairman put the proposed text to the Executive Committee. Its approval was required before there could be any commitment to changing the PLO Charter. The Israelis wanted the PLO to declare the relevant articles of the Charter 'non-operative and non-valid', but the Palestinians balked at this, suggesting that the Charter should instead be 'not in effect'.

At midnight, in the Bristol Hotel, as Savir and Abu Ala were locked in verbal combat, a small but highly significant incident occurred. There was a knock on the door of the suite and in burst five familiar faces. Uri Savir's eighteen-year-old daughter, Maya, was on holiday in Paris with her boyfriend, celebrating the end of her compulsory military service. They had come down to the Bristol to find her father. At the same time, Abu Ala's wife, Heyam, was visiting two of her sons, Amer and Isam, who were in Paris. They had all come to the Bristol to see Abu Ala, but it had taken them some time to find him, as he was checked in under the name of Larsen. And so the families of both men found themselves in Suite 119 together. They were all introduced. Abu Ala could not resist a quick dig when he presented his sons to the Israelis, explaining that the family complained because they never saw him – he was always shut away negotiating. 'You see, here they are, fatherless – and stateless too!' he said.

The sons and daughter recognized the importance of what their fathers were doing, but they made light of it and teased Savir and Abu Ala. 'If it was up to us, we should get a very quick decision on a declaration of principles,' said Maya, laughing.

'Yes, especially it if was was about which discothèque to go to!' added Isam.

And, ignoring their parents, they began to debate the merits of various clubs in Paris. Watching them, both fathers were forcibly reminded that this was what the younger generation wanted: fun and friendship and a common future, not war and hate and military service. At last the families departed and the negotiators got back down to business. Savir and Abu Ala told each other that it was for their children and the millions more in Israel, the Occupied Territories and the Palestinian diaspora that peace must be made.

There were still two major points of disagreement: the wording of the changes to the Charter and the vexed question of the rejection of violence and terror. Arafat was reluctant to accept that he should call upon his people inside the Occupied Territories to stop the violence. He made the point that the PLO outside could not undertake to control the Intifada within the Occupied Territories. It was agreed that this contentious point should not be included in the text of the letter to Rabin but should be articulated in a separate letter written by Arafat to Johan Jorgen Holst. But then Abu Ala argued that, while they were prepared to say the people on the West Bank should renounce violence, they would not state that they should renounce terror, since that implied that all Palestinians living on the West Bank were terrorists. On the sofa Joel Singer pondered the problem, playing with the ebony and silver Arab worry beads that Abu Ala had given him. Finally he came up with a compromise that worked. They would use the word 'reject' instead of 'renounce'. That way the statement would suggest a more objective, less involved, stance. At last, in the early hours, Abu Ala indicated to the Israelis that this would be acceptable to Arafat and the Executive Committee.

At this point I tried to reach Larsen by telephone in his room. Luckily he was passing through and picked up the phone. 'What the hell are you doing here?' he hissed, terrified that my presence might blow things at this delicate stage.

By now journalists were searching systematically through all the hotels in Paris looking for the team. Jerusalem had called to say that the Israeli embassy in Paris had had over a hundred demands to reveal where the group was holed up. I calmed Larsen down and told him that I would not leave my room, that Savir knew I was here, but that Abu Ala had no idea and I was not about to tell him. Then Larsen said, his voice shaking with excitement: 'I think they are about to do it! I have been sent down to fetch some papers so the draft of the text can be finalized, and then I will deliver a copy to both sides. I can't believe I am about to do this.'

I wished him luck and he rang off. And now the final point, the wording of the letter referring to the PLO Charter, was all that was left. Arafat told Abu Ala to convey the final decision of the Executive Committee: the wording could only be that the Charter had to be declared 'not in effect'. It could not be 'non-operative and non-valid', Savir and Singer were told. They called Peres in Israel and he consulted the Prime Minister. Back came the answer, a flat refusal accompanied by instructions to pull the team back home at once. Abu Ala passed on the response to Arafat, and the Chairman agreed to abandon the phrase 'not in effect', but made a subtle change to the Israeli wording. Now the final expression would be that the relevant clauses of the Charter 'are now inoperative and no longer valid'.

It was now past 4.00 a.m. and everyone was exhausted. Savir and Singer had a few drinks, and Larsen, as he passed the door, noticed that they looked absolutely shattered, lying back in their chairs in silence, their eyes closed and heads thrown back. Shimon Peres has a favourite saying: some lawyers know their clients and some lawyers know their files. His own pair of negotiators fitted that description. Savir was the man who concentrated on the clients, Singer focused on the files. The other members of the channel said they thought the two Israelis were as different as chalk and cheese, and wondered how they would ever get along. At the start Singer and Savir had disagreed over their negotiating strategy, but as the weeks passed they became close friends and formed a very effective partnership. And by the end, when they were locked in argument with the Palestinians, they hardly needed to communicate with each other verbally. Just a look or a gesture was sufficient.

Meanwhile, on the floor above, the camera crew and I were having difficulty keeping awake. I called room service to ask for coffee, and within minutes an elderly and very formal-looking waiter in a black tail-coat appeared at the door. It was nearly 5.00 a.m. The poor man must have thought the scene extremely bizarre. The room was decked out with a camera, microphones and lights. I, carefully made up and wearing high-heeled shoes and a smart business suit, was standing in the middle of the room while across the king-size bed sprawled two bleary-eyed French technicians, somewhat underdressed in jeans and T-shirts and with bare feet. The waiter, carefully averting his eyes from what looked like the set of a rather suspect movie, murmured '*Merci, madame*' and backed hastily out of the door.

Downstairs, Savir remembered that I was waiting. He showered and changed and presented himself for the interview. He was exhausted but elated, his voice hoarse and barely audible, but his words and his feelings clear and strong. I questioned him before the camera and then we talked on afterwards. He was greatly affected by the meeting between the children, and emphasized that it was for them that he and Abu Ala knew they had to make the peace deal work. Finally, at 6.00 a.m., he departed to take a dawn walk by the river with his daughter and one of the Norwegian security men. I threw my things into my bag and took the tapes from the crew. I knew *Panorama* had a scoop and, hoping our office manager would forgive the astronomical hotel bill, I hailed a cab for Charles de Gaulle, from where I took the 7.00 a.m. flight to London.

We all thought that the negotiating was now over. Savir had told me at 6.00 a.m. that the agreement was settled. Holst and Marianne Heiberg had gone to bed and Larsen and Mona were deep in an exhausted sleep when a security man woke them at seven o'clock.

'You must get up. I'm not sure what it is, but there is something wrong,' he warned.

Abu Ala was looking gloomy. He told Larsen: 'Everything is catastrophic. It's all over.'

Arafat had just called to say that he would now not agree to the clause calling on the people of the West Bank and Gaza to reject violence and terror. Joel Singer was on the phone trying to reach Rabin in Jerusalem. Savir was looking grim. The Israeli Cabinet was due to meet to approve the text in less than an hour and Rabin would delay that discussion unless Arafat gave in. There were now just four days to go before the Washington signing.

'Are you serious?' demanded Larsen.

'Absolutely, we can't get hold of Rabin at the moment, but the minute we do this whole thing's finished,' said Savir.

Abu Ala got up to go to his room. Larsen followed him into the bedroom, and on into the bathroom, refusing to go away, cross-examining the adamant Palestinian.

'Yes, I called Arafat. Nothing can be done.'

'You have to do something. Can't you call back? Don't you see that after all this, all we've done, it won't be of any use?'

Suddenly Abu Ala turned abruptly to face Larsen, just inches away from him in the confined bathroom. His hard, set look changed miraculously. He grinned and said conspiratorially: 'They're fishing! They're fishing – just wait and see!'

Then Larsen understood once more that it was brinkmanship at the final hour and that both sides knew the deal was all but done. Holst was awakened and Larsen told the security men they could order up champagne. Then everyone assembled in the main suite and Abu Ala made a final call to Arafat telling him the Israelis were threatening to postpone the Cabinet meeting. Then he turned round and said abruptly: 'It's agreed.' Marianne Heiberg began putting the final changes into the computer. When the time came to print out copies there were problems, as usual, and the security man with the user-friendly touch came once more to the rescue. Now everyone read the text. There was still a word that Abu Ala and Savir could not agree on, but everyone knew that the bargaining was, in reality, over. Then Savir, using the common language that he and Abu Ala had developed over the many months of arguments, made a casual reference to 'twenty seconds': 'Give me twenty seconds, will you, Abu Ala? You and I need to resolve something in private.' The two men went into the bedroom of the suite and closed the door. 'Abu Ala, we have to finish this,' said Savir. 'OK,' was the simple answer. But Abu Ala of course made one final condition. The word Savir wanted would be adopted but the Palestinian would be the one to tell the others outside. They shook hands and left the bedroom. Now Arafat would call on his people to reject violence and terror, the letters could be signed and the Washington ceremony could go ahead.

Both Savir and Abu Ala knew that the mutual recognition pact would ultimately prove even more significant than the Declaration of Principles they had reached in Oslo. It was the ideological breakthrough which transcended even the political breakthrough of the Declaration of Principles. The Gaza/Jericho accord was a more technical answer to the long-standing problem of how to return the Occupied Territories to Palestinian control gradually, without endangering Israel's security. But mutual recognition addressed a hundred years of conflict – the philosophy and the prejudices that had developed behind the history. It was the real basis of a new relationship, and signified a commitment to making that new foundation irreversible. By the texts of the two letters, the Palestinian national movement and the Jewish national movement recognized each other. They tacitly accepted that both could have a country, that both could live together side by side in the area between the Mediterranean and the River Jordan. In a way the mutual recognition agreement, with its wider implications, actually made the Declaration of Principles redundant. For it opened the way to a meeting and a dialogue between the leader of Israel and the leader of the PLO. After that, anything was possible. Even with setbacks, there could never be a return to the dark days of the past.

The champagne was opened and a call was made to the pilots of the Norwegian government jet standing by at Le Bourget Airport. They would leave for Tunis immediately, carrying the letter for Arafat to sign so that they could deliver it quickly to Jerusalem, getting Rabin's signature on the letter recognizing the PLO. The pilots explained that they had missed their early morning slot and were now trying desperately to get another take-off time for Tunis. Savir and Singer packed and went downstairs to pay their bill. A few reporters had arrived outside by now, and the Israelis just got away before the mob descended. The Palestinians, with Holst and Marianne and Mona, were taken out through the garage by the security team. One man remained with Larsen and they went to settle the hotel account. The hotel's computer was out of order, and the Norwegians had to wait downstairs as the lobby began filling up with reporters, who were trying to find the Norwegian Foreign Minister. Finally Larsen told hotel staff to send them the bill and the two men rushed out to find a cab. This took some time, and they just made it to Le Bourget as the plane was about to leave.

On the journey the pilots brought out caviare, goose liver pâté and champagne, which they had laid on specially. Everyone had been up for more than twenty-four hours, but they were too excited, too keyed up, to take a nap. When they arrived in Tunisia, a humid tropical dusk was setting in, and on the tarmac Hassan Asfour and Yasser Abed-Rabbo were waiting to greet them. In the VIP lounge, which was packed with press, they gave a hurried news conference and then set off at top speed in a huge motorcade, with horns blaring and lights flashing, to the Hilton Hotel. Hassan Asfour was riding in the back of the second car with Mona and Terje. He was in a highly emotional state, talking and crying, his head on Larsen's chest as he tried to explain what this moment meant for him. The transformation of the Communist from the Gaza Strip was now complete; he realized that the recognition pact had brought the PLO and his people back into the international fold. Less than a year before, the PLO had stood on the brink of political and financial extinction, its leader facing oblivion. Now that the way was open for the United States to recognize the PLO, it stood centre stage with a real future ahead for all the Palestinian people. Hassan Asfour was intensely proud that he had been one of the small Palestinian team who had made it possible.

As the motorcade drew up at the Hilton, the Norwegians were shocked by the sheer number of journalists gathered there. In the open-plan lobby, an Arab-style dining-room and lounge, there were literally hundreds of photographers and journalists. Larsen gave up counting but thought there must be a hundred and fifty TV cameras. The journalists thronged around the Norwegians, who began to fear that in their exhausted state they might fall and be trampled underfoot. Holst was pushed down into a chair, invisible behind a forest of microphones and cables and a blizzard of flashing, clicking cameras. Larsen and the burliest Norwegian security man fought their way to him, grabbed him under the arms, and lifted him to his feet. Then they ran down the corridor to the lifts, which they found were out of order, and then around the back to find the service elevator. At last they reached their floor, which was cordoned off, and found sanctuary in their rooms. They were sweating and shaking uncontrollably, and it was then that they realized the magnitude of what Norway had helped to achieve. But they were still afraid that this media circus might be for nothing. In his brown briefcase Holst carried the two letters, but neither of them had yet been signed.

Late that night, Arafat emerged battered but triumphant from the latest round of PLO meetings, which authorized him to accept the text and sign the letter. The Norwegian team again ran the gauntlet of the world's press. They made their way back to Arafat's villa, whither they had come, so full of doubts, in July to try and fathom the Chairman's intentions. For the first time they all met the mysterious Abu Mazen.

'It's a great pleasure meeting you, Mr Holy Spirit,' said Larsen. 'Did you know about your nickname?' Abu Mazen laughed delightedly. The rather machiavellian tag had pleased him enormously. Abu Ala, Hassan Asfour and Yasser Abed-Rabbo greeted the Norwegians excitedly. The visitors, still anxious that Arafat might not sign, noticed with relief that there was a PLO video outfit and a stills photographer in the room. Then Arafat came in and, without ado, went quickly to the long meeting table. Holst sat down beside him with the others assembled behind. Then the Norwegian Foreign Minister drew the letter from his briefcase and the Chairman quickly signed. There were no speeches, just handshakes. But everyone knew that in those fifteen seconds history had been made – in a plain and rather shabby room, the inner sanctum of a government-in-exile, soon to be returning home. In a touching moment, the members of the Norwegian security team asked to be presented to Yasser Arafat. These were men who for years had shadowed suspected PLO terrorists in Scandinavia, and now one of the most famous guerrilla leaders of all time kissed them on the cheeks.

The pilots of the Norwegian jet were now told to file the flight plan to leave Tunisia for Cyprus. Although a letter had been signed which the Norwegians hoped would usher in a new era of peace, it was too soon to expect that the ban on direct flights between Arab countries and Israel could be lifted. Once over the Mediterranean they changed their course for Tel Aviv, arriving there as dawn was breaking. When the jet taxied to a halt before the sign 'Welcome to Israel', a black Cadillac at the head of a motorcade moved towards the plane. Out stepped Shimon Peres and the Blazers, who had come to greet their Norwegian friends. Then, at breakneck speed, they drove the thirty-five miles to Jerusalem. Security was very tight, with armed men along the route and two helicopters flying overhead. When they arrived at the King David Hotel that Friday morning they encountered more journalists. It was the second day without sleep for the Norwegian peacemakers. Mona Juul was getting desperate; she had gone for forty-eight hours without a pause for breath or even time to pack and unpack properly. They had no clean clothes left, so she hung up their crumpled ones in the bathroom and turned on the hot taps, to try and steam away the creases. But the clothes dropped down on to the wet floor and she burst into tears with fatigue and frustration.

After having breakfast with Shimon Peres, they all departed for Rabin's office. Outside, there were banners and demonstrations. Angry settlers and opponents of the peace plan shouted at the Norwegians. In the large office the press and leaders of the government were assembled. At the table Holst sat in the middle with Rabin on his left and Peres on his right. It was significant that both men were sitting there, side by side, as Holst brought out the letter. Just below Peres were seated the full contingent of the Blazers: Beilin, Savir, Gill and Shlomo Gur. And with them sat their newest recruit, Joel Singer. Without much ceremony Rabin took out a cheap government-issue blue ball-point pen and signed his name. Everyone suspected that the choice of pen had been deliberate. Then Peres leaned over and said something to Rabin who nodded in agreement. At this point Peres addressed the others in the room: 'I would like to bring to your attention, ladies and gentlemen, the team who really did the job. I would like you, Marianne and Mona and Terje, to come to the podium and greet the Prime Minister of Israel.'

Somewhat embarrassed, the three Norwegians got to their feet and squeezed past all the journalists to get to the front. When it was Mona's turn, Peres gave her a big hug and kissed her on the forehead, his sign that, for him, her contribution had been a special one. And to Larsen he said loudly: 'Terje, thank you.'

Arafat's letter was given to Rabin, and then the letter signed by the Israeli Prime Minister was faxed to Arafat in Tunis. The original was kept by Holst to be delivered at a later date. The next day Avi Gill realized that the Israelis had not taken a copy and, belatedly, one was made before the Norwegians left. After the signing Peres took the Norwegians to his favourite restaurant for lunch. Sitting there gazing out over the old city of Jerusalem, the Norwegians and the Blazers and Yair Hirschfeld and Ron Pundak ate salmon and then steak, and toasted the further success of the Oslo Channel. But the atmosphere was not as convivial as it should have been. Already there were fears about the future. The agreement could now be signed, but there was further negotiation to be completed before the withdrawal could get under way in December. The violence was continuing: killings by Hamas and a corresponding crackdown by the Israeli army. And although the majority of the Israeli public supported the peace initiative, Beilin and Peres knew that it could very quickly turn sour.

There were tensions too within the group, exacerbated by the mounting media coverage. As in Norway, the press had had a field-day with the story of the secret negotiations. Hirschfeld and Pundak had not been hidden away in Paris, like Savir and Singer, and they had received the lion's share of the attention. Some stories had been wrong or slanted: it had been claimed that Rabin had been kept in the dark, that high-level officials had only been involved at the very end. There was annoyance and rivalry within the Israeli team, just as there had been the week before among the Norwegians in Oslo. Here, too, the close-knit secret circle was breaking up under the pressure of public exposure.

The White House signing was just three days away and, when their task in Israel had been completed, the Norwegians hurried back to Oslo. Mona went shopping for an outfit for the ceremony but, despite the shop assistants' eagerness to help, she could find nothing she liked or which fitted her. It was apparent to everyone in the channel that relations between her and Terje had reached a low point now. They were both physically exhausted after four days without any sleep and many months of round-the-clock phone calls, meetings and travel on the emotional roller-coaster of the channel. The endlessly gushing, and often inaccurate, media coverage of the two Norwegian husband-and-wife teams was insulting to Mona's professional abilities. Larsen was attracting a great deal of attention, and in his open, sociable way was thriving on it. But Mona was the professional diplomat and expert on the Middle East, even if in her more reserved manner she did not make a great show of it. It was inevitable, and only human, that there should be resentment and rows now between the two people who for so long had sacrificed their own personal lives, their family commitments and their deepest feelings for the Oslo Channel.

That Friday night it was still not clear who would attend the ceremony in Washington, and who would sign the agreement for Israel and the PLO. Rabin was in two minds about being present. The Americans feared that if Rabin stayed away so might Arafat, and then the PLO leader could later disown the deal, arguing that it was Abu Mazen's initiative and not his own. Arafat sent a message to Washington, indicating that he would like to come but that he would only do so if Rabin attended too. So Bill Clinton took the initiative and told his advisers that he intended to mend America's broken links with the PLO. This made it easier for Rabin to decide to attend the ceremony, and then Arafat agreed to come also, to meet his lifelong enemy. For the Americans it was a big relief; now there was far less chance of the parties reneging on a deal made publicly, with the backing of the superpower.

'It feels like a gift,' Clinton said. And indeed it was, a present on a silver plate held out to a beleaguered President who badly needed a public success. Just nine months into office, his Administration was floundering. There had been blunders over foreign policy in Bosnia and Somalia, and at home trade ills, the health care reforms and the deficit loomed large and threatening. Then the Gaza/Jericho agreement fell into his lap, a foreign policy triumph that he could make the most of. It was only fair, he said, to remind everyone of the enormous investment that both his and the Bush Administration had made to solve the problems of the Middle East. They had pushed both sides in the direction of a Declaration of Principles, even if they had not been able to make it happen. Oslo had come in with the magic touch, but America's muscle was still needed to remind the parties that this agreement must be made to stick. Both the Israelis and the Palestinians wanted the American seal of approval on their work, in the form of a White House signing before the cameras. And so that weekend Clinton's aides gathered to plan the set-piece ceremony, the entrances and exits, the desk and chairs, and, most importantly of all, to choreograph that delicate piece of political theatre – the handshake. Rabin had been sounded out about his willingness to participate in this act. All he would say was that if there was a hand to shake then he would shake it. But he urged the Americans to make sure that Arafat did not show up in his usual military uniform with a pistol on his hip. He was assured that the Chairman would be wearing a safari suit instead.

On Sunday, 12 September, the Norwegians left for Washington. There was quite a party on the plane. Holst had magnanimously suggested that as well as Marianne, it was appropriate for Egeland, Mona, Terje, Geir Pedersen and Even Aas to come too. As usual they were accompanied by their six friends from the secret service. The Palestinians set out from Tunis on a plane provided by King Hassan of Morocco. Abu Ala, Hassan Asfour and Mohammed Abu Koush accompanied Abu Mazen, Yasser Abed-Rabbo, Arafat and the other dignitaries. But at the last minute one VIP was left behind at Tunis Airport with all her cases: Suha Arafat, the Chairman's wife. Abu Mazen argued that the American media would focus on Arafat's attractive Christian spouse rather than the leader of the PLO and the peace deal itself. And so Mrs Arafat remained at home and watched the ceremony on television.

In Israel a sombre but forgiving note was struck when Peres and Rabin invited widows and victims of terrorist attacks carried out by Palestinians to accompany them to Washington. Three brave women took up the challenge: Elisa Ben Rafael, whose husband had been killed in 1992, in the bomb attack on the Israeli embassy in Buenos Aires; Dalia Ya'iri, whose husband had been killed in a PLO beach raid near a Tel Aviv hotel in 1975; and Hanna Maron, who had lost her leg in the PLO grenade attack on an El Al bus at Munich Airport in 1970. A fourth woman came to the airport, Smadar Haran, whose tragic and shocking story is engraved on Israeli hearts for ever. Her husband and four-year-old daughter were murdered by PLO terrorists who stormed their apartment in 1979. Smadar hid upstairs and, in a desperate attempt to stop her baby's cries from giving them away, accidentally smothered the child. She told Rabin, that morning at Ben-Gurion Airport, that she could not face going with him to Washington to see the PLO, but she encouraged him to meet Arafat and make peace with her family's killers.

'It demands a transformation in all our souls,' said Smadar that day. 'I don't forget. I don't forgive. But they are our enemies and we must take the chance to talk to them ... Israel has to have the strength, and I personally have to find the strength, to undergo an emotional revolution and to speak to the Palestinians. Our nation is destined to live alongside them.'

The Norwegians arrived in Washington on Sunday afternoon to learn that their Foreign Minister had been given a very minor role at the White House signing. The bureaucrats in charge of protocol had decided that Holst and the Egyptian Foreign Minister, Amr Moussa, who had worked tirelessly for peace, would be allowed to attend the gathering before the ceremony. But then they would be ushered out of a side entrance to their seats on the lawn, while Clinton, Secretary of State Christopher and other American luminaries escorted the main Israeli and Palestinian figures out through the portico to the audience of three thousand people. Back in Norway there was already resentment at the way America seemed to be stealing the limelight. The very day of the Washington signing there was to be a general election in Norway, and it was not the time for one of the country's most important politicians to be pushed into the background. Larsen was deputed to try and get the protocol arrangements changed. There was resistance, for the State Department and the President's PR advisers feared that the Norwegian presence would draw attention away from the President and from America's role. Finally a direct appeal to Dennis Ross was successful, and at 3.00 a.m. it was agreed that Holst and Amr Moussa would walk out on to the lawn with the other VIPs.

No sooner was that sorted out than Larsen received an ominous call from Abu Ala, whom he had been expecting to call with some last-minute 'cosmetic change'. And sure enough the Palestinian wanted to know what Larsen could remember about an agreement to put direct references to the PLO into the text of the Declaration of Principles. Larsen said that he was not sure any such agreement had been made. 'There will be no signing unless the PLO is written in,' snapped Abu Ala.

It was at about this time that the Israeli delegation landed in Washington and Peres and his entourage went to their hotel to catch a few hours' sleep. At 5.00 a.m. Avi Gill was awakened by the phone. Hassan Asfour was on the line. 'We are in big trouble,' he warned. 'The Chairman doesn't want to sign.'

Arafat was insisting that the Israelis should agree to initial 'PLO' in pencil at every point in the text where the expression 'the Palestinian team' was used. This time his go-between was Dr Ahmed Tibi, an Arab physician from East Jerusalem. Privately Peres and Rabin decided, after consultation, to concede the point – since they had recognized the PLO there was no reason not to. But Peres was not about to let the PLO know that, with all of four hours to go before the ceremony. His message back, through Tibi, was that the Israeli Cabinet had approved the Declaration of Principles word for word, and it could not be changed now.

'But the Chairman does not agree,' said Tibi. 'He is packing now to leave.'

'Tell him,' said Peres, 'that we just arrived and we have not even begun to unpack yet. We can leave even quicker still!'

At nine o'clock Peres calmly kept an appointment with Warren Christopher, then returned to his room with less than an hour to go until the signing. With twenty minutes left, Tibi came to Peres's suite in desperation, and Peres said: 'OK, we will let you write in "PLO" in one place only.'

Tibi then tried to squeeze out one last concession, that the correction be typed in, not pencilled in the margin. Peres acquiesced. Then Tibi picked up the phone and called Arafat who agreed to Peres's condition. The Arab doctor turned round smiling, with one last message for Peres before the ceremony: 'The Chairman is delighted; he sends me two kisses, one for each cheek, and a third one for you, Mr Peres.'

The ceremony was about to get under way, and all the Blazers, including Yossi Beilin, the Deputy Foreign Minister, were still at the hotel. Peres had been whisked away in an official car but there was no transport left for the others.

'It seems the ceremony will go on without us,' said Savir, in the ironic, understated manner of a Blazer.

'Never mind, let's go to a movie instead,' was Beilin's quick reply. But they ran to find a car and hitched a lift with some security men. And so the Blazers, hot and panting, their immaculate suits for once all awry, made it to the White House lawn with only minutes to spare. The first person Beilin saw there was Dr Boutros Ghali, the UN Secretary-General, a friend and fan of the young Israeli minister.

'You naughty boy,' cried Boutros Ghali. 'You should have told me what you were up to. I had an idea you were behind it all the time.' Beilin was touched to see the joy on the face of the veteran Egyptian statesman, who was telling everybody around him that it was one of the happiest days of his life.

Terje Larsen, however, did not seem to be having such a happy day. He and Mona and Jan Egeland had been assigned seats at the very back, at the furthest point of the U-shaped stand around the podium. Consequently all they would be able to see would be the backs of the people conducting the historic ceremony. Larsen found some friends among the crowd; he stopped to talk to Savir and Singer but they were preoccupied with the details of the ceremony. Abu Ala and Hassen Asfour greeted him but Larsen was somewhat sore at the verbal lashing he had received yet again the night before, over the final textual changes. Yair Hirschfeld and Ron Pundak were nowhere to be seen. No room had been found for them on the official Israeli flight, another snub for the professors. They had made their own way to Washington by scheduled airline, and Avi Gill had arranged for them to get tickets to the ceremony. Like the Norwegians, they were squeezed in somewhere at the back. Thousands of miles away in Geneva, Thorvald Stoltenberg, the former Norwegian Foreign Minister, turned on his television in the UN building where he was still striving to broker peace in Bosnia. He was happy that day that at least one conflict appeared to have come to an end, even if the killing was continuing in the former Yugoslavia. He was proud to know that he too had played an important part by offering Norway's services to bring about the peace accord.

Back on the White House lawn Larsen looked tired and jaded and uncomfortable too in his thick suit. He was becoming flushed and hot as he and Mona and Egeland waited in the blazing sun. The scale of the scene before them reflected the huge sums – billions of dollars – that America had spent over the years trying to solve the Middle East problem. The Norwegians calculated that their secret channel had cost a mere half a million dollars, a very modest amount in terms of government expenditure. At last, the Marine Corps snapped to attention, and the ceremony began with Tipper Gore, the Vice-President's wife, dressed in shocking pink, leading the cavalcade of dignitaries, Holst amongst them, who stepped out in twos and threes on to the White House lawn. The last three to appear were the men at the heart of the symbolic ceremony. Bill Clinton walked forward in the middle, fulfilling the pledge made by George Bush in the wake of the Gulf War to seek a meaningful solution to the problem of the Holy Land claimed by Jew and Arab. Beside him strode Yitzhak Rabin and Yasser Arafat, the two men who had risked all in pursuing this accord.

As Peres and Abu Mazen signed the Declaration of Principles, Yossi Beilin felt a sense of fulfilment but regret as well. It could have been done much earlier, he told himself, but at least we have made a start. Standing beside Peres and in front of Rabin, Joel Singer turned the pages of the Declaration. Proud to have been the only one trusted by both men, Singer had skilfully played on two chessboards at once. He had both confronted the PLO and negotiated an Israeli position acceptable to his two, very different, political masters. Way beyond the podium Yair Hirschfeld craned his neck to catch a glimpse of the Declaration of Principles which he had first discussed with Abu Ala at Borregaard, and which was now the foundation of a peace accord. And down in front, amongst the Arab diplomats, the Palestinian banker smiled. It had been worth all the efforts, the emotions and the games he had played with the Israelis to shape this deal.

And then the moment they had all been waiting for came at last. The crowd held its breath, and Terje Larsen, Mona Juul and Jan Egeland had a good view of Clinton's back as he raised his arms, in the much rehearsed gesture, coaxing the two men together for the handshake. Arafat was smiling broadly, his stocky figure standing proud, as he reached for the Israeli Prime Minister's arm. Rabin was hunched, his head was tilted and his whole manner spelled reluctance. Then Arafat relinquished Rabin's arm and stepped boldly forward to greet Shimon Peres too. Rabin appeared to shake his head in disapproval, but his lips were saying: 'Now it's your turn,' as he too acknowledged the new partnership with his old political foe.

Mona and Terje, watching Arafat with Rabin and Peres, were close to tears. They had helped to bring about a miracle on the White House lawn and, like the other members of the channel scattered throughout the crowd, they felt honoured and gratified to have been able to play their part.

The crowd began to break up and the President walked back

into the White House for the reception. Holst found Larsen and insisted that he come in with him. There was no room for Jan Egeland and Mona Juul; they returned to their hotel with the Norwegian security men. Egeland cut short his visit and flew home that afternoon. Back at the White House a guard tried to stop Larsen coming in without a proper pass. But finally Dennis Ross got him through and there in the hall Larsen recognized many of the world's great statesmen gathered to celebrate the achievement of the unknown Oslo team, even though they were not included in the party. At the end, as the limousines lined up by the door to collect the ministers and ambassadors and former presidents, Larsen saw Bill Clinton enquiring who this unknown visitor was. The President came up smiling and said: 'You did a great job, Mr Larsen . . . '

But before he could continue a small figure launched himself from the shadows and grabbed the Norwegian in a bear-hug. It was the Chairman of the PLO, exclaiming with delight. For Larsen it was a suitably exotic ending to the day on which a dream had come true. For he had seen a peace deal signed and then been kissed by Yasser Arafat, in front of the President of the United States, in the portals of the White House.

Epilogue

The members of the Oslo Channel were swept up in the euphoric activity that followed the Washington signing of the peace accord. Joel Singer and Hassan Asfour were appointed to the Israeli and PLO delegations charged with settling the details of military withdrawal from Gaza and Jericho. The two men met again in Egypt – in Cairo and at the Hilton Hotel in Taba, on the Red Sea's rocky shore. The talks, reported daily by the media, soon ran into trouble. The old problems, so familiar to the secret channel, returned to haunt both parties. They could not agree on the size of Jericho and the question of who should control the borders. The date set for the start of the withdrawal, 13 December, passed without agreement and Israeli troops remained in Gaza and in Jericho. But the respect and friendship between Singer and Asfour endured, although Asfour found himself under increasing pressure from more radical elements in the PLO.

Uri Savir, Terje Larsen and Abu Ala met again in Paris. They headed delegations to an international forum convened to disburse two billion pounds in aid and development funding for the Occupied Territories. With the approval of the World Bank, Abu Ala began to shape a Palestinian Economic Council for Development and Reconstruction. The PECDR was intended to be practical, professional and open to scrutiny. But within weeks Yasser Arafat stepped in, determined to take control of every detail and appointing his own cronies to head this important and influential body. The international community became alarmed: there were reports of Arafat's aids conducting secret meetings with businessmen in hotel rooms to carve out deals with hefty commission payments. Abu Ala had warned that the peace deal would depend on swift action to bolster the Palestinian economy.

But his best efforts were continually frustrated by the old guard in the PLO.

Yair Hirschfeld and Ron Pundak took no further part in the many official committees that sprung up around the peace process. They went back to forging links with local Palestinians and continued their quest for funds to run their small research programme.

By late December, Johan Jorgen Holst had collected thirteen peace prizes from around the world. From Los Angeles to New York, from Canada to Germany, the awards for Norway's Foreign Minister were announced. Marianne Heiberg too was honoured on some of these occasions. The crowning glory, commissioned to commemorate the Norwegian's subtle diplomacy, was a massive steel sculpture donated by the Carter Center in Atlanta, Georgia. The Americans planned to hire a jumbo jet to fly it to Oslo, where it would be erected with pomp and ceremony in the city centre.

Terje Larsen still had no time to return to his regular academic work. He was given the title of Ambassador and an office at the Foreign Ministry. He and Mona Juul longed to take a break, but found themselves inexorably caught up in the process they had helped to launch. The requests came flooding in for their assistance in solving many of the world's most intractable problems – from Northern Ireland and Bosnia to Guatemala and East Timor. FAFO became a well-known research institute in the Middle East, and the Norwegians even heard that Palestinian babies born that September had been christened Fafo.

For the Blazers, Yossi Beilin and Uri Savir, and for their mentor Shimon Peres, there were difficult times ahead. The militants of Hamas quickly learnt that targeting Israeli settlers in Gaza and on the West Bank touched a raw nerve in the body of the Jewish state. Public approval for the peace plan plummeted and the Labour Party looked increasingly exposed. Rabin trod the tightrope of placating domestic outrage at the violence while maintaining the new dialogue with the PLO. He took a stand over the question of Israeli control of the borders but allowed the final batch of Palestinian deportees to return home.

Yasser Arafat flew around the world courting its leaders, promising democracy and collecting many offers of financial help. But the PLO still faced bankruptcy, and international donors balked at the idea of releasing funds to the Chairman's autocratic control. Hard questions were being asked about PLO Swiss bank accounts and about Arafat's increasingly arbitrary demands. Some people even questioned his sanity. Others criticized an extensive shopping trip that Mrs Arafat had taken to the boutiques of Paris. Meanwhile Palestinian widows went without their pensions and the refugees in Gaza waited for the economic miracle. Once more it seemed that Yasser Arafat would prove the truth of the famous Israeli taunt that the PLO has never missed an opportunity to miss an opportunity.

The discreet Abu Mazen retreated once more into the shadows, disillusioned by his leader's antics. He had endured a brief and unwelcome spell in the spotlight which dented his confidence in his new neighbours-to-be, the Israelis. Just two weeks after the Washington signing, Abu Mazen's office was provided with a new chair and lamp by the PLO official in charge of refurbishment. A month later, strange radio traffic was detected in that part of Tunis. The helpful Palestinian official was unmasked as a Mossad mole in the heart of the PLO establishment; the signals, it turned out, were emanating from Abu Mazen's chair.

The members of the Oslo Channel had never expected their peace deal to receive a universal welcome. They knew there would be rejection, anger and recriminations in the weeks ahead. It rapidly became clear to them that the circle they had successfully formed to hammer out their differences could not be recreated at the official Israeli and Palestinian level. Rabin and Arafat, and their new and extended teams of representatives, could not agree on the final details to make military withdrawal a reality. And so on 18 December the secret channel reconvened back at Borregaard. Peres was there, along with Uri Savir and Abu Ala; they were joined by Joel Singer and Hassan Asfour and other Israelis and Palestinians from the new negotiating team. An atmosphere of sadness hung over the gathering, for Johan Jorgen Holst had suffered a serious stroke and was unable to attend. Terje Larsen and Mona Juul hosted the meeting at the old manor and tried once more to foster a special atmosphere. They all knew that they were the only ones who could save the agreement now. The outcry in their own communities was undeniable, and so too was the sour sense of disappointment that now permeated the political arena and the columns of all the newspapers. But they were all still optimistic that their achievement could in the long term transcend the present difficulties.

The small group trusted that what they had learnt about each other could somehow be transferred to the wider stage, and that what they had done would prove irreversible.

The success of the Oslo Channel had been the result of a combination of both local factors and global forces, and the members of the channel believed those essential ingredients were still in place. The end of the cold war and the break-up of the Soviet Union removed a principal player from the drama of the Middle East and also withdrew the patronage enjoyed by several states in the region. Russian was now intent on attracting American assistance, not on challenging American interest in an area of strategic concern and importance. The Gulf War had changed the whole atmosphere of the Middle East: new fears had been aroused by Iraq's aggression while a number of old fears had been somewhat allayed by the unlikely sight of Israel restraining its forces. The demonstration of American power and will humbled Arab pride in some quarters and gave impetus to the rising tide of fundamentalist rejection. The isolation of the PLO, an isolation increased by Arafat's support for Saddam Hussein, brought financial repercussions which threatened the very foundation of the organization. At the same time the talks in Washington proved that Arafat could not be sidelined.

Israel was reluctant to accept that message, but the Jewish state increasingly came to recognize that in a changing world heavy military responsibilities – which drained the country's economy, its youth and its hope – could no longer be sustained. Israel could not remain the pariah in a region where, in order to survive, a country had to be a part of a communality of economic interest. Israeli priorities had to change, for hundreds of thousands of Russian immigrants needed to be absorbed into a society afflicted by isolation and the burden of its large army. And Israel's great protector, the United States, had made it clear that continuing support was dependent on genuine attempts to resolve the territorial problems. The growth of the settlements on the West Bank would have to be halted; the expansion of the Jewish population on Arab land could not go unchecked. The election of the Labour Party, with a mandate to seek peace, was the signal to enter into dialogue with the PLO. And the decision of Rabin and Peres to bury their differences and work together at last for peace was the final element in the Israeli equation.

The interests of both the PLO and Israel came together on the streets of Gaza, where the youths of Hamas roam. For the PLO the increasing strength of those extremists threatened its claim to represent the Palestinian people. Arafat feared that by the time he had a state to call his own he would not be the power in the land; the terror which had once been the weapon of the PLO was now being used against it. In Israel the voice of mothers grew difficult to ignore as they cried for something to be done to end the killing of their sons. The Israeli sense of moral outrage over the continued occupation of the West Bank grew stronger as the Intifada flared, claiming yet more Israeli and Palestinian lives. The demon with Arafat's face was being replaced by the demons with black masks who attacked the settlers. There seemed to be no end to the cycle of death and bloodshed.

When the Oslo Channel was tentatively launched, some on the Israeli side believed they had seized the best moment to exploit the weakness of the PLO. Others countered that, by offering the olive branch to a desperate Arafat, Israel might well have foolishly saved her enemy. But the reality was that both sides had no alternative. Peres and Rabin realized the PLO might not be there much longer to do a deal with, and there would never be accommodation with the extremists. As one member of the Oslo Channel succinctly put it, 'The truth is that they need us, but we need them.' Both sides knew they had exhausted all the other possibilities, but it was not clear at the beginning if that alone would spur the channel to success. For Israel's psyche was deeply scarred by terror and rejection, and the Palestinians were haunted by their homelessness and the humiliation of occupation.

The Israelis and the Palestinians, as they sat face to face through all those long days and nights in Norway, identified the key to lasting peace. It was to build mutual trust on a strong foundation of shared economic interest, to be a bulwark against fanaticism and the tide of history. The idea they first set down on paper around the fire at Borregaard, a joint Declaration of Principles, was the means by which they attempted this, refining those principles through the process of negotiation. By rejecting the historical perspective, they cut through the Gordian knot that had tied the Washington talks in limbo. And they decided to postpone decisions about the most difficult issues: the future of Jerusalem and the settlements, and the existence of a Palestinian state. Instead, 'graduality' became the guiding principle, which would allow Gaza and Jericho to become the first experiments in peace. Then the group's priority became to establish the economic concerns on a par with those of security. As Abu Ala often said: 'This agreement can only walk on two legs and with a clever head. One leg is security, the other is economic development.' By building democratic institutions and encouraging a parallel infrastructure of interlocking industry and communications, they hoped to bind the peoples of the area together in economic interdependence. They knew that only if new employment, housing, schools and hospitals improved the quality of both their peoples' lives would there be hope of holding the foundation-stones of peace steady against the earthquakes of the future. For they were fully aware that the Oslo process was just a stepping-stone along the road to peace. That road leads to the divided Holy City of Jerusalem, brooding on the hills. And on across the broad sweep of the West Bank of the Jordan, the land the Palestinians call home, the final status of which is as yet undecided.

In the aftermath of the White House signing the flaws in the Oslo agreement became apparent. Critics said the agreement was more favourable to the Israelis, who maintained their grip on overall security, while all the Palestinians gained was two small pieces of land freed from military occupation. The difficulties with implementing the Declaration of Principles brought the accusation that there was a looseness in the wording, leaving room for argument and stalling. It was claimed that the small team had been overoptimistic, indeed somewhat amateurish, in their approach. They had evaded the hard questions, which returned to dog those charged with actually implementing the accord. The truth is that the negotiators had no choice, if there was to be any agreement at all. The Washington talks had shown the dangers of getting bogged down in the details. The members of the Oslo Channel took a risk; through the Declaration of Principles they sought to demonstrate that a broader understanding could be achieved, one that went beyond the drawing of lines on a map around the city of Jericho. In retrospect, the optimism that swept around the world in the wake of the accord created the illusion that a single peace agreement could be a panacea for all ills in the region, that it could change the reality on the ground for ever.

The quiet diplomacy of Norway was a new and significant

part of the forging of the peace accord and may well become a model for mediation in other conflicts. The Norwegians would be the first to deny that their presence influenced the talks. The condition they always set for their involvement was that the parties should be ready to negotiate in good faith. The political climate was right at the end of 1992, but this small Scandinavian country pushed strongly for a role that enabled it to facilitate the agreement. Carefully balanced between the sides, Norway had the signal advantage that its own strategic resources of oil made it independent from the maelstrom of the Middle East. The small country's unbiased reputation, its generous aid policy and its uniquely intimate governing circles were all factors in the creation of the secret channel.

The negotiators claimed that they all became a little 'Norwegianized' as the talks proceeded. Larsen and Juul bypassed all the paraphernalia of modern conferences: the limousines, the impersonal hotels, the posses of security men and translators. Instead the country homes, good food and intimate walks in spectacular Nordic surroundings all helped to create a collegiate sense, a feeling of camaraderie. Much has been made of this aspect of the talks, although the participants themselves are reluctant to attribute too much influence to the style of the negotiations. But they have talked about the strange impact on their spirits of discussing death and conflict in the sunlit, tranquil surroundings of the fiords. It was undoubtedly surreal, but perhaps necessary, for them to be distanced from the Middle East in order to make sense of the problems there. Only in a different environment could they find the solutions which had evaded so many of their predecessors. And only in a place like Norway could they be sure of hiding from the outside world. The Israelis and Palestinians often joked with their hosts: 'No one will think of looking here. After all, who would think of anything happening in Norway?'

Throughout the talks their greatest fear was discovery. Only in secrecy could they demonstrate that real compromise was not only necessary but possible. Their isolation from the demands of the media and the scrutiny of critics back home meant they could function as real negotiatiors rather than as the mouthpieces of political dogma. The function of the Israeli and Palestinian individuals was both to confront each other and to argue the case for the Oslo Channel to their political masters. The seven men who met in Norwegian log cabins and walked in forests never forgot that they were just the instruments of those who had sent them. The real responsibility was taken by the leaders, but those leaders themselves needed skilful handling to persuade them first to come on board, and then to take the ultimate decision to endorse the peace deal and commit themselves to its implementation.

When the scholars come to write about the lessons the Oslo Channel has for the techniques of negotiation they will doubtless focus on the intensity of the talks. The teams spent days and nights together, with no excuse to break away when the discussions came up against a wall. Eating, talking, walking and driving together, they had no chance to evade the issues or to allow passions to cool. This was essential for creating the sense of mutual dependence and the intimacy that were the talks' special trademark. In conversation every single member of the channel talked about the baby they had created and would carefully nurture. The struggle over mutual recognition was likened to the pain of childbirth. They all feared what would happen when the fragile infant was exposed to the harsh judgement of the outside world, but that fear did not stop them from creating it.

Uri Savir once told the others: 'You will see, Hollywood will never make a movie about us. We are all such unlikely characters, no one would believe it.' But Savir may yet have to eat his words. His remark was true in part, for at first sight the characters were unremarkable: no statesmen or famous peacemakers with a public vision. But they all had qualities that set them apart as individuals. And within the group those qualities combined to create an understanding and then a momentum that proved unstoppable. There was Abu Ala's pragmatism, Hassan Asfour's courage to change old ways, Joel Singer's hard-headed but practical approach, Uri Savir's moral sense and intellectual perception, and Yair Hirschfeld and Ron Pundak's devotion. And behind them all there was the humanity of Larsen, 'the existentialist', as they called him.

These men who lived together for intense periods during a nine-month span had a strong perception of their own self-interest in a changing world. Israel had thought that by exerting tough controls over the rebellious Palestinian population in the Occupied Territories it could somehow ignore the deeper problem of its border conflicts and its relationship with neighbouring Arab states. The Palestinians had tried to remedy their stateless condition by appealing to their Arab brothers to weaken Israel or push it off the map. Paradoxically, they discovered that in the end their best chance of partnership lay with Israel.

And finally the personal contact between the small group of individuals in Norway proved there was a natural empathy beneath the suspicion and distrust which might with time erase the images of war and terror. It was an empathy created by their shared experience of exile and persecution and their long-standing geographical closeness in the biblical land of Palestine. The likeness in their character and experience was not something they would readily admit to, but it became undeniable. The common language they all developed in the channel was proof of this, and gave hope that their peoples too might develop a way of communicating.

It is possible that the understanding these men reached to help them fashion a peace accord is but a cruel trick of fate which cannot be repeated between their peoples. But the world can only try to have faith that the story of the Oslo Channel gives real hope for the future, hope that the enmity between Israel and the Palestinians can be overcome. The two sides broke down a psychological wall just by talking to each other. It is rare in long-standing conflicts for there to be no direct communication between the antagonists, but that had been the situation with the PLO and the Israeli state. When Savir and Abu Ala shook hands in the Thomas Heftye cottage, with Larsen's introduction ringing in their ears, they began to break the cycle of suspicion and distrust. And that handshake has already been mirrored many times over, as former Arab terrorists have met Jewish soldiers, Israeli journalists interviewed PLO officials, and Palestinian and Israeli businessmen sat down to discuss joint ventures.

The overriding image left behind is that of a Palestinian guerrilla leader and an Israeli general standing together on the White House lawn. The Oslo Channel made that meeting possible, and the greeting 'Shalom, Salaam, Peace' reverberated around the Middle East. More blood would yet be spilt but something fundamental had changed. The demon of hatred, fear and suspicion had been confronted, and life in that arc of land between the Mediterranean Sea and the River Jordan would never be the same.

Johan Jorgen Holst appeared to be recovering from his stroke and left the hospital for a rehabilitation center. But he suffered a setback and died in the early hours of 13 January, just two days after he learned that a group of German politicians had nominated him for the Nobel Peace Prize. A state funeral was held on 22 January. Yasser Arafat, Shimon Peres and the members of the Oslo Channel attended. In Oslo Cathedral, Warren Christopher paid tribute to Mr. Holst's contribution to building peace in the Middle East.